The English Golf Coast

Phil Dowell

Published by

MELROSE BOOKS

An Imprint of Melrose Press Limited
St Thomas Place, Ely
Cambridgeshire
CB7 4GG, UK
www.melrosebooks.com

FIRST EDITION

Cover designed by Amanda Barrett Creative Design
Photographs by courtesy of Lyme Regis and Bridport & West Dorset Golf Clubs

ISBN 1 905226 43 8

Printed and bound in Great Britain by:
CPI Bath, Lower Bristol Road,
Bath, BA2 3BL, UK

With thanks to everyone who contributed, knowingly or otherwise.

"Drink to me only with thine eyes,
And I will pledge with mine."

CONTENTS

THE WARM–UP

Just inside the entrance to the car park, there is a slate plaque on a rough stone plinth which reads as follows:

Teignmouth Golf Club
Founded 1924
Course designed by the
world famous architect
Dr Alister Mackenzie
also designer of
Augusta National USA

I like the use of "also". What a proud club!

The weather is less than welcoming. Indeed, it has been getting ominously worse on the run down from North Dorset to South Devon. Though we try to deny it, it is definitely raining. It won't stop us playing, of course.

But first, we need lunch, and in the pro shop we almost have an argument with the proud young assistant about whether we need to pay green fees at this private club before or after we eat. I don't know why we are bothering – we are obliged to play, of course, whatever the weather. This is day one of the West of England Senior Challenge, one of the foremost biennial golfing events in the calendar of, well, ours. The defending champion has returned the replica claret jug, and it is temporarily reunited with its little brother, the trophy for the runner-up. The contestants are all here, and if not straining at the leash, none-theless determined. And that goes for both of us.

Obviously, the young pro is not aware of this and remains sceptical, but he comes off the phone to the steward to report that though the kitchen is busy, we can indeed be accommodated for lunch. When we enter the clubhouse, there is no-one else to be seen, and we are served an excellent meal without fuss.

Refreshed and fearless, we then don waterproofs, pointedly purchase green fees, and proceed to the 1st tee, one of the most inviting opening drives down a long secluded fairway to a distant green. It is played along the side of the hill, high above the river Teign just before it meets the sea, and there are glimpses of the estuary town of Teignmouth to be seen when cloud cover permits. We drive off safely, and then watch as a man emerges onto our fairway through some trees. He has an iron club in his hand, hits a ball with it, and disappears whence he came. This sight is reassuring; otherwise, from what we can see, this could be the only one-hole golf course in the world.

Actually, I know it isn't. I have played here before, as part of my "collection" of all the seaside courses in the west of England. Nevertheless, it is unusual to see just one hole at the start of a round. Perhaps the trees have grown since Dr Mackenzie laid it out.

Personally, I have not visited his project in Augusta, USA, and right now it would be nice to have some August weather for our august competition, but it will not help to complain. Neither of us wears glasses, so it will be, as the cliché has it, the same for both of us.

The defending champion is Jim Rafferty, aged 62, handicap 15, of The Buckinghamshire Golf Club; I am ten years younger and three strokes lower, formerly of The Buckinghamshire, and now a member of Sherborne Golf Club. As our birthdays are close together, we arranged two years earlier to celebrate Jim's achievement of (amateur) senior status coinciding with my (strictly theoretical) eligibility for the seniors' pro tour. There have been some important changes in our lives since that first encounter. Jim has in a sense gained a wife, for he has finally persuaded the hard-working Jacqui to retire. In stark contrast, I am a widower of some three months, after death finally parted my wife and me after twenty-five years of mostly blissful togetherness. But life has to go on, and thankfully, there is golf.

As I mentioned, this is day one of the West of England Senior Challenge which, with reference to the conditions, we have deemed the Stableford round. Tomorrow, it is match play at Perranporth, reaching a climax with stroke play at St Enodoc on the third and final day. There are no incidental prizes for nearest the pin, longest drive, closest to the green in two at a par five, or shortest putt holed after a bunker shot. This is pure golf.

I have little sense of direction, certainly when playing golf. This is one respect at least in which I "play each hole as it comes". The layout at Teignmouth goes back and forth across an area of land fairly near to the clubhouse, before appearing to set off across country. There are a number of two-tier greens, and this, plus the fact that the two hardest holes on the front nine are par fives, would appear to be hallmarks of its eminent designer.

Teignmouth is essentially parkland, with nice springy grass which should be very good to hit from in summer, but this is May following the wettest winter on record, and we get the impression that the greens are only playable because they are being kept very grassy. The biggest immediate challenge is to hold on to our clubs, for the rain has worsened. At the 10th tee, I wonder aloud if we should call it a day, but since we don't know the way to the clubhouse,[1] and can't see it, we have no real option but to continue – with another par five – stroke index 3 – into the elements.

Looking back, I made the serious mistake of trying to use an umbrella in cold driving rain. Without gloves, the hand holding it is exposed to everything that is going, and soon loses all feeling. The scoring – which had been going remarkably well – became patchy, and in coping with the elements, it was a case of every man (or in our case, both of us) for himself. Still, we played on, and then – horror of horrors – we came upon a series of fourballs playing a match. We knew it was a match, because we met a couple of spectators – non-playing captains, perhaps – who told us so. Nor was it just any match, but an advanced round of the Devon County Seniors Knockout and very serious stuff. Funny how everyone gets on the bandwagon with this seniors' thing, isn't it? It looked like we were going to grind to a halt behind the match on the 13th tee, and be held up. Bad news; if there is one rule for playing in foul weather, it is to keep moving.

Then, a minor miracle happened. The people ahead of us shook hands on the green, turned about, and walked back towards us. It was a victory – 7 and 5 – for the home side. Two or three times more this

---

[1] I have since had a feeling that it might actually be just across the road, but this is not how one arrives at it from the 9th hole.

happened, we weren't held up at all, and as the last group passed us, they mentioned that soon we would be turning to have the wind at our backs for the closing holes, which we played almost with relish.

I'd like to tell you who won. Normally I keep score, but on this occasion, I did not have a pencil. Well, this is not strictly true. I had – that is, I possessed – about 45 pencils. There were about 30 in a drawer in my bedroom, where my wife put them. The rest were scattered about the house, or maybe in the boot of the car. I just did not have one with me. Not that it bothered me. Normally, I remember the scores well enough to be able to corroborate with someone else who is writing them down. Jim was scoring. Unfortunately, on this occasion I did not register his scores on the nasty part of the back nine. He wrote them down, but the rain washed them from the scorecard as he continued to use it! So, we had played through conditions more suited to a car wash, and we did not know the result. But, we had responded to The Challenge, which was the important thing. We decided to declare the match a half – which we could have done before starting, of course.

Then, without taking off our sodden, dripping waterproof clothes, we went and looked around for a few minutes at what was on sale in the pro shop – not that either of us wanted to buy anything. The proud young pro probably thought we were a right pair of drips.

I

THE CHALLENGE

Driving down through northern Cornwall to Port Gaverne, Jim told me that he had just about retained enough sanity to appreciate Dr Mackenzie's handiwork, but was a bit mystified about why it belonged in my collection of West Country seaside courses, as it was on top of a hill a couple of miles inland. I explained that there had been some "slippage" in the rules for "the project", and a sea view counted. It was just as well, otherwise we might have been obliged to stop off at Lyme Regis, exposed in effect directly to the Atlantic Ocean, at an elevation of a few hundred feet.

"The project" had started a few years earlier when my wife and I had moved from West London to North Dorset. It seemed a natural thing to do to explore the local golf courses, and also the coastline, and combining the two became a consequential pleasure. So, we took to making short trips beyond Somerset and Dorset to Devon and Cornwall, and I undertook to play all the golf courses on the coast from Bristol to Bournemouth, via Land's End – entirely for my own pleasure, and not in any particular sequence, just as the opportunities arose and the circumstances permitted. Some middle-aged men collect miniatures, or motor bikes, or mistresses. I collect golf courses.

'And,' said Jim, 'when we have played St Enodoc, you will have finished?'

'Yes,' I said.

'What will you do then?' he asked.

'I'll play my way round the rest of England,' I replied.

And this, dear reader, is my personal account of the experience. It is not a travelogue or gazetteer of golf courses, and I certainly do not give each course a rating on the Richter scale. I just recount what happened, what I saw, or what struck me about each place I visited. I try not to mention too often what club I used for each shot. I will get some things wrong, for which I apologise in advance, and I am certain that you will want to disagree with me at some point, whether over a matter of fact or opinion. If so, live and let live, or – golf and let golf...

I will explain more about this grander project in due course, but first I am sure you will want to know what happened on day two of the West of England Senior Challenge...

PERRANPORTH

Perranporth Golf Club is laid out on the cliff tops to the east of the town, overlooking the enormous sandy beach, where to stand alone at low tide is to realise one's insignificance in the overall order of things. On the course the land moves sharply up and down, being presumably created by a thin layer of soil and grass on top of granite. (Whether the land can actually "move" is a moot point. We were much amused by the legend in the course planner informing us that the 16th green "slopes violently to the right". We were almost afraid to step on it in case it tilted suddenly and threw us off.) The greens however are not the trademark feature of Perranporth; this accolade is reserved for the drives. One can see all of the 1st hole from the tee (not to mention the town of Perranporth and the cliffs leading to St Agnes' Head), but thereafter, on eleven or twelve of the remaining holes, one aims for a marker. Lest there be any doubt – and there would be otherwise – each marker takes the form of a large silhouette of the number of the hole. For good measure, the 7th hole bears two large figure 7s, one white, and one yellow, indicating the lines from the different tees. To survive, one must generally drive over these posts.

Fortunately, the Reverend (as Jim is affectionately known at his club) and I did just that – in weather as contrastingly brilliant as yesterday's had been awful – so I am unable to tell you what happens if you have a vicious hook or a severe slice. It could soon become tedious. If having played there before gave me any advantage over my fellow Challenger, on the tees it was limited to pointing to the marker post.

There are golfers who would criticise such a layout, maintaining that one should be able to see one's ball land, but I don't subscribe to that view. Provided one is consistently able to find the ball after driving roughly over the marker, I think it is fine – and this was certainly the case for the three rounds I have witnessed at Perranporth. Indeed, it is arguably more satisfying to see a well-directed ball disappear over a numbered marker post than it is to see it land some indeterminate distance away on a fairway. It excited me, and I was really looking forward to Jim's reaction, which did not disappoint me. It is perhaps a place to visit, though; being a member might be frustrating. There were an awful lot of second-hand clubs for sale in the pro shop.

Indeed, it is true that in addition to hitting the fairways, some of the plateau greens require precision approaches. Plateaux are not uncommon, but one or two of these in the middle of the round are from The Lost World, with sheer drops at the edges. This is where I got the better of the Reverend, or rather, he got the worse of himself. We both took seven on the 9th, so the Rev's net six won that to leave him one down, but I then played the next four holes in one over par gross, and won them all, so by the time we reached the 16th, the only short hole on the inward half, its violent leanings had no bearing on the match. I had won, and the Reverend needed to win at St Enodoc to retain the trophy. We were to play the Church course the next day, so perhaps the force would be with him...

If our match was over by the time we reached the 18th the same was not true for those behind us – and we became aware that we had been caught up. Behind us on the tee was a female player – we could not call her a lady – in a shocking pink top and very short shorts. She was half the first pair of a ladies' club match which must have progressed at a startling rate, given our respective starting times. We had finally fallen foul of Perranporth's blind tee shots on the 18th, where local knowledge probably advises an iron – certainly not the driver we both hit – off the tee. As we searched in vain for Jim's ball, the colourful player behind us on the tee launched into a massive drive which pitched on a downslope, bounced on a track crossing the fairway, and flew over our heads into oblivion beyond the green. No warning, no apology, no appearance. The perpetrator marched straight off the course to the clubhouse. In the car park shortly afterwards, her visiting opponent apologised to us, and rather meekly explained how she, playing off 16, had just beaten a 2 handicapper by two holes. One down on the 18th tee, her opponent had "gone for it". As she spoke, the losing tigress emerged from the clubhouse, climbed into her lime green, original VW

3

beetle, customised to multicoloured surfing trim, and drove off with familiar reckless abandon, leaving much of the tyre rubber behind. Whether she was heading back to California, I don't know – but I guess Cornwall was a good place to start if she was – and Perranporth is a frustrating place to be a member.

Whenever I travel, I take with me three volumes: *The Royal & Ancient Golfer's Handbook*, which, amongst lots of other interesting things, lists details of all the golf clubs in England; the *AA Easy Read Britain Road Atlas*, self-proclaimed as "Britain's Clearest Mapping", with generally helpful blue flags indicating the whereabouts of golf courses; and *The Good Pub Guide*. This last work is not always as reliable as the other two, but it is good fun choosing somewhere to stay from its contents. On this occasion, it had done us proud. The Port Gaverne Inn is to be found clustered with a few houses in a cove just east of Port Isaac, and proved to be idyllic. On arrival, however, we were not so sure of our welcome. We asked the man at reception if there was somewhere to dry our stuff after its soaking at Teignmouth. He replied 'No'. We could not dispute his honesty, but he might have let us down more gently, perhaps by adding the word 'sorry', or better still, explaining that our rooms would be nice and warm and do the trick. As it was, it was almost as if it was our fault that our stuff was wet!

That evening, however, we became favourites of the landlady (who had long since left behind the epithet "of a certain age"). In our time at the Bucks, the only thing Jim and I had ever actually won together was a quiz, held after the club championships were abandoned one year because of heavy rain. (Remarkably, this was in late June. The previous year it had been so hot that the management had come out onto the course with cold drinks. It was not unknown for this to happen, but on this occasion they were free, which was rare indeed.) After we got back from our day out at Perranporth, we found there was a quiz in the Inn – and we won. The landlady was delighted, because she provided the prizes, and was fed up with giving them to the same group of people who sat with a half of cider and four straws all night, and took away two bottles of wine as their prize.

The other thing we did was to discuss the "rules of engagement" for my coastal tour, which I later expressed as follows.

THE RULES OF ENGAGEMENT

I feel a need to explain the rules of my engagement, as it were, if only to prevent some readers from being disappointed that there is no mention of, for example, Royal Porthcawl.[2] It's in Wales, and I am touring the coast of England.

My undertaking tends to come up in casual golfing conversation, and can result in exchanges like this:

Keith	'Hey, John, have you heard what Phil's doing?'
John	'No, what are you doing?'
Me	'I'm playing all the golf courses on the coast of England.'
John	'Are you? That's very interesting. Have you played St Andrew's?'

Such confusion would not happen in Scotland, where folk are sensitive to the distinction between the concepts of Britain and England, a notion which often passes Englishmen by. I don't know why the Scots make such a fuss. It reminds me of Rugby League fans, always telling us how superior their game is to the version for 15 men. If it's so great, why don't they just ignore the other code, like Union fans do?

The stipulation to play the *English* coastline was important in limiting the scope of my undertaking. Judging by the coastal courses I've played in Scotland, I would love to play the rest in that country, but I wanted to embark upon a task I could see myself achieving without having to sell my house and set off in a camper van. Starting from Dorset, Scotland is not very accessible. I once drove up to Royal Dornoch, a distance of 1,024 km. I know we use miles in this country, but this makes the point – and there are more northerly courses than Royal Dornoch.

I then eliminated courses of only nine holes. This was something of an arbitrary decision, but in terms of travelling, it felt like it was not worth going a distance (and paying a green fee) just to experience nine new holes when there are eighteen-hole courses going begging, and I am not getting any younger. Speaking of which, also barred were courses that are younger than me. As far as I know, this only makes

---

2 Apart, obviously, from this one.

a difference of one,[3] that being Cape Cornwall near Land's End, but I have heard decidedly mixed reports about it, and I did not want the westernmost course in the tour to be disappointing.

The final criterion was the most significant. On my tour of the West Country, I had included courses from which one could see the sea, as well as those which were next to it, even if it could not be seen. This came about following a conversation when someone said 'Have you played in Looe?' to which I replied 'In lieu of what?' but my inter-rogator was of course advising me to play the excellent course which is named after, but a couple of miles inland from, Looe in Cornwall – nevertheless with a good view of the sea. Looking at a map, there were several courses, particularly on the south coast where residential development arrived before the golf boom, whose qualification would be subject to this rule. It would not be easy to assess in advance whether they offered a sea view. I suppose I could always have asked, but I am an Englishman, and felt that saying 'Erm, excuse me, but can you see the sea from your course?' would appear a little impertinent – or indeed, brainless. In any case, there was another reason supporting this decision, namely finance.

It is known as a seaside course, but Royal Lytham & St Anne's is not actually next to the sea, and I have heard it said that it is "awesome", and this by a friend who hits it a lot further than me. I was also once told – by the Rural Dean of Wimborne Minster (who, as All-Diocesan Champion of the Church of England was once invited to play there for nothing) that the green fee is £140. Well, it might be nice to play there one day, but £140 to be intimidated?

So, the courses must be strictly on the coast. Literally littoral, in fact, the second word meaning "of or relating to the shore of a sea, lake or ocean" according to my Collins 21st Century dictionary. Actually, I thought of calling this book *Literally Littoral*, but then I remembered that I wanted it to be bought by golfers, who might need a certain four letter word in the title to gather what it was about. But, if anyone reading this plays at a course where the beach is treated as a water hazard, did you realise that you have a *literally littoral lateral*?

Even this specification requires some qualification; what is the ruling if the course is next to the sea but there is a track between it and the

---

[3] Actually, there are others in Yorkshire. See Number 15.

seawall, say? Here, I decided to apply the rule of equity, whatever that may be; if whatever intervenes is natural, undeveloped land, then the course qualifies. If there is a road, it does not, but a railway line (which would have been put there before the golf course) is OK, as is an unpaved track, which may have been there for centuries.

The final question was: what if another golf course intervenes? This had particular relevance in Merseyside, where Southport & Ainsdale butts onto Hillside, which is in turn adjacent to Royal Birkdale. (I think it would also apply to the Old Course at St Andrew's, but in case we need reminding, I'm not playing there. It's not in England.) I left the Birkdale question unresolved until one day I went there and discovered a road passing between the Open Venue and the shore. That saved two hundred and fifty quid at a stroke.[4]

So, those were the rules – and what was the journey to be called? Well, it was not *one* journey, it was many, and there should be no suggestion that I was setting out to play in any sort of sequence, to "circumnavigolf" the country, as it were, which "journey" or "voyage" would imply. I wondered if it were a pilgrimage, for as we all know, there are distinctly religious elements to the ritual of golf, but a pilgrimage is "a journey to a shrine or other sacred place". I wondered if it could be an odyssey, but that too is a single, if eventful, journey (and also, I feared puns such as 'Is 'e odd, then?')

Eventually, I came across the word *peregrination*, which *Chambers Dictionary* – self-styled as *The* Authority on English Today – defines as "travelling about; wandering; a complete and systematic course or round". "A complete and systematic course or round" – perfect!

So, you are at this moment reading about a personal peregrination around the literally littoral linksland of England, but don't worry about it. I will still miss two-foot putts.

******

Well, they say that the important thing about rules is to know when to break them, so when we set off the next morning, and we arrived at St Enodoc, we found that while you can see out to sea, and you can go down to the water's edge without crossing a road, strictly speaking it is on an estuary. I decided to treat estuaries on their merits using, as the

---

[4] Mininum Green Fees at Birkdale £125, Hillside £65, Southport £60.

R & A would have it, the principle of equity. St Enodoc was clearly a literally littoral course on the line of sight rule. In fact, it was two courses, the Church, and the Holywell, which qualifies by virtue of being inland but contiguous with the Church course. We had actually warmed up on it the previous day, after Perranporth.

ST ENODOC HOLYWELL

The Holywell course at St Enodoc Golf Club is short, some 4165 yards, SSS 61, par sixty-three. It is adjacent to the Church course but is more reminiscent of meadowland than mound-and-sandhill linksland, being therefore consistent with the notion of the linksland linking the good land to the shore. The longest hole of the nine par fours is 399 yards, but there are only two others over 300. Similarly, only two of the par threes are over 160 yards. Consequently, it does not take long to play, but apart from that, it is a little difficult to understand its purpose. Perhaps it was intended as an "apprentice" course where one can learn the basic skills of the game before taking them out onto its big brother, but if so, it would be like switching from a Honda 50 to a Harley Davidson.

At one point, we were waved through by a man playing with at a guess his ten year old son. With no children of my own, who am I to pass judgment, but it seemed from watching them that it would be quite discouraging for the child, as he would have taken about six shots by the time he reached the green of a par four. And, on a busy day, he would be standing by idle letting better players through a few times. And idle time passes oh so slowly when we are ten. Perhaps this was "competitive dad" from *The Fast Show*, but perhaps he was genuinely hoping to cultivate a new playing partner. Perhaps he aspired to an ideal of being able to play golf under the guise of – sorry, that should read "while definitely" – making a contribution to family harmony, as in 'I'll just take Tristan to the golf course while you and Isolde go shopping, dear'. Whatever, this is surely not the way to go about it. It must be quite depressing for Tristan, and he might end up hating the game. Far better to follow Harvey Penick's advice, and "play from the hole backwards", ie learn the game by holing out from whatever is a reasonable distance for your age. How about dad driving, and both players playing in from that point?

After our round at Perranporth, Jim and I played this "junior" course using only four clubs each, to save energy for the morrow. We fancied that the course was pronounced holly-well, until we came upon something on one of the later fairways which looked remarkably like a shrine, or holy well. I suppose the course might be described as pleasant enough but innocuous, and it is remarkable how well one can perform using only four clubs. Depressing is another way of looking at the same phenomenon; why do the other ten make so little difference? And why is it so important to carry them? I suppose it must be golf; like all the best religions, it is strong on ritual.

There are times when the human race does not tend to acquit itself well. Take airport departure lounges, where everyone tries to ignore the fact there are so many other people around, all of whom are just as simultaneously nervous, excited and powerless as they are and, in the case of Gatwick, half gaga for having got up at 3.30 AM. Then there are motorway service areas, where stressed families get out of their motorised confinement and fail to notice anyone else doing the same; and finally, there are golf clubs. Take a group of grown men, perhaps successful enough in life to be able to afford golf holidays with "the lads", dress them in golf gear, and I guarantee you any semblance of intelligence will be left behind in the locker room. We arrived the next day at St Enodoc for The Grand Climax – the final day of the West of England Senior Challenge – secure in the knowledge of our 9.30 tee off time. I don't follow the argument against having tee reservations. It does not prevent anyone turning up on the day and playing if there is space, but the other way round, one might turn up to find the course overrun by pillocks. Unfortunately not even the reservation system could prevent that very thing happening as it did this day. There were about eight of them, milling around inside the very spacious pro shop, generally getting in the way.

From their accents, we deduce that they are Yorkshiremen, something Jim Rafferty claims to be, so they have all come at least 400 miles, by road no doubt, and they do not know what is happening. They do not know when they are to tee off (not for at least 40 minutes, it transpires, so why do they get in our way?), what the competition format is, and whether they will play a second time in the afternoon. When later some of them appear in the clubhouse at the end of the morning round, they do not know *whether to eat lunch*. It is very tempting to ask them all for their twenty quid for the special "sweep" we are organising on their behalf. Instead, we are obliged to tee off with these pillocks now milling around the tee. There are enough people around to bring to mind the touchline of an American Football game.

ST ENODOC CHURCH

The omens are not good. The 1st hole on the Church Course at St Enodoc Golf Club is a very attractive par five and, as we observe on the way back in playing the 18th alongside, it is really quite manageable. A chance for a comfortable opening par, indeed. We both take nine, but at least, as this is the stroke play round, no-one has an early advantage. After four holes, the score reads Rafferty 29, Dowell 28. I am told that these opening holes are made for strategists. Number 6 features a giant bunker with the choice of an easy drive round it, or a tough one over it. We both drive into it. We aren't playing like strategists, we are playing like pillocks. It is several holes before anyone starts to score real golf numbers, and I think we are in awe of the course, with its gigantic mounds, and its wonderful views. As I have stated, technically, the latter might be of the estuary of the river Camel rather than the sea itself, but that is OK with the Rules Committee. Estuaries count as sea. There is no way I am leaving this place out of my collection. It is not so much a church as a golfing heaven, and we are playing it on a glorious day. Only the golf is disappointing, but who cares?

I am even intimidated by the speed of the greens at St Enodoc, which does not help the scoring. They certainly seem to suggest a better climate in Cornwall. Seaside greens tend to overwinter well, and apparently especially so in Cornwall. I say "even" because after seven years at The Buckinghamshire, fast greens are not a problem for me. There they often read 12 or 13 on the stimpmeter, and for good measure, are mostly over 40 yards long. We once played a friendly match away against Wentworth, and those first-time visitors amongst our team came away saying that the West course is much more interesting than it looks on TV, but the greens are a little on the slow side.

At St Enodoc, the 9th hole is particularly gorgeous. One sees it in the distance, but the course turns away again before finally arriving at the tee, allowing one to admire the prospect of a distant plateau green set against a backdrop of a kind of "residential compound – strictly private" surrounded by tall conifers. The estuary is on the left, and there is a private lane down to the estate. Perhaps it can also be reached by boat. Either I have seen many photos or paintings of this green, or I have played it in another lifetime. It is only stroke index 10, but it seems a lot harder, and I get a par. It is only the third such proper golf score between us.

The 10th hole goes inland, and is a little odd. It is a long par four, and the fairway is a narrow strip of flat land with a steep grassy bank to the right, and a small ravine to the left. It is like playing through a mountain pass, and there are people walking along a footpath, which adds to that feeling. I have since heard criticism of the course as a whole, based on this hole, but dismissed it as the complaint of what when I was a child we called a mardy[5] player who had had a bad round there. Most of the holes are beautiful, so what is one blemish? Isn't the Mona Lisa's smile crooked?

Naturally enough, the course planner describes the 10th hole, at 457 yards, as an outstanding par four. I suppose it would say that, wouldn't it? However, when it states that the uphill 17th at 206 yards is another championship par three, I have to agree entirely. I got a two. This sealed the fate of the second biennial West of England Senior Challenge, increasing as it did my already substantial five-shot lead to nine strokes, thanks to Jim Rafferty's unfortunate six. Not even I could squander a nine-shot lead in one hole.[6]

But I am getting ahead of myself. It is when we reach the 10th green at St Enodoc that we understand why there are people walking along the footpaths, and why this is called the Church course. There is a church, entirely surrounded by the golf course. The story goes that it somehow became entirely covered in sand, until it was excavated in 1864. The people on the footpath are now walking to it from the private lane, primarily to visit the grave of Sir John Betjeman. This former poet laureate was a member for many years, and loved the place enough to request to be buried in the churchyard. In the clubhouse there is a framed enlargement of a hand-written poem penned in tribute on the death of a former secretary of the club. Despite the very plain language he uses, it is somehow very moving, particularly to a man whose wife has died less than three months previously. As far as I know, Betjeman never attempted to describe the course in verse, limiting himself to rapture

---

[5] Meaning someone unwilling to take the medicine of defeat.
[6] In case there are any children reading, I will not disclose the final scores.

at his birdie three on the 13th hole. So, if he could not do justice to it, you will have to excuse me if I don't try. You will have to play it.

Thus, I became the second ever winner of the West of England Senior Challenge, after the inaugural victory of the Reverend J R. On the first occasion, the only coastal course we played had been the great links at Burnham & Berrrow. At University, having just started playing golf in the summer before my first year, I was alarmed to meet someone who had already given the great game up. He said he had developed the "Burnham hook". This sounds like something you might use to hang the Dunmow Flitch on, the latter being a side of bacon, but that would be the wrong Burnham, on Crouch, in Essex. This is on Sea, in Somerset – or perhaps more accurately, on the mud of the Bristol Channel.

I never really thought about the Burnham hook until I heard about The Open Championship Pre-qualifying of 2000. About 100 profes-sionals competed for six places in Qualifying proper. On a practice day, the 1st hole played a driver and a 7 iron. On the day of the event, the wind was up, and it required the same clubs, with a 3 wood in between. The first sign of difficulty was when an early starter came in with a score of nineteen over. He was an amateur, a club member, handicap plus one. One of the pros eventually qualified with a 79, and when he went on to get into the Championship proper, this was thought to be the highest recorded qualifying score in modern times. I fancy that the Burnham hook is a consequence of trying to hit low topspin drives into winds like this. Fortunately, the wind was moderate when the Reverend and I played there.

BURNHAM & BERROW

There is something exciting and classi-cal about the scene outside the clubhouse at Burnham and Berrow Golf Club. You can catch a glimpse of a practice ground beyond the putting green, and apart from that, you see the 18th green, isolated from its fairway by a series of mounds, and the 1st tee, from which the target is a saddle shaped area of lush green fairway between tall mounds of natural grassy vegetation. If this is your first encounter with true links golf, you know how you feel about it. If you don't fancy it, it is best to say so at this point, as you are about to grind your way in a northerly direction along the Somerset coast for two miles or so, and the prevailing wind – or so I believe – which blows directly against you on the 1st hole – will be off the sea, and across from about 45 degrees against. It will be a while before you see the clubhouse again. Stock up with balls now.

You won't actually be close to the shore, which might be a blessing at low tide, as there is a nine-hole course[7] to the seaward side of this great links, which looks interesting. None of the four par fours in the first six holes is over 400 yards, even from the white tees; they just feel as if they are. There is a big premium on driving well. There are also some very forward blue tees, and when I later enquired as to their purpose, the reply came "to enable some of the elderly members to enjoy their rounds". A touch of Harvey Penick again – playing the game from the hole backwards – at the other end of life. The 4th hole offers possibly my favourite type of tee shot, an elevated tee playing to a fairway laid out on a left to right diagonal. I don't call this a dogleg, which should have a more abrupt turn around the landing area; this is more of a straight hole with an offset tee. You look at it and wonder how much of the fairway you can cut off. Your natural left to right shape will help – if you hit, as you do when you are playing well, a fade. A slice, on the other hand, will leave you in the sandhills. A hook, on the "wrong side" of the wind, will be a disaster. A draw could run out of fairway. Such thoughts would have been fairly academic to the Open qualifiers, many of whom could not reach several of the fairways on that fateful day.

The greens were superbly true, as one tends to expect from links courses, but I was a little surprised by the bunkers. There was a fair smattering around the greens, but not the usual trouble lining the fairways. After the round, I checked through the course planner. There are only two bunkered fairways in the first nine, and three more coming home. Not that it matters. If the ball is on a bank, in rough, 18 inches above your feet, you are still not going to reach a green 180 yards away.

It is fun but challenging, and there comes a time when you start thinking that it will be nice to pass the turn and play some holes wind-assisted. Indeed, at the 10th hole, Jim drove successfully over a large mound which obscures the landing area, hit a wedge close and holed the putt for the only birdie of the day, but this proved to be a false dawn. Whether the wind direction changes with the tide, or it is just

---

[7] Possibly a better apprentice ground than St Enodoc's.

happenstance that the natural way of laying out the course in an out-and-back loop along the coast conspires with the prevailing wind, the fact is that the holes still seem to be wind-against on the way back. The course Jim and I played was 8 yards shorter than the yellow course at the Bucks, but it seemed a good deal longer. Well, they do say that seaside golf is all about the wind. I think on balance we enjoyed it. We drove home happy, but tired.

When I spoke to the Reverend a few weeks after The Challenge to suggest a pilgrimage to Royal St George's, at Sandwich, in the County of Kent, I was surprised to hear him announce that he would love to go, as he was born in Canterbury. I thought he was a Yorkshireman. Anyway, if you are going to be ordained, then I guess Canterbury is as good a place as any to be born, and better than most, though it has to be said that Jim was not ordained by the mother church, but by the Brother-hood of the Buckinghamshire, on a trip to Portugal. Indeed, he was revered by all, and made one of the captains. As it was not a members' club, we did not have elected officials as such, but someone was nomi-nated for the role when we had a match against another club. There are quite a few of us who can casually mention in the right company that we were captain of the Buckinghamshire.

There is a village near Sandwich called Ham (or perhaps it is a hamlet) and somewhere, there is supposed to be a road sign bearing the legend "Ham Sandwich". I have never seen it. Nor have I seen any signs in Royal Tunbridge Wells, where I stayed the night before our assignation, that indicate how to get out of the place in a direction other than for London or Hastings. The people of Kent can be a little insular in outlook. They recognise East Sussex and have heard of Surrey, but mostly they argue amongst themselves about whether they are Kentish Men or Men of Kent, and my guess is that the people of Tunbridge Wells do not often travel to Sandwich.

Thus with a mixture of disgust and anxiety, I phone the Reverend who is on his way down from Buckinghamshire, to announce that I might be a little late. I ask him where he is, and then I need to ask him to repeat the statement that, though he has been on the road for 90 minutes, he is currently approaching South Mimms on the M25, at a speed of zero miles per hour. Somewhat unhelpfully, I realise afterwards, I make a comment to the effect that I would not have chosen that way to go round.

Even a genuine man of the cloth might not have shown the restraint that Jim did in his reply.

Rather than phone ahead and ask if it is OK if we are delayed by an unspecified length of time, I make my way to the venerable club. I have been there before, by train and double decker bus to watch The Open, and this is totally different. Then there were avenues of artificial walkways through tents and things, but no real sign of a golf course. Here there is a drive, a modest clubhouse, but no real sign of a golf course. After furtively checking with Jim (he is through the Dartford tunnel) lest my mobile be confiscated, I park and approach the club-house. There is a bell push and a discreet sign "Members only. Visitors please ring." Surely not? I turn towards another building, and take in a view of an expanse of long grass as far the eye can see – as far as the sea, indeed, but it looks a long way off. I stumble into the pro shop and blurt out something, but a charming Scotsman puts me at ease and directs me next door to the caddie master. He too is Scots: 'Aye, well, we had ye doon for 11.30 but dinna worry, we'll get y'off anytime.' This seems highly plausible, as I seem to be the only person there. I decline the offer of the practice range, but I try the putting green which is about halfway to the 1st tee, and therefore a quarter of a mile from the clubhouse door.

Then I try some chipping. Over to the left there is what looks like a practice chipping green with a couple of bunkers, an unusual, thick-ish fringe and an odd-looking slope to pitch into. I play around, hitting a couple of balls onto the green and casually flicking them back off with my wedge. Then I wander off to meet Jim, and as the Revmobile heaves into view, I realise that there was only one flag on that green, and the bunker was not adjacent to it like a normal practice hole. I have just been practising on the 18th green. The slope was that which Sandy Lyle famously failed to get up the year he won The Open! It is so revered it has a name, Duncan's Hollow. Of course, it all looked different as a great amphitheatre with stands and scoreboards. Now it is just a golf green. Frankly, I have seen more imposing-looking finishes on pitch and putt courses.

After we negotiate some sustenance for Jim,[8] we finally make our way to the 1st tee.

ROYAL ST GEORGE'S

You do not so much stroll to the 1st tee at Royal St George's Golf Club as cast off and set sail for it. You are leaving civilisation as we know it firmly behind. You may recall that in the 2003 Open, Tiger Woods lost his ball on the 1st hole. Jim Rafferty lost the fairway. We simply could not work out where it was within the vast expanse of green gleaming in the bright sunlight. We only settled down when Jim got the first par on the short 3rd, but this proved something of a false dawn. His problem was the greens. The slopes were as irregular as the surface of a poppadum, though much more subtle. When the ball hit a green it would run in an unexpected direction, and Jim simply could not get his first putt close enough to hole the second. My problem was getting to the greens in the first place, as something unpleasant was happening to my clubface as it encountered the ball. Our joint problem was divining where to go next from the green we had just played. There was one where a sign read "High tees" – not a catering offer, but an indication of which alternative box was in use, always assuming you knew where it was.

Perhaps because the back nine are more familiar to me from having been a spectator, things did seem to ease up, but the front nine were awkward and awesome. I do not think there are many 28 handicappers in the club. The fairway on the 4th hole – the one with the giant bunker where they have had to move the tees forward from time to time – is not too difficult to find from the weekday tee, but where is the green? The 5th has mounds interrupting the fairway, and the 8th does not really bother with a fairway at all. There is just a landing area, and another shot to a half-hidden green.

The putting problems continued for the Reverend, and I stayed in the match. I was pleased to get a par on the 510 yard 14th, the one with the out of bounds down the right, as there was a photograph in the clubhouse officially identifying it as having been voted "one of the world's great golf holes" and – despite my earlier comments about it – I also parred the 18th – definitely a great finishing hole – to halve the

---

[8] We were caught in a kind of time warp. We could order toast and anchovy paste from the lounge as it was 10.55 AM but by the time it was to be served, we would have to remove ourselves as we could not sit wearing golfing clothes after 11.00 AM. Jim asked for the toast "medium rare" as a compromise.

match. We both agreed that if Jim had been able to hole anything, he would have murdered me.

Changing in the clubhouse, we spoke to a member who agreed that it could be a little tough first time out. He was also a member at a course down the road at Deal. 'On balance, I think I prefer it,' he said. 'It's called Royal Cinque Ports.' After he had left, Jim said to me, 'Phil, did he really say there was a golf course called royal sink putts?'

I do not think that it was the proximity of the English Channel that planted the idea in the Rev's mind, but we never did get to play Royal Cinque Ports together, just down the coast. Jim and his wife Jacqui went off to Belgium to become tax exiles and, in his case, a football coach. Having once scored a goal past Gordon Banks in a serious match, the Rev's first love was always football, and perhaps the idea of coming back to Blighty for golf dwindled. Or maybe, it was because he was a Sheffield Wednesday supporter that he stayed away. Later, they moved to Portugal. I am grateful for Jim's enthusiasm and inspiration at a difficult time, and maybe one day it will be necessary to play the coastal golf courses of Portugal. Who knows – but first, rather a lot of England awaits me.

2

PLAYING ALONE

In order to stay happily married to a non-golfing wife, while also indulging an enthusiasm for visiting different golf courses, it is necessary to cultivate the art of playing alone. Otherwise, imagine the sort of conversation that might take place on a weekend trip to Cornwall, just the sort of opportunity my wife Celia and I would take after we moved from London to Dorset.

Celia:	'Er, Phil, there's someone in the back seat.'
Phil:	'Yes, I know. That's Arnold.'
C	'Arnold?'
P	'Yes. Don't worry about him. He's come for the golf. He won't be any trouble.'
C	'But where's he going to sleep? Does he have his own room?'
P	'No, I couldn't afford it. He can sleep in the bath.'
C	'Oh no he can't. I booked a room with a shower.'

Celia tolerated my golf – in fact, she approved of my playing, observing that I used to come home with a kind of glow, even if I had not played well (which was often the case). She loved pitch and putt, but found a full-sized course a little frustrating, following a bad experience in Ireland. Occasionally she would accompany me round a course, even more rarely playing, but later in life she preferred to spend her green fee money on other luxuries available in hotels, or to read a book on a beach somewhere while I investigated the local terrain.

But, time was of the essence. I always felt I didn't have an hour or so to hang around waiting for a chance partner, and playing alone – subject to who else was on the course – was the fastest version of the game.

Actually, I used to play alone a fair bit when I lived in London, it being just about the only way of getting any golf into a busy working schedule. Opportunities for weekend play outside of becoming a club member were fairly non-existent, and so were opportunities for club memberships until the expansion of the early 1990s. It was possible to get one person to a golf club after work on a summer's evening, but meeting anyone else was usually logistically a step too far. So, I played alone.

I would not say I cultivated the art in those days. Desecrated it, more like. I used to have a rule that if I did not see where a ball went, the shot did not count (unless I happened to find it subsequently) and I could play another. I have since come across people who have the shot again when they *do* see where it went. Such "rolling mulligans" are tempting when playing alone, but no-one should delude themselves that they are scoring well if they employ that tactic. In those days, I would have found it difficult to play a strange course on my own. As a beginner, *everything* about golf is difficult, including navigating one's way around. (Driving – a car, that is – is like that. Do you remember how impossible it was to read road signs the first time you drove on your own?)

On my home course in the winter, I sometimes play two balls over nine holes, which is a way of fitting eighteen holes' worth of play into a short time, but I do not recommend that on a strange course; there is too much emphasis on where the balls are, and not on where *you* are, which is the point of the exercise. I have also played a personal Texas scramble, where you play every shot twice and take the best result. This is brilliant, particularly with holeable putts (carry a spare ball and drop it if you miss with the first, but don't move anything else), and you can break par – but it is a recipe for disaster when the first spring medal comes round and you can only hit the ball once.

Celia died in early 2001, having been ill throughout the previous year. I found golf by the seaside especially comforting on occasions when she was in hospital and, looking back, I suppose that this project has subsequently filled part of the vacuum that remained after she departed this life. She commented to a consultant one day when discussing the seriousness of her illness, 'I can't die, otherwise there'll be nothing to stop Phil playing golf all the time.' Well, I am not playing golf all the time; I am writing about it as well.

MULLION

Mullion Golf Club is situated to the north of the village on the clifftop on the rugged western side of the Lizard Peninsula looking directly west at Nova Scotia, although you can't see that far. Nevertheless, you might have thought that the prevailing recollection of my visit there would be the views, although if there is an English county in which to get blasé about coastal views it is Cornwall, with or without golf courses.

Mullion is proud to be the most southerly course in England. As such, it is a little off the beaten track. Possibly for this reason, my abiding memory of visiting there is actually the gents' locker room not, I hasten to add, for any sinister reason. Celia was with me throughout, except when I went in, of course. We had cause to return to the club the day after playing, as there was a second-hand driver in the pro shop of a type a friend had asked me to look out for. I had also come away without one of my Buckinghamshire Fifth Anniversary souvenir wood covers, about which I enquired. I was directed to a cupboard in the locker room.

It was enormous, and when I opened it, an avalanche of shoes and other golfing paraphernalia came tumbling out. You can imagine the scene. Get some golf in on holiday in Cornwall; after a fine round, put the clubs in the car, change the shoes in the locker room; sit outside the clubhouse watching the sunset, a couple of pints of beer, or maybe scrumpy cider; perfect. Then, some weeks later, back in Halifax or Bolton: 'Maureen, have you seen my golf shoes?' 'No, when did you use 'em last?' 'When we played that course down in Corn...Oh, bloody 'ell!...' Hence, a cupboard full of shoes; as noted, Mullion is a little off the beaten track.[9]

Mullion GC starts unusually with a par three, and then goes back and forth on fairly level terrain with a par five interrupting a run of rather innocuous medium length par fours. I found these holes a little confusing, as they are mixed up with some of the closing holes and there are understandably few features like trees to help identify the target lines. At the 6th hole, the course goes rapidly downhill, literally. People play from the 6th tee and just disappear from view. So did my

---

[9] My wood cover, incidentally, was on a table in the passageway. The cupboard was full to bursting.

game at this point (go rapidly downhill). There were very tempting tee shots to be played down towards a cove, and my ambition got the better of me. Well, I have to be honest, I had already breached the rules. I duffed my opening tee shot. Instead of going 176 yards, it went about 176 feet. It was a nice day. There was no-one about. The course was called "Mullion". What would you do?

The Mulligan hit the green, and I holed the putt, and wrote two on the card. So, when I was tempted by the extraordinary slopes of the holes from 6 onwards which take you down to a cove and their potential for outrageous bounces, I "went for my shots" as they say in cricket. I enjoyed it, but did not achieve any special results, other than to dispose of a few used balls. There is a mysterious abandoned chapel in the cove, but I did not have a prayer of recovering my concentration, and although I played the rest of the holes, the round did not register in my mind with the clarity the course deserved.

I remember thinking it was a very interesting place. I must go back. The trouble is, it's a little off the beaten track...

It is actually likely that we would have visited Mullion some time. There are the village's non-golfing attractions, the magnificent Kynance Cove, and the ultimately disappointing Lizard Point to see. The same may not be said for Bude, to which we deviated on our way back from deepest Cornwall in the year of the total eclipse of the sun. The roads were surprisingly empty, and we reached it with time to spare. Celia offered me the chance to play, and I of course jumped at it. As with all things in golf, there has to be a "principle of equity", and equity on these trips involved my knowing from a marital perspective how many times it was reasonable for me to play. This was a bonus offer, and I did not hang about.

BUDE & NORTH CORNWALL

For the town with possibly the shortest name in Cornwall, Bude boasts the longest club name – but that matches the prominence of the course, which may be unrivalled outside Scotland. Bude & North Cornwall Golf Club is like a giant village green, with one of the beaches at the lowest end, and a road running through some way inland uphill by the clubhouse, and the rest of the course bordered by roads, or rather residential streets, on the other sides. Celia and I had lunch in the "bottom corner" at a hotel, watching people play the short 4th. Almost no-one we saw hit the green, yet doesn't it always look so enticingly easy a thing to do when one is merely watching? In due course I paid my green fee, and when I got down there, my beautiful 7 iron didn't just find the green, it found the narrow gap between the flag and the windward side bunker to which it was tightly cut. I walked proudly forward to the green (I was sure there were people watching) and the putt was almost, but not quite, a gimme. When inevitably I missed it, I had the presence of mind to stroll up to the ball and pick it up as if I were retrieving it from the hole. Hopefully, they were not watching too closely. As I walked away, I wrote down a 2 on the card!

The next hole took me back to the clubhouse where I endeavoured to rectify the oversight caused by my enthusiasm to play. In my excitement I had forgotten that I had taken my woods out of the bag so it would fit more easily into the car. Now I needed them. Playing a bouncy, humpy links course without long woods is like playing cricket with a tennis racket.

So, I nipped into the pro shop, where someone very kindly lent me a driver. I think it is probably illegal to add another club to the bag during the course of the round. It is certainly illegal to do what I did next: attempt half-heartedly to hit a shot with it off the fairway, then – with the words 'if you're going to hit it, hit it' still leaving my lips – drop another ball and swing at it. It flew like a cross between an Exocet missile and a Barnes Wallis bomb, ran up a steep bank and finished on the elevated green, about 250 yards away, uphill. That was it. Like a chance encounter with a girl at a party, the driver and I just hit it off for the "night". We didn't even ask each other's names, and would probably be embarrassed ever to meet again. It was the same with the course. I'm sure the members regularly play the bump and run shot, but not the way I did on the long holes, with a driver from the fairway. Very effective into the wind!

There were a number of blind shots to play which required hitting a second shot into a central area of mounds that concealed a green or two, after which one played away to the edge of the course again. Each time, my ball did just what was expected of it. When I finally hit a wayward approach into a burn on about the 15th, I nevertheless found the ball, playable on a ledge half way down the bank. I chipped out and then holed a curling putt to save par. On the 18th tee, I needed a par five for my (notionally) best ever score. I duck-hooked into scrub. Annoyed,

I tried to find some rationale for a mulligan, but when I finally took it, I lost the ball, so I de-rationalised quickly! Still, somehow I managed to play the original through the practice ground and rough, onto the green, and into the hole in four more shots. It may not have been strictly according to the rules, but it was brilliant. Three over par.

Or was it brilliant? The point about the "retrospective gimme" is this: how upset might I have been not to get a two after my brilliant tee shot on the 4th, and how would it have affected my subsequent play? It is all very well saying that one should play each hole, each shot indeed, with no mental reference to those already played, but we all know – to use the technical term – that is a load of bollocks. It may be that the very few tournament professionals who become champions can do this, but that is what makes them special. But, in the way that petty crime can lead to more serious stuff, so during this round that "pip" (I will explain the term later) gave way to the kathleen,[10] the replayed shot with the driver.

Still, it was a great round, and I was aglow with the way I had responded to what is probably quite a difficult, certainly unusual, course. It is always a good idea to praise a course when visiting it, especially to the people who work there, so I told them it was great, and I had gone round in net 61. They asked if I would like to buy the driver. I said thanks but no. It wasn't the moment to put our relationship onto a legal basis.

Actually, the rules did *not* prohibit me from playing another ball. I just had to declare the first unplayable, but still count it, and take a penalty shot. Also, I *was* allowed to leave the course provided I did not cause undue delay. It is not a case of automatic disqualification, as once happened to Heathcliff, a colleague at the Bucks, playing at his previous club, West Middlesex. The 1st hole plays alongside the clubhouse, with the tee to the left, and the green to the right. The pro shop is between the tee and the clubhouse and, realising he was short of balls, he popped in for more, to face immediate disqualification from some over-zealous official; possibly a football referee getting mixed up with "leaving and re-entering the field of play". Of course, he could still play, it just did not count. Neither does a player playing alone. According to the rules, he has no standing, so in a sense, he can do whatever he likes. In all

---

[10] From the lovely Irish song "I'll take you (home) again Kathleen". This shot was from the fairway; a Mulligan is played off the tee – strictly speaking (if it is possible to be strict about illegal plays), the 1st tee.

honesty, I would not say that I took extreme liberties, but I did have one problem.

Playing a strange course with one ball is entertainment enough, and they say that even in match play you should play the course and not your opponent,[11] but where I have trouble is on the greens. Some people suffer from the yips, I get the pips – a "pip" being an acronym for a "psychologically impossible putt". What happens is that from a distance, the ball looks close, and I think "that's a gimme" – or maybe just "I hope that's a gimme". As I get closer, the ball seems to get further from the hole, and the thought occurs that it is eminently missable. Once this happens, I am in two minds, neither of which is exactly capable of holing the putt. The rules of golf state that a concession may neither be declined nor withdrawn. That's true inside my head as well; once the thought occurs even that it *just might* be a gimme, it's too late. At Newquay, it happened on the 1st green, and in a sense spoilt another good round.

NEWQUAY

There is another walk-on part for Sir John Betjeman in the description of this visit to Newquay Golf Club. The adopted Cornish golfing laureate was an enthusiast for Victorian architecture (I think St Pancras station was one of his favourites), and he left his mark on Newquay with his description of the Headland Hotel as the ugliest building in Cornwall. There was subsequently only one thing for the proprietors to do – proudly proclaim their "accolade" to all-comers. It is an odd location, since it is in one sense remote (being as you might guess, on a headland) but otherwise in the "middle" of Newquay, as there seem to be parts of this sprawling and somewhat run-down town in all directions.

Actually, the weather tried to spoil the round for me before I even started it. Unless you are one of those people who only carries waterproofs if (a) it is actually raining, or (b) you have received a personal email from John Kettley instructing you to do so, it may be some time

---

[11] Actually, it's Americans who say this. Maybe that's why they lose the Ryder Cup.

since you were drenched on a golf course. Here, it happened to me in the car park. It was April, and periodically black clouds were flying over at some speed, when one elected to empty its contents there and then – just at the exposed moment when I had got all my stuff out of the boot of the car, to discover that the entrance to the clubhouse was on the other side of the building. I should have got everything, including myself, back into the car, but before I could think of it, this localised shower made me generally wet through. Of course, I proceeded with my mission, having to gamble that there would be no more cloudbursts, or that at least I would have time to see the next one coming. I needed to dry off in the wind. If there is one thing worse than being wet without waterproofs, it is being wet inside them. I used to have a pair of "waterproof" trousers which through some kind of remarkable capillary effect, accumulated water on the inside, in the crotch, where it was then soaked up by my conventional trousers. Excruciating.

If the view of the hotel is not good, the same cannot be said for the view from it. What is remarkable is that one can see not only the whole of a magnificent beach – which, extrapolating from the length of holes on the golf course, must be at least three quarters of a mile long – but also, the whole golf course. The latter is a privilege usually reserved for the pilot of the Met Life blimp. Actually, it makes the course look rather featureless, for the land is not pure links, with its colour contrast fairways; there is a hint of lush pastureland, and in April, anyway, it is green all over. Fortunately, to play it is to experience it on a different scale, and the land provides a very pleasant playing area, a sort of oasis of calm within an otherwise strangely urban environment.

The area slopes down fairly sharply towards the beach, with the holes being played mainly across the gradient rather than up and down. I suppose in the final analysis you would call it links, but there has been a fair amount of earth moved to create greens so they do not have severe sideways slopes. There is also a kind of gully running through the course, which turns out to be a public footpath down to the beach, which you cannot actually see from the course, because of a line of sandhills covered in shrubs. No fewer than six holes feature this gully as a kind of obstacle, although it is not exactly "in play" (probably wisely, given how many people must use the path in the summer), other than at the short 16th where it's possible to bounce a ball off the protecting mesh above the path and onto the green.

The hole I remember best is the 8th, a par five down at the farthest point from the clubhouse, playing up to a plateau green actually quite near to the Headland Hotel. From a good position off the tee, I played my second shot over the footpath, leaving a wedge to the green which stopped pretty close to the hole. I duly walked up towards the green, and raised my putter to acknowledge the applause from the hotel. I was fairly confident no-one would be watching, in fact. Then, I hope to God no-one was, for I suffered an attack of the pips, and "sort of" missed the putt. I actually made a note on the scorecard – it was four feet, to accompany the five foot pip I had taken on the 1st. I kept other data in those days, and apparently I hit nine greens in regulation, and eleven out of thirteen fairways (no mention of any mulligans or kathleens either). Shame about the pips.

When I got back to the clubhouse, I noticed that it had a round tower with battlements. What did the poet laureate think of that, I wonder? I also noticed that you cannot even see the course from the clubhouse, never mind the beach. Possibly the only place you can see both from is the Headland Hotel, which is of course fully visible from the clubhouse. I have a souvenir, the scorecard. It features an aerial photograph of the beach, the course, and, in all its glory, the Headland Hotel.

After the round at Newquay, gazing out at the course from our room in the Headland Hotel, I though it would be nice to return some day – but there were a lot of courses still to play. As I have mentioned, my excursions in the West of England included courses not only literally littoral, but also within sight of the sea, a total approaching forty. When I extended this to the rest of England, even acting most strictly, I added close to a further fifty. Unless I had any particular reason to return anywhere, it would have to wait.

Another factor that enabled me to play golf this way was that we had no children, so there were no other family responsibilities to consider. In the earlier days when we lived in London, we tended to work hard, with one or the other of us coming home late in the evening. Staying out for golf was not a problem, but the prospect of "golf widowhood" never reared its head. There was simply no chance of playing at weekends without paying a fortune and waiting an age to join a club. At Ealing Golf Club, which I used to visit, you even had to become a social member before you could become a golfing member and, judging by some of the conversations I heard in the bar, this method of joining was a modern version of trial by ordeal.

Talking of ordeals, my solo expeditions were not always a success:

STADDON HEIGHTS

At Staddon Heights Golf Club, I was off my game, and while I try not to let this affect my judgement about a course, inevitably it must do. I was at least fortunate that it was not played clockwise around the strange plateau where it is "tucked away", despite being really quite close to Plymouth, the biggest English city west of Bristol. It seemed remote.

I had just bought a new driver, and it was hitting everything thirty degrees left. (Notice it was the driver's fault. Straight down the middle, it would have been me doing the hitting.) The ball was flying straight, though, and not over the cliff edge, but onto an adjacent fairway. The course was laid out in a sequence of back-and-forth holes, which is not a feature I generally care for.

If my drives were going straight, the same could not be said for my irons, as I was fighting off an attack of the "unmentionables". Hence, a straight left would be followed with a right cross, and with the odd hook thrown in, the round began to sound like it was from a boxing match. With that aggravating 'Why is this happening?' feeling, I did not exactly sail round the course. Rather, I tacked.

Still, if there is a course on which to emulate a sailing ship, Staddon Heights, overlooking Plymouth Sound, is probably it. But, if Drake had been playing as badly as me, it is doubtful whether he would have seen off the Armada. I suppose we would have got Spaniards into the Ryder Cup team that much earlier.

The course included a number of water hazards, and was surprisingly moist, featuring the sort of lush grass which I imagine Devonian cows eat to produce their famous clotted cream. At the 18th, the second shot is played across a road to a green edged by a bank of thick grass, US Open-style. My ball went into it, and I could not find it. Quite the closest to a hole I've ever lost a ball, to end a thoroughly quirky day.

I had lost the plot long before that. Talking of Spaniards, maybe Seve Ballesteros in his prime appreciated a course when he played it from the wrong fairways. I did not.

When it comes to choosing somewhere to visit for a short break, where better than a hotel which also has its own golf club? It did not take me long to spot the Whitsand Bay Hotel Golf Club in my *R & A Handbook*, and we arranged to go for a few days, taking along my widowed mum. It sounded like a brilliant scheme, until I was required by a client (I used to work occasionally) and had to leave early by sleeper train – a misnomer if ever there was one. Is anything more guaranteed to wake someone up than a sudden deceleration accompanied by a violent clanking of buffers? The location for the Whitsand Bay Hotel itself is pretty good – overlooking Whitsand Bay actually, just west of Plymouth Sound. If they were after the off peak, mid-week leisured classes (sometimes known as Saga louts),[12] then they also did well not to name the hotel after the village in which it is located – Portwrinkle. I am not sure though that the land used for the golf course is the best choice, but then nowhere's perfect.

Except Turnberry. There can be no better place on earth for a golf course than the land occupied by the Ailsa course, and no finer spot to locate a hotel to overlook it, sheltered at the back by the hills keeping out the evil east wind, gathering the warmth of the Gulf Stream and basking in the glow of the evening sun. They start digging Ayrshire tatties on Whit Monday, you know. Some people say Gleneagles is better, but how can it be? It isn't by the sea.

Anyway, they are both in Scotland, and I could actually afford to stay at the Whitsand Bay. I could not remember much about it, though. The visit was an early one, possibly before my intention to "collect" Cornish courses was fully formed, so I decided to pay another visit.

WHITSAND BAY

Most visitors to Whitsand Bay Hotel Golf Club come from the east, but can still end up approaching Portwrinkle from the west. It all depends whether you take the Tamar Bridge or the Torpoint Ferry. Have a look at a map. I actually consulted an ordnance survey map I happened to have from the earlier trip (essential to find your way around the lanes and creeks in that area). On the western approach to the hotel you

---

[12] Except when they are from the Shires, when they become Aga louts.

pass a fairly nondescript few golf holes, and although the sea is visible, it is not particularly near. A right turn down to the hotel reveals a few more holes on the other side of the lane looking, I thought, a little like an afterthought. I was wrong.

I remembered the 1st hole. In some innovative places like Lynton (or perhaps it was Lynmouth) they used funicular railways to link the cliff top and the shore. Here, they used a 366 yard golf hole. No real problem if you take it steady; more of an issue if, having forgotten your tee time, you arrive to find that you are two minutes behind a fourball you should be six minutes in front of. They were milling around as fourballs will so, following instructions from the pro, I asserted my priority and teed off. Up the middle went the ball, with considerably greater ease than its owner who felt obliged to follow as fast as he could. I am not too bad on the flat, but I am not built for gradients, and I have walked up shallower staircases. A few minutes later, having had to ask the whereabouts of the 2nd tee, hit two balls across the lane from it (this is required), lost them both (not required), I stopped hyperventilating and found myself on the 3rd tee, a 190 yard par three, looking out to sea to the left, and also out to sea to the right, with a strip of land about 20 yards wide offering a home to a green which was not so much sunken as quarried. My second ball found it (I did not see the first land, but if it got a good bounce, it may have reached the sea to the left). The green is actually surrounded with mounds, is pear-shaped, and a mere 17 paces along its longest dimension.

After three holes, my game was also pear-shaped, but there are more things to a round of golf than the score, and some of them were here – namely magnificent views in both directions of Whitsand Bay, with its sandy beaches and standing rocks and craggy cliffs, and points east. My OS map subsequently indicated we were about 200 feet above sea level at this point. Amazingly, there was space on the seaward side of this green for another tee, for a 300 yard uphill par four. Again I was hurried, as a man and a small boy asked me to play through, and I was a little confused by an apparent choice of tees for the 5th hole.

I chose the right one. The South West Coast Path follows the "edge" of England fairly faithfully whenever it can. Here, you use it to walk from the tee to the fairway. The teeing ground itself is between the path and the cliff edge. This hole too is uphill, with the land rising to 280 feet. I enjoyed the views, but remained confused by the alternative tees – confusion is a feature of navigating one's way as a lone player around a strange course – until I finally noticed a small green between the fairway and the cliff edge. At a point when vertigo sufferers would already have left the course, the designer had squeezed in a modest 190 yard par three, by virtue of having excavated the cliff to a depth of about 15 feet to reach the horizontal for his green. This was the only horizontal bit of the hole. I played it from the white tee, back towards whence I had come, and I would say that in any serious westerly wind – ie about every other day – it is broadly impossible. Indeed, broadly is not exactly the word for it – it is narrowly, slopingly, impossible. I felt that a step in the wrong direction on the tee could have proved fatal, but that was before I spotted the ladies' tee. OK, it is "only" 143 yards, but it is several feet lower, and (you've guessed it) between what passes for the men's fairway, and the cliff edge. It could easily be lower than the green. You may not even be able to see the green, just the top of the flag. I might have gone to check, but I needed to keep moving, honestly.

This explained the other teeing ground (although one could easily play the wrong one in bad weather say) which is the 7th, a 400 yard par four yet again uphill, but slightly inland, and although pretty good views remain in sight for the rest of the round, the course thenceforth loses its brilliance. The golf was a little idiosyncratic perhaps, but the first six holes were, first literally, then figuratively, quite breathtaking.

In fact there are three par fives in the next four holes down, back up, and again down this sloping cliff top. At the summit, there is the 150 yard, par three, 10th where my 6 iron appeared to pitch on the green, bounce like a tennis ball, and bounce again even higher a second time. A second ball hit with a 9 iron bounced short, but had still run through the green when I reached it. Here you can see inland, with views of the St Germans river and what I imagine must be Dartmoor beyond, though if your ball like mine has just bounced off the course and onto a road running behind it, you are not too bothered about whether it is Dartmoor in the distance or the Himalayas. I tried the revised pitch-it-short technique at the short 12th hole. The 9 iron left me 15 yards to the front of the green!

The course crosses back over the lane to the side where it started, and it is rather these holes which are the afterthought, so to speak, being played across side slopes, with "terraced" greens. Finally, what goes up must come down, and Whitsand Bay Hotel Golf Club conforms to this adage in spectacular fashion with its 199 yard 18th hole, though whether that yardage is of the base of the imaginary triangle through the earth or its hypotenuse through the air, it does not say. You do have to ring a bell *before* playing, something unique in my experience, and guaranteed to mean absolutely nothing to a first time visitor down below. As for what club to use, I cannot say. The one I chose sent a first ball left, and over the lane into the nether regions of the land below the 3rd hole (which looks even more unlikely in side elevation), and a second one aimed absolutely straight at the hole high into the air until it came down somewhere I didn't see. I looked in the hole. It would have been a spectacular par three finish. It wasn't there, of course.

Cornwall has a number of resort hotels and courses, some fairly modern, some older. Given its topography, that is no surprise, but there are only three inland courses which date from before World War 2. Perhaps it was like Spain is today, with golf primarily as a tourist attraction rather than a pastime for locals. Being a golfing resident at a resort is fine, but if one is not, the following is a reason for preferring visits to members' clubs.

CARLYON BAY

According to my map, "Carlyon" is part of St Austell Bay, an area of Cornwall which, when Mother Nature doled out her generous helpings of attractive coastline, rather missed the boat – if those metaphors may be mixed. At Carlyon Bay there are low level "cliffettes", ten to thirty feet high, sporting scrubby growth like a teenage beard, and somewhat silty-looking sand on the beach.

I had been looking forward to this visit for the fanciful reason that it represented my best ever chance of going round a golf course under par. That should read "under Par" for, again according to my map, in the same way that Barton is under Needwood and Ashton under Lyne, Carlyon Bay Hotel & Golf Course is under (the town of) Par. I have to admit to disappointment; OK, the scoring – above par – was to be expected, but also the experience was not the greatest. If you have visited the St Austell area – if not for golf, then to see the Eden Project – you will know that if nature was unkind to it, man has been positively brutal. Unless you like docks and heavy industry, Par is a serious mess. True, after following the docks for half a mile, you do catch a glimpse of the end of the golf course, as you pass alongside the mineral processing plant, thence past the euphemistically named waste water processing plant and the unnamed construction site, under the main Penzance to England railway line (via a tunnel which you subsequently use again while out on the course), and into an area which seems to be the edge of a large private estate, where you find this commercial venture. I did not visit the hotel, but there is a modern clubhouse reminiscent of those found in courses abroad – ie primarily designed for taking your money, with good bars, and his'n'hers' pro shops.

The course stretches out along the "clifftop" but that is about the limit to its seaside nature. In an early, abandoned version of this text, I wrote that I had reached all the par fives in two. I think that unlikely, but I do remember the 2nd hole, because I reached the back of the green in two – and the flag was on the front. At the 10th, I reversed the process, reaching the front with the flag at the back. Both times I took three putts, because the greens were exceptionally tricky, with hidden contours making it difficult to get the ball close to the hole. There is an old saying that the way to get really subtle greens is to hire a bunch of Irish labourers, take them to the pub, and stress that you want the greens to be perfectly flat.[13] Considerable care was taken in the construction of the course, but possibly the pressure of operating as a commercial venture has prevented the same level of care being maintained...

During this round, I enjoyed what seemed like extensive conversations with the people playing behind me, because the fourball in front had no intention of waving me, or anyone, through. This was the opinion of the twoball behind, who kept arriving on the tee while I was still waiting to play, and their annoyance at the people in front was seemingly on my behalf, which was rather charming. We discussed my joining them, but as they were playing from the whites, but hitting the ball nearer to the green than me (this on a course where I reached two par fives in two!) and playing match play, we decided against it. I invited them to play through, but they declined, on the grounds that if the group ahead would not call me through, it would not call them. I am not so sure this would have been the case, but it was chivalrous of them. Have you noticed how – broadly speaking, of course – the better golfers are, the more time they have for other players? The guys behind me were seriously good.

Overall, I did not enjoy the experience. However nice the guys behind seemed, when my time finally came to play, I sensed a need to

---

[13] These days, this kind of statement is of course politically incorrect. Rather than apologise, I will compound the offence by observing that, were they English labourers, you would also have to specify that you wanted the turfs laid "green side up".

hurry, exactly the opposite of the way to cope with slow play – to play slowly oneself.

One thing I learned is that while it is a good idea in principle to visit courses which welcome holidaymakers, in practice it is a bad idea when they welcome them indiscriminately, if one intends to play alone and enjoy oneself. It is OK being resident at a place to find quiet times to play, but on flying visits the chances of enjoying the "freedom of the course" are much greater in winter (weekends excepted) when the limited hours of daylight are more than compensated for by the limited numbers of golfers who take five hours over a round. Having said this, I realise that if this were Spain, my only chance of playing at all would probably involve joining up with a mixed threeball riding buggies, possibly from some Nordic country – but this is not Spain. In case we need reminding, it is England.

Gradually, I have accumulated a set of "rules" for playing alone, which I present here for anyone thinking of golfing their way single-handedly from John O'Groats to Land's End.

RULES FOR PLAYING ALONE

The fundamental rule of golf is to "play the ball as it lies" with subsequent rules being derived using the principle of equity. The fundamental rule of playing alone is "look as if you know what you are doing". Subsequent rules are derived from the principle of Equity, as in the actors' union – ie, if you don't know what you are doing, nevertheless act as if you do.

In fact, this first rule used to be expressed more succinctly as "do not look a prat", but modern sports psychologists say we should avoid negative thoughts. I tried this for a while, with a personal mantra of "whatever you do, do NOT allow a negative thought into your head". It did not work. Express this principle in your own words, and with it firmly in mind:

1. Try and pick a time to play when the course is quiet.

At your home club, you know when this is. When visiting, ask ahead of time in the pro shop. In my experience, no one minds lone players, even though technically they have no standing on the course, but being "sandwiched" is horrible. Remember that with solid fourballs up ahead, you run this risk even if it is quiet when you tee off as faster people my come up behind you.

2.   Find your way around the course intelligently.

If you usually depend upon your playing partners to tell you where to go, you will have to become self-reliant. This involves *using your eyes* to identify visual clues, incorporating any assistance available such as maps, signposts, etc. If you can, work out where the next tee is before you get to a green, so you can leave your bag somewhere handy. Look at other bits of the course as you pass them, so they will be less of a surprise when you play them.

3.   If in any doubt, hit another shot.

You have no-one to help spot your ball, so if you don't see where a shot goes, or where it finishes, hit another one. This will help you with the distance, so at least you have some idea where to look for the first. It is up to you and the circumstances as to whether you search for the first ball. Whatever you do, do not wave anyone through. You will look like a prat. If the first ball is not available, you decide whether it counts or not (see rule 4).

4.   Try not to cheat.

If you want to play a practice round where you can repeat bad shots, do so – but do not count the score on a kind of personal scramble basis. Otherwise, play according to the rules of golf. Decide in advance if you are going to have gimmes, and what criteria you will use. The usual is "inside the steel", i.e. shorter than the length of the putter minus the grip.

5.   Do as I say, not as I do.

It makes little difference if you do cheat, because no-one will believe you anyway, but *you will know*.

6.   Be prepared to be called through.

This is quite a complicated rule, as it represents the situation where the fundamental principle is most exposed to scrutiny.

      6.1   Unless it is chock-a-block ahead, do not decline an invitation to play through. Your hosts will think you are a prat. If you do not want to be called through, do not catch up with the group ahead. Play a practice round, or pretend to gather blackberries.

6.2 Assume you will be invited through, as most times you will be. Do not think too many unkind thoughts about the people ahead if they do not appear to have it in mind to issue the invitation, in case they then do so.

6.3 You are most likely to be invited to play a tee shot. This is great, because you do not have to play the ball as it lies. Because you should be ready, you can take your time while appearing to play quickly. Few things are more annoying than someone who dawdles through.

6.4 Remember to take aim. This is the most important shot of the round.

6.5 If you should happen to hit a rank bad shot, do not be tempted to play another ball. Get your bag and walk forward in the direction of the next tee. Shout out something like, 'Thanks. Put me down for a double bogey'.

6.6 If you hit a moderate shot, decide before you get to the ball whether you want to play it or pick up. If it is for example a long putt, which is basically a hiding to nothing, say something like, 'Will you give me two from there?' and pick up.

6.7 If you hit a good shot, make sure the next one is good as well. There is no finer feeling than playing really well in front of an audience. If you make par, or better still birdie, make sure to wave your thanks extravagantly.

3

DESIGNED BY JAMES BRAID

Meeting strangers on golf courses, it is a common occurrence to be asked what brings you to their course. On hearing of my tour of the south-west coastline, my two non-playing companions at Carlyon Bay singled out Perranporth as somewhere to enjoy, adding that it was designed by James Braid.

This name rang a bell. For some years, I used to visit south-west Scotland, and of all the courses I have played in the Galloway Region, and I have played most of them, my favourite is Stranraer – designed by James Braid. Indeed, the 18th hole is called "Braid's Last", which I understood to refer not merely to the last hole at Stranraer, but the very last hole JB worked on anywhere.

Unless you are taking a ferry to Northern Ireland, you are unlikely to come across Stranraer GC by accident. It is on the shores of Loch Ryan, sheltered from the ravages of westerly winds, and there is something very appealing about the way the course has been laid out to make best use of the natural features of the terrain, including frequent changes in the direction of play, use of slopes, and the hazards created by the burn and some spinneys. On hole number three you have to decide whether to hit over the tree-lined burn, or lay up. It runs diagonally, at about 30 degrees to the line of the hole. All the holes have names; this one is actually called *Bluidy Burn*.

If all this rang a bell for me, I then proceeded to drop a clanger when I recalled that Sherborne was designed by James Braid. I am of course a member at Sherborne. There is a similar theme reflected in how the northern part of Sherborne is laid out, where the holes will fit, on the northern and western sides of a hill. It gives rise to some odd stances, which is not to everyone's liking.

I wondered how much of a coincidence this appearance of Braid's name was, so using my "bible" – *The Royal & Ancient Golfer's Handbook* – I looked at who had designed which courses. Not every course lists a designer – Burnham & Berrow prefers to describe itself as having evolved, for example – but without going into the history, the name of the designer voluntarily listed by the management of each course would be the one to use. This is despite some apparent discrepancies over dates. Sherborne was founded in 1894, when Braid was in golfing terms still in nappies, age 24. Stranraer was founded in 1905, so if it was his last work, how does one explain Perranporth, founded in 1927? No doubt the explanations would emerge in due course.

Meanwhile, the interesting discovery was that of the eighty[14] or so courses in my littoral peregrination, Braid was listed as having designed no fewer than twelve of them, including St Enodoc as well as Perranporth.[15] I thought this impressive, until I worked my way through the listings for the whole of England, and came up with a total of 109! Well, he did live to be 80, but up until the outbreak of the first World War, at which time he was 44, he was busy winning the Open five times, when he was not coming second or third to Harry Vardon or J H Taylor.

These other two members of "The Great Triumvirate" did not stay at home all the time either. Vardon is credited with thirteen English courses, and Taylor possibly thirty. (I think there may have been another designer of the same surname, so there is doubt.)

Obviously, Braid did not originate most of these courses, although he might have done so at Perranporth, given the date, and it would have taken someone with considerable imagination even to think of creating a golf course on the land. Possibly, he may have been involved when clubs moved to new land, or acquired more. I fancy this did not happen too often, if at all, with coastal courses however; having visited them, it is fairly clear that they are on the best available land for golf, and generally this is the worst land for any other purpose, classically so when it is linksland. In Skegness, they did not have quite enough linksland, so Braid improvised.

---

[14] This number became oddly subject to minor changes as time elapsed. Road atlases are not the perfect indicator of whether a golf course is literally next to the sea.

[15] See Index of Courses Visited for details of course designers.

NORTH SHORE

The North Shore Hotel and Golf Course are found in the northern part of Skegness in Lincolnshire, between the Mablethorpe road and the sea. The part of the course that is visible from the road looks green, flat and extremely lush. This is because apart from the odd obviously man-made mound, the land is level, and it is indeed lush. This is the sort of soil that produces fields of Brussels sprouts in profusion, so it is not surprising that grass grows well. I believe that if it rains after they have cut the fairways, they play winter rules to allow the removal of grass clippings that adhere to balls. You cannot see the sea from this part, because there is a large natural mound or ridge which runs the length of the course. The hotel is located on this mound, so the 1st hole, a par five, is gently downhill. Otherwise it is straight and flat. From the green, the 2nd tee, unlike the 8th, 13th, and 17th tees, as well as the 7th and 12th greens, is nowhere to be seen. The map on the card is indispensable, and even then it is confusing because the number of the hole is shown in a green circle, in microscopic type, representing the green and not the tee of the hole. So far, if Braid were being marked for technical merit and artistic interpretation, he would lose point one for each.

At hole 2, you drive across a not very intimidating unnatural mound-like ridge. On closer inspection, this turns out to be a sort of excavated footpath to the beach. If it is intended as a safety measure, I am not convinced of its efficacy. A "runner" – a bounding mishit – off the tee, normally no real threat to mankind, could easily fly up this ridge and take someone's teeth out. From the green, it looks like the next hole is a blind par three, but on (eventual) arrival at the tee, there is a gap between two small hillocks, and the green is in full view. We have rapidly reached the far end of the course, and so the 4th hole turns back towards the clubhouse and immediately looks more seasidey. The big natural mound, covered with rough, runs the length of the left hand side. I passed some people searching for a ball playing the other way, but in my rough; they were at least thirty yards off line, yet one of them was insisting it should be easy to find. One of the others was clearly not amused, and it did not seem to occur to any of them that they were in my way. Some people! I tried to keep a low profile as I passed; they were playing ahead of me. The next hole, number 5, stroke index 1, reverses direction again and plays on the other side of the big mound, with only a few yards of rough between the right edge of the fairway and the beach. This is a good hole; the tee is elevated by the mound so you can see the green, but a sort of carbuncle protrudes into the fairway over which you may have to play your second shot blind. With the wind against and off the sea, fearful of the beach, I hooked my tee shot over the mound (the big long mound, not the carbuncle). I played another, and appeared to push it onto the beach, but as I walked forward, there seemed to be something that looked like a ball in the middle of the fairway. Was the wind strong enough to have blown it back?

The answer was no; it looked like a ball, but it was a mushroom. There was another up ahead. I saw a ball on the beach. It could have been my second. I don't think it was a mushroom. Mushrooms don't grow on tidal patches of sand. I clambered up onto the mound on the other side of the fairway. There was a ball, a long way over, on the other side of the 4th, which I had just played. Could it be mine? It was a long, long way over, but I suppose that a hooking ball with wind assistance might have made it there. Or it could be a mushroom, though it did look like a ball? I had a trolley which wouldn't traverse the mound easily, it was raining, and I didn't fancy walking over there to find it was my ball, and then having to walk back for a club, so I grabbed a 3 wood, and set off, head down. When I looked up, there were two balls (or mushrooms) in view. What was happening? Eventually, it dawned. This was another fairway, sharing land with the 4th. (The 15th, in fact, with an invisible tee.) These were other people's drives. Obviously. Remembering the maxim that a lone player should always look as if he knows what he is doing, I nevertheless walked up to each ball and checked the markings. As I did, players emerged onto the fairway. 'Some people!' – they may have said.

After the 5th hole, the 6th plays at right angles, back inland. It is a short par four, only 255 yards off the yellows, downhill, tempting despite trees on the right and bunkers, and it reveals the nature of the big mound. Depending on how you wish to look at it, either there is one mound which has two ridges – a major, higher ridge on the seaward side, and a minor, lower ridge inland – or it is two mounds separated by a valley. Either way, Braid makes good use of it for the back nine. Numbers 7 and 8 however are on the flat part of the course near the road. If 7, a par five, had a name, I would call it "Frog Eye" as it features a pop-up bunker near the green (basically, a small pimply mound with the front excavated and filled with sand). Number 8 doglegs round the tree-lined edge of the course, and then number 9 plays back to an excavated green near the clubhouse. Again tempting, only 251 yards from the whites. I didn't make it, but made sure I cleared the front bunkers with my pitch...Aargh, there's a bunker at the back as well!

If you have got a mental picture of the role of the mounds or ridges (and if not, you may well have stopped reading by now), I can explain how hole Number 10 makes a fine 400 yard par four along the valley between the major mound and the shore. Number 11 is a par three from the major mound over the minor mound to a green beyond, and 12 another short par four (281 yards from yellows) into the confusing flat part near the 1st green, 8th tee etc. Number 13 reverses direction with a shortish par where the second shot is played blind over both mounds (long hitters need to lay up from the tee to stay on the fairway), and then 14 is a par three played from a tee in the major mound to a green in the minor mound. Number 15 goes out (as you know by now) sharing a wide fairway with the 4th, quite some challenge into the wind. Number 16 comes back again, with a tee in the minor mound playing diagonally to a flat fairway with the excavation I mentioned several pages ago running an awkward distance in front of the green, and then possibly the piece de resistance is a sharp dogleg left, only 349 yards (whites) with a semi-blind shot to a basin green nestling between the mounds. Finally, number 18 tees up on the major mound for a closing valley fairway – only 260 yards from the yellows – and, with the wind behind, and whether you have taken three on the last or an equally probable six, it really invites you to welly it.

At first you might think that the great James Braid had designed a somewhat monotonous course, with only two par fives and three par threes, but at the time he worked, the concept of par was yet to come. Using the white tee yardages, he has produced a layout with three holes between 140 and 190 yards, four in the range 250–320, another four less than 400, four more between 400 and 430, and three over 470. And, though I won't go into detail, I suspect the longer ones play up and downwind, with the shorter ones having crosswinds. As for number 18, I like it. If it had a name, I would call it "Home James"!

Whenever Braid worked on a course, he did not arrive with a fleet of bulldozers. He used the land that was available to him, and to my mind there is something natural and hence essentially fair about the courses even if, and notably so at Perranporth, there are blind shots involved. If you do not like playing blind shots, steer clear of James Braid's seaside courses – but also remember that at the time he worked, it was customary to play with a caddie, who would have known every inch of the course whether it was in view or not.

This perspective contrasts rather sadly with the work of contemporary designers such as Robert Trent Jones, who appear to work on the assumption that it is customary, or even obligatory, to play with a buggy, or cart, as he would call it. With no limit to how far apart holes need to be placed – there is a Trent Jones course near Biarritz where there is sometimes a walk of 400 metres from the green to the next tee – and no limit, other than financial, to how much earth may be moved, the relationship between golf course and terrain is lost. There is a course somewhere in the US made of eighteen "famous" holes, each copied from another location around the world. Just imagine if you could "design" yourself a spouse in a similar manner – or less fancifully, a house. We play golf one hole at a time, just as we occupy one room at a time, but to make a proper house, the rooms must be coherent, they have to fit together. So must the holes on a golf course.

For further diatribe against "modern" course design from a more authoritative source, see five-time Open Champion Peter Thomson's foreword to *Classic Golf Links of Great Britain and Ireland*.[16] Not that Braid confined himself to linksland.

WALMER & KINGSDOWN

No doubt because my visit was in the week following the 2005 General Election, it struck me that Walmer & Kingsdown sounds very much like a parliamentary constituency. If it were, the winning candidate would be returned by a "hillside". I had idly supposed that, being one of four clubs on the eastern coast of Kent between Dover and Ramsgate, Walmer & Kingsdown Golf Club would resemble its linksland neighbours at Sandwich. I got a hint of the difference from the directions in the *R & A Handbook* – "on the cliff top south of Deal". And indeed, on the cliff top it is, and also the cliff bottom, side and back. I presume that the cliff in question is a Dover White, but of course, I did not see the front of it, if that is the part which faces out to sea. I can tell you that from the back, it is formed by an escarpment, with the land rising not so gently towards the sea, and the cliff top itself varying in height above sea level. In America and elsewhere, courses have something called

---

[16] By Donald Steel, Chapmans 1992.

a slope rating, which is supposed to measure their relative difficulty. If there was a slope rating which measured the extent of the slopes on a course, Walmer & Kingsdown might well be world champion.

For reasons which will shortly become clear, it is impossible ever to identify a golf course as "trademark James Braid", but if his intention was always to use the land as it lay rather than adjust the landscape to accommodate his personal style, then he was true to his ideals here. The problem he had was finding sufficient flattish areas for the greens. Often, the solution is to build plateaux, but here, the major-ity are chiselled out of the fairways. I doubt that the word "chiselled" appears in the modern – or even the ancient – golf architects' glossary, but if you imagine sliding a blade horizontally into a wooden wedge (or a spade into the side of a grassy bank) and removing it vertically, there would be left behind a roughly flat, roughly square area, edged on two adjacent sides by a roughly vertical bank. This is a fair descrip-tion of most of the greens at W & K – small, squarish, flattish, and chiselled...

Which makes the golf fun, because you have to decide whether you want your ball to pitch on one of them, or to pitch short and bounce or trickle over one of the banks, or even to hit a bank and bounce sideways. Then, when you have decided this, you have to execute the shot. To get to this position, you have first had to drive up, down, across, through, over and round some very attractive, sloping fairways with a fair smattering of copses and shrubberies (for a cliff top course, there is a surprising amount of thriving tree life; this is not the bleak landscape of Royal St George's). Unfortunately, I cannot tell you what happens if you drive badly, because I didn't (what a shame!), but it is when you reach your ball that the fun really starts. When you thin your third consecutive pitch-and-run on a short par four after a good drive, you finally realise that you are doing it because the ground behind the ball is higher than the ground in front of it. Then, on a longer hole, you calculate that the extra club you need because you are playing uphill will be offset by following wind (there is, inevitably, a wind). Only afterwards do you work out that your 7 iron came up short because the sloping lie turned it into a 9 iron. There is a certain respite on hole number nine, a fairly flat, straight par five. Then, when you think you may have "regrouped" ready for the back nine, JB takes you along the *side of the back* of the escarpment, as it were, and the ball is some inches above, or perhaps below your feet. I fancy he knew what he was doing.

I have seen enough of life to know that it is not fair, that first-past-the-post electoral systems laugh in the face of democracy, and that there is no such thing as a free lunch or a level playing field, and I can tell you something. I bet the representative teams of Walmer & Kingsdown Golf Club do not lose many home matches.

I have occasionally participated in the Drambuie Scottish Golf Classics, four-day handicap Stableford competitions held over four different courses, which are tremendous value and, depending on the weather, fun. The Highland Classic is based around Royal Dornoch, and at nearby Brora I discovered the existence of the James Braid Golfing Society. This is a group of like-minded people dedicated to preserving the spirit of the game played by James Braid. Membership is by invitation only. If I may, I will quote from the Society's web site:

The James Braid Golfing Society exists not to try to save wayward golfing souls or bring the forces of reaction to bear on what some see as the threat of deteriorating standards. What it does seek to do is preserve the values and dignity that James Braid himself brought to this noble game in the eighty years of his life, and by so doing, at least attempts to give a lead by example.

I was told by the Society's Secretary that JB only spent half a day at Brora, in which case his journey would have taken him longer than his assignment (unless he was on a tour of Scottish coastal golf courses – now there's a thought). Records of Sherborne Golf Club were destroyed in a clubhouse fire, so it is not known exactly what work James Braid did, but he certainly visited more than once. There are some pages from the *Sherborne Post* on display today in the clubhouse, all from 1936. The 26th February issue announces Braid's impending final inspection, the construction work having been carried out by the "well-known firm" of J R Stutt from Paisley. Well known to whom, one wonders? The visit is subsequently reported in the March 4th issue with a photograph. He is wearing a trilby hat,[17] a tweed jacket with all three buttons fastened, and swinging a club.

The issue of the 8th July covers another Braid visit, this time for an exhibition match between JB and Meredith Thomas, a Sherborne amateur, against Ernest Whitcombe, a Somerset professional, partnered by the Hon Sec of the Dorset County Union. Ernest was the eldest of three brothers, all of whom played in the 1935 Ryder Cup in Ridgewood, New Jersey. At the time of this match, he was 46, twenty years junior to Braid. The match is reported hole by hole, and includes a note of cheering from the onlookers when Braid finds one of his "own" obviously controversial bunkers on the 7th hole. He nevertheless makes his "bogey" (my quotes), a term which equates to "par" in England at this time. The reporter also employs the terms "birdie" and "eagle", but puts them in inverted commas himself. What is of particular interest in these days of talk of restricted balls and banned drivers is that on the 292 yard 8th hole, Whitcombe's tee shot finished in a greenside bunker. Hit, no doubt, while he was wearing a buttoned-up tweed jacket.

As I have mentioned, Sherborne golf course is on the top of a hill. Meanwhile, back at sea level:

WARREN

WARREN GOLF CLUB
18 HOLES SEA TURF

is the legend inscribed in six foot high letters on the roof of a large green corrugated iron shed. The advertisement is for the benefit of passengers whose train has stopped at Dawlish Warren station, the excitement of whose journey is about to be enhanced as the line will shortly turn to the right to run along the seashore. (Unless they disembark to play, of course.) The station is literally adjacent to the golf course, so much so that one bank of the sunken 18th green is actually its retaining wall. To reach the course, one passes through a small tunnel underneath the embankment and turns sharp left. The path to the course passes between the 1st tee on the right and the 18th green. The shed was once the clubhouse, perhaps, as it is sensibly placed to the right of the 1st fairway. The "modern" clubhouse, with its car park protected by high fences, is rather less sensibly positioned, since it turns the 18th hole into a sort of chicane. But in truth, there is probably nowhere else to put it.

The fairway of the short par four 1st hole is a wide expanse of bobbly land – the term "sea turf" comes to mind – and in late June it is pretty parched. This means that a drive down the left to leave a short

---

[17] It isn't a trilby, but you know what I mean.

lob from a tight lie over a half hidden bunker is not a good experience early in the round. There is a walk back to the 2nd tee, set among some tall bushes, to a fairway lined with gorse on the left and out of bounds in the scrub between the course and the dunes of the shoreline. More bobbly sea turf. The par three 3rd has a similar set-back tee, and another set of bunkers lurks up by the green, which typically emerges naturally from the surrounding ground. The bobbliness is just smoothed out to produce attractive borrows on true surfaces.

There is a small observation platform by the 4th tee to which is attached a notice reading thus: "Please ring bell before playing to alert players on or near 9th green". If you did that with some of the players I know, you would have to spell "alert" e-n-r-a-g-e. It might be the same here; there is no sign of a bell. Holes continue along the dune side of the course until at the 6th green, one can hear the roar of the sea. The line of dunes is quite close by now, and I pop up to have a look at an expanse of sandy beach with remarkably small waves for the noise they generate. On the opposite side of the course is the estuary of the River Exe, while ahead of us, and getting closer throughout the journey so far is the town of Exmouth, on the opposite bank of the river.

This is as close as we get, and there is a hook-shaped end to the promontory creating a small bay, too narrow to provide any more golfing land. The bay provides an opportunity for a dogleg, or rather a sickle-shaped 7th hole. My deliberate fade slices a little, and ends up on the bank, just inside some red stakes. I am lucky; my ball is in play, and this is a literally littoral lateral water hazard. It seems natural for the course to play back towards the dunes with a long par three, and then the 9th hole, the longest of the par thirty-three outward half, turns back towards the clubhouse, playing alongside the 4th fairway. There is not so much a lurking as a downright hidden bunker beyond a mound which I find off the tee. When eventually I reach the green, no-one sounds a bell.

The 10th, the longest hole so far, continues back homewards towards the 1st green, which is as close to home as it can get, as there is barely room for the 1st and the 18th holes in the final section of the course. Design-wise, I tolerate the fact that this 434 yard hole follows the 424 yard 9th into the prevailing wind on the grounds that (a) they are on separate halves of the course, and (b) my second shot swerves round a bunker in best wing three-quarter style and leaves me a 10 yard chip which I hole. Stroke index 1 birdies are rare animals.

I am not sure that I approve aesthetically of what happens next. Number 11 turns back towards Exmouth, followed by number 12, and both are par fives. Off the yellows, the first eight holes measure 2164 yards, the next four measure 1761, and the final six 1619. I wonder if these four big ones are known as the "something" mile? I don't think the word would be "Royal". But the scheme certainly works in terms of using the available land, the nature of which has changed by the time we get to the 12th green, and the lurking bunkers have been replaced by small water hazards. We are back near the 8th green, so it is natural to include another short hole back towards the estuary and its salt marsh. The grass here is much greener, and the finishing sequence is a series of holes played from set-back tees to maximise the available length, which is not great. They play a little left to right, and local knowledge of club selection depending upon wind strength and direction may be a decisive factor in scoring well. Although there is lots of evidence of "civilisation" with the boats moored in the estuary and the views of Exmouth, this is a very natural place to be – until reaching the 18th tee, where a series of portacabins announces the view from the other side of the clubhouse, just about the most unnatural hazard one could imagine. Playing in, I wondered if one should hit into the wall or the net above the 18th green, but the golf course is only 30 yards wide at its very end, so you would probably bounce out of bounds.

"18 holes, sea turf" or perhaps James Braid's motto was "See turf – 18 holes". Given the available land, a design triumph, and right next to the railway station. A little unbalanced perhaps, but genius often is.

Another Drambuie Classic event I played was in Ayrshire,[18] the closest I was likely to get to Stranraer short of needing to take a ferry to Larne, so I dropped by, played the course, failed for the umpteenth time to par or even bogey the 17th hole, and also acquired a history of the course. Sure enough, the course was designed by JB in his final, 80th year, he having been tempted out of retirement to reposition Stranraer GC as the disruption caused by the Second World War was cleared up.

It is quite remarkable that Bernard Darwin wrote a biography of JB which does not appear to mention Braid's design work, considering that he kept at it for so many years. Indeed, is he the world's most prolific course designer?

---

[18] On the Ailsa course at Turnberry which hosts the Open, playing from the members' back tees, I parred all four par threes, but no other holes, and thus produced a card without a single four on it.

There is an easy way to pose such unlikely questions these days: type the phrase into Google. I did. In the UK, there were references to the possibility of the famous landscape gardener Capability Brown qualifying for the title, because one in seven of the grounds he shaped in Yorkshire now has a golf course. A way to go, I think! The US name that cropped up most was in fact Pete Dye. I wondered exactly how many he could claim, but the web site www.petedye.com was still under construction! Probably, the designers are having difficulty deciding where to put the cart paths.

How many does Dye have to beat, anyway? How significant is hole number 18 at Stranraer, aka "Braid's Last"? I turned again to my *R & A Handbook*, and while I was at it, decided to look for the work of the Great Triumvirate. Braid was a Scotsman, so one would expect him to have worked in his native land. J H Taylor was an Englishman, so perhaps unwelcome in Scotland, or perhaps he did not care for the climate. Either way, he designed no courses there. Vardon, from Jersey, did – but only two. He also has three credits in Wales. In addition to 109 courses in England, Braid has 13 in Wales, 6 in Ireland, and at least 77 in Scotland – a grand total of 205. Eat your heart out, Pete Dye.[19]

In Edinburgh, there is a public course dating from 1893, called Braid Hills. The designers are listed as Ferguson & McEwan. Never heard of them. Besides, sometimes, it does not matter who designed the course...

KNOTT END

Talking of in-laws, I had been looking forward to playing Knott End Golf Club, as it is where Neff's Granny (Neff is a son of Celia's sister, and this was the granny who was not my mother-in-law) used to play. That story goes that after leaving school, she had wanted to work, but her parents – strict if generous – considered such an idea infra dig. So, she took up golf

---

[19] Actually, I heard a comment during The Open that Jack Nicklaus has designed over 300 courses worldwide, so we need to make allowances for the differences in conditions. Nicklaus and Dye might technically boast more courses than Braid, but I bet they haven't done it all in person travelling by train.

instead, and became club champion and a regular with Lancashire Ladies. Quite some feat at five feet nothing.

As it happens, this trip was with Harrison, my golfing nephew from the other side of my family (and therefore even less related to Neff's Granny than me, if that is possible). The weather had worsened overnight, and it was blowing mightily in Fleetwood where we were staying. Our hotel was only about a decent par five from the Knott End Clubhouse, but the Wyre estuary intervened. So we had to drive south to a place called Thornton (or perhaps it was Cleveleys[20]) to cross the river. The quite heavily built-up surroundings on this peninsula north of Blackpool masked the true extent of the weather, but it asserted itself with a vengeance in the car park of the golf club, as spray came over the wall to greet us. We mistook this for breaking waves, but it was just the wind whipping up the estuary. I contemplated a rule change (estuary, not sea, but amongst other effects, that would have ruled out St Enodoc) – anyway we had come to play, so what the hell... That is a special feature of a golf holiday – sometimes when you would not dream of going to your local club and playing for nothing, you pay money to play whatever the weather. When I was little, my dad used to have the same approach to seaside holidays. We spent some weird days on the beach.

Unfortunately, we got out just after a fourball, and I dreaded the thought of being stuck behind them in such conditions. "Keep playing" is the maxim in bad weather, to which should be added "Keep your grips dry". In other words, do NOT – as some meticulous players tend to do – take "extra care" in setting up and practice swinging. Hit the f—ing thing before your hands, gloves and grips get soaked.

We need not have worried about the fourball. As they left the 1st green, there was a sort of cloudburst – only the rain was mostly horizontal – and they quickly left the course. As indeed did everyone except Harrison and me. We had started, so we would finish – but we had to shelter for a few minutes behind a rather inadequate clump of bushes. For a while the rain might have extinguished hell.

When it abated, we tried to play the 2nd hole, 216 yards directly towards the shore, and directly into the wind. It was difficult, because the shot needed a driver, and the ball was simply blown off the tee peg before we could hit it. The course layout was across undulating parkland, and probably quite interesting, but the wind was across all

---

[20] It seems the town formerly known as "Thornton Cleveleys" is in fact two places.

the time, and it was impossible to hit the ball straight. (There was in fact only one downwind hole on the course – number 17, 306 yards. I drove close and birdied it. Harrison, now tired as even fit but occasional golfers become, skied one into a field. I gave him a mulligan. He topped it.)

There were some inexplicable changes to the sequence in which the holes were to be played. The sequence on the card actually reads 1,2,3,7,6,4,5,8,9,15,14,10,11,12,13,16,17,18. Now, many times in my life I have been thought stupid by someone who did not understand the perfectly sensible reason behind my actions, but can there be a serious explanation for (a) playing the holes in the wrong order, and (b) printing scorecards to reflect this sequence, when the alternative would be to *re-number the holes* and play in the same sequence as they do in St Andrew's and everywhere else in the world? While it meant nothing whatever to us as first time visitors what order we played the holes in, the evidence helped us realise that we could skip a couple of tough ones by the shore, and get sooner over the brow of a hill, to a more sheltered – no, sorry, that should read less exposed – area. The conditions there were merely extremely challenging. One hole does not really start unless you can first drive to a diagonal fairway across a track. We couldn't.

By the time we rejoined the windward side of the course, there was bright sunshine, and it was infested with fair-weather golfers, so we could not as planned pick up the pair of holes we had missed. Only sixteen holes, then. Sorry, Neff's Granny.

Did you understand the throwaway comment about the impossibility of identifying "trademark James Braid"? With so many in his portfolio, there could never be a single style. I fancy that if people showed him their land, and asked him for a golf course, he gave them one. With Braid, what you get is what you see – unless it's over a hill, when you get a marker post.

4

AWA' THE LADS

The first "official expedition" after I decided to extend my peregrination in fact took place with Neff, my nephew with the golfing granny, no relation to Harrison. It was to the furthest destination, Northumberland. As we drove into Alnmouth, we got our first glimpse of the sea. It was very calm, and the same colour as the road, which was wet from the rain. We headed straight for the golf course, which was not necessarily a straightforward thing to do, as the positioning of the blue flags in my *AA Easy Read Britain (Giant Scale)* is somewhat approximate. Either that, or Neff, who was using it, took after his aunt, my late wife, in being a less than brilliant navigator.

The road we took actually went through a golf course, which is sheltered from the sea behind high dunes. We passed a man waiting to play two balls, reached the beach, turned round, and passed him again. He had only played one of them. This turned out to be Alnmouth Village Golf Club, and although it dates from 1869 and is clearly littoral, we were not scheduled to play it, because it is only nine holes. (Perhaps the man with two balls was economising on walking, but staying away from home for the requisite time of a full round. Golf helps keep some people out of the house.)

Neff is a rugby player, a second or back row forward, and tends to play golf like one, so our first challenge is to devise a scoring format to ensure that he wins the trophy, which is his grandfather's monogrammed silver hipflask. (All the time I knew Harding, Neff's grandfather, he was teetotal, but the hipflask was probably a twenty-first present, such was his family background. One of his brothers still gave him whisky for Christmas when he was 75.) Neff is keen to play golf when he can, and significantly for this choice of venues, grew up in

Newcastle, so he speaks the language. Accordingly, he nips into the Village Club and enquires where the other club might be. He is given directions, but also told that the Alnmouth Club might be flooded! Well, this is August.

We duly locate the Alnmouth Club, which itself dates from 1869. It is therefore the second oldest on the coast of England, but this fact passes me by at the time. On what might be the original clubhouse, I observe a notice stating boldly that green fees should be paid in strict priority of availability to: The Hatch opposite the Office, *failing which*, The Secretary's Office, *failing which*, The Bar. I am surprised when Neff correctly judges that we pay in the pro shop. Perhaps there is more to speaking Geordie than just pronouncing vowels twice and putting "like" on the end of sentences. In fact, there was a small amendment in blue biro to the notice that was only visible close up.

ALNMOUTH

Alnmouth Golf Course is gloriously green, and not apparently flooded. I hit a 5 wood second shot onto the 1st green and hole the putt. I like this place. It is gently undulating pasture land on top of what might be called low cliffs of say 20 feet. The greens are fast, true, and generally flat. I hole several putts of what I call a "pro" length, i.e. ones I usually miss, but tournament players frequently seem to hole, particularly to save par. The ones I miss are short ones, which I don't seem to hit properly. The course loops back to the clubhouse at the 6th hole, and again at the 9th. This is probably handy for some weather conditions. As Neff explains, this is Northumberland, and weather can change quickly.

It is not actually raining when we start, but we need waterproofs for the first few holes, only to play the back nine in glorious sunshine. The sea is now the colour of my car, which I believe the manufacturers call Mauritius, after the colour of the Indian Ocean, no doubt. This second loop of nine holes follows rising land away from the sea and, for some reason, the 10th and 11th greens are almost waterlogged. The ball makes a very satisfying gloopy noise as it plunges into the water in the hole. As the sun shines, so Neff's game starts to appear (mine is doing very nicely, thank you). He mentions that it seems easier in sunshine, echoing the opinions of a group of former test cricketers I had heard on the radio the previous day discussing run-scoring. Personally, I never stayed long enough at the crease to find out.

At its far end, the Alnmouth Course meets the Village course, separated by a fence. We face a prospect like those on spoof calendars of the world's toughest holes, where from the elevated 16th tee, it looks as if one plays to an impossible "island" green which seems to be slightly out to sea. In fact, that green is on the other course. Our hole is a downhill par five, and Neff hits a screaming drive, followed by a 3 iron, leaving us both a few yards short of the green in two, with me to play first. Should I pitch, or run it? 'Pitch,' says Neff, 'or it will run through the green.' I duly pitch, but he chips, and it runs through the green! 'Why did you do that? I ask. 'I didn't want to leave it short,' is the reply. Sometimes, one forgets what a difficult game golf is for the occasional player. 'I was trying, you know, Unk,' says Neff later.

Happily, Neff gets his par, and follows it with another at the splendid par three 17th, and a bogey at the 18th. This is a delightful spot, if not a particularly typical seaside course, and as I have finished with three pars for a 79, we are both pleased. There are a few houses bordering the inland part of the course, including one with a gate onto the 11th green. 'What a great place to live.' 'Yes, Unk, except for the weather. This is Northumberland.'

Northumberland is richly endowed with castles, among which Bamburgh is remarkable for being intact and, indeed, inhabited. It towers over the village in what seems to be a reassuring fashion. Perhaps it would be threatening in bad weather, but the weather for today is splendid, with lots of cumulonimbus clouds, while the sun manages to shine through the gaps most of the time. The sea is very calm, and resembles smoked glass, at times even assuming a pinkish hue. When the sunlight reflects from the clouds, the effect is like moonlight.

We drive through the village without seeing a sign to a golf course. This coast differs from the Costa del Sol in a number of ways. In Spain, there are signs marked "Campo de Golf" every few kilometres – but you have to set off early to find the right one. The sign never states *which* "Campo de Golf" it is referring to. In Northumberland, one finds the course by a process of elimination. Here, we have clearly gone too far and turn round. I notice what I think is an observation platform, but Neff says this is merely a beacon. Then he spots a flag, and we are on our way, by turning left towards the sea as often as we can.

BAMBURGH CASTLE

The castle itself is obscured by the clubhouse of Bamburgh Castle Golf Club, until we have played the 1st hole, whereupon it watches over us for a while. The course is unusual in starting with a par three, and unique in also having a par three 2nd. The latter, into a seemingly gentle wind, measures 209 yards. My driver doesn't reach the green. The next holes are both par fives, with the 3rd being also unusual in measuring only 422 yards. It still takes three good hits to reach from the yellow tees; I would not care to play it off the whites. At the 4th I get a members' bounce and secure my first par. We have left Bamburgh Castle behind, and are looking instead at glorious views of Holy Island, Lindisfarne Castle, and the estuary at Budle Bay turning into golden sands in the ebbing tide. We turn back for the 5th, the first par four, starting to go uphill. Another members' bounce gives me a birdie putt, which I hole despite the best efforts of a greenkeeper on a mower to put me off by pretending I don't exist. (This reminds me that I forgot to read through the notice at Alnmouth asking members to refrain from verbal abuse of green staff. A reason for returning there, perhaps?)

Neff meanwhile has announced that he does not intend to give up rugby just yet for golf. He is playing like a rugby player, to be precise a hooker, and though the fairways are lined with generous cuts of semi-rough, Neff is persistently reaching the hay beyond them with his ball. If he finds it, by agreement he throws it like a hooker at a line-out into the fairway – but he does not throw in the towel. Once again – this is becoming commonplace – the 6th hole at Bamburgh is unique in my experience, a par three, but stroke index 1 – 224 yards, uphill. Then another uphill, par four hole takes us to "the elevated section", where the views of Lindisfarne are if anything even better. It is from here that the sea seems to change to its pinkish colour. As we step forward, the magnificent sight of Bamburgh Castle again heaves into view from behind a large mound, and we also see a group of what appear to be phantom golfers silhouetted against the sky, playing tee shots to an invisible green which seems to boast about a 14 foot flag.

At the 8th – yet another par three, across a valley, protected by a granite outcrop – I get yet another members' bounce, while Neff's better struck shot sticks on a ridge. After the 9th we round a corner to the 10th tee, and there – to my great satisfaction – is a solid brick-built staircase, very solid indeed, about ten feet high! It is not, I point out to Neff, a beacon. He replies that were it further south, by the Tyne, it might be a stairway to Hebburn. It enables one to see if the green is free. That is apparently all it does, save to commemorate the contributions of the members who funded it. This is the fifth par three in ten holes, 197 yards from the whites, and played blind. From the 188 yard yellows, we both get pars. There is also a substantial drinking fountain at this tee, so given the presence of running water, all it needs now is for a flushing toilet to be installed "below stairs".

The 11th is a dogleg left round a hillside, and I hit my second shot – followed by a provisional – too far left of the green. I meet Neff scrabbling about on the scrubby bank – he has hooked his way round – and we are both obliged to abandon our balls. On the way to the next tee, remembering my members' bounces, I sneak a look into the hole. The ball is not in there. We go downhill, then uphill again, and now we are once again in the elevated section, at phantom plateau, the 14th tee. This is named for its view of the Farne Islands, including Grace Darling's lighthouse, which continues to shine brightly despite the sunshine. This is positively the last par three (of six, total 1149 yards), and another blind shot. Neff gets another par. Are shots easier to play without the intimidation of a target?

At the next hole – called with great imagination Castle's View – we drive straight, but downhill and out of sight. The second shot requires me to clear a deep gully in front of the green, which I am pleased to do with a 5 wood. Although the ball clears it, players have to walk through the gully. This course may be short, but it is demanding to walk. Standing on the green, Neff stares into the middle distance and remarks "that's interesting". Wondering what panoramic spectacle I can have missed thus far, I turn, to realise that he is referring to the necessity of clearing the gully uphill with the next tee shot. This time the player is assisted by a flight of twenty-four wooden steps; the ball has to make its own way. Neff is, of course, intimidated.

We finally turn our backs on Lindisfarne and the estuary, where the tide has now turned, as the course threads its way back to the clubhouse round the landward side of a young mountain. The 17th only measures 238 yards, but it is a par four, despite playing from an elevated tee. This leaves some unanswered questions about the prevailing wind. Finally, I get my last members' bounce of the round to within 10 yards of the 18th green, which means I have hit about a 270 yard drive. The chip almost goes in for an eagle, and I get a closing birdie. The whole thing was most enjoyable, but I fancy it is more of a brilliant party fling than love at first sight. To return might produce a tearful ending.

Some months later, I finally stopped humming "Meet me on the corner".

Dunstanburgh Castle is as ruined as Bamburgh is intact, with two vertical structures rising ominously from a rocky headland. They are some distance apart, with the effect that the overall profile changes according to one's viewpoint. It looks decidedly eerie through the slight haze created by a sky of solid, pale, high cloud. The sea today resembles rice pudding – without a skin, obviously – except that if anything, the surface is smoother.

As is now customary, we find the golf course at the wrong point, down a cul-de-sac where people park to walk across to the sand dunes. There is also a path along the edge of the course and, unusually, a notice inviting non-golfers to take advantage of the catering facilities at the clubhouse, half a mile along the path. This makes quite a change from other places in England, where one feels that The Committee would ideally like to put up signs saying "non-golfers will be shot on sight". As in Scotland, golf in Northumberland is clearly the people's game; everyone is welcome, with or without a handicap, and indeed, playing partners. This is a busy Saturday, with a ladies' medal and men's scramble, but there are still lone players to be seen.

DUNSTANBURGH CASTLE

What cannot be seen from the clubhouse of Dunstanburgh Castle Golf Club is the eponymous castle, which is obscured by two enormous sand dunes to the south. To the north, there is an elevated tee about thirty feet up in the dunes; the southerly ones must be at least fifty feet above the course. We set off, and I am driving superbly. I miss only two of fifteen fairways, one because I drive through a dogleg, the other which I attribute to the distraction caused by the sudden appearance of a female jogger clad in Lycra. When I ask Neff if he saw my ball, he admits that he was watching the jogger instead. I feel slightly thwarted. I was trying not to look.

Neff tells me how he knocked eight minutes off his best time for a half marathon when he found himself following a shapely – and obviously athletic – female, and determined not to lose sight of her. It would have been ungentlemanly to overtake. He needs all his stamina today for his hooks from the tee have turned into scythes, by which is meant viciously curved shots which fly knee high into the hay beyond the left hand rough. With a swing like mine, it is not easy to give advice to others, even occasional players, but something has to be done. I usually limit myself to repeating "turn, don't tilt", but this is no help, for Neff is actually hitting his irons rather well. But then, after his tee shots, he needs to.

In the course of the first six holes we establish clearly that if he moves the ball forward in his stance, he gains elevation. To prevent the hook, he needs to release and re-grip his club a few degrees clockwise. This results in a straight, high flight. The bad news is that, in cricketing parlance, everything now goes over extra cover. The good news, if it may be called that, is that the course is laid out in a St Andrew's-style loop, but with the other fairway to the right rather than the left. Neff can at least find his ball. Towards the end of the round, I point out we have in fact cured his hook, which represents some kind of success.

I am not so "successful" with my own game. Despite beautiful driving, I struggle to find greens. The only thing that golf and school have in common for me is that I am averse to lessons, but I had recently found it necessary to consult Big Al, my teacher, for unmentionable reasons. He tried to give me only one swing thought, but currently, I am finding it difficult to follow his advice to hit my irons "with my right buttock", and they are either going long and left, or short and right. The greens are slower than recent days, and I seem unable to get the ball in the hole. Putts either lose their line as they slow down, or I don't find the line in the first place. Towards the end of the day (we play thirty-six holes) I start to get quite annoyed, even throwing a club when a rare shot that hits a green runs off the back. It's ages since I did this, and it reminds me how anger can start to dominate all other perceptions, leaving the "poor" golfer to feel persecuted by the elements.

Fortunately, this doesn't happen during the first round, when the sun comes out to create one of the best days Neff can remember in Northumberland. The course may not be the best prepared overall, but it is delightful. Classic linksland, with undulations, and bigger humps and hollows, which you either love or hate. The unexpectedness of some features might be thought unfair, but I would once again point out to non-believers that when the course was laid out, visitors would have invariably played with a local caddie who would have explained where to go and what to avoid. (I sometimes add the observation that there are plenty of nice new flat layouts with plantations of saplings next to motorways to play on for those people who don't like hundred year old links.)

At Dunstanburgh Castle, you could not get closer to the sea. After three holes northwards, the course turns, and from holes 3 to 10, one steps from the green a few yards to the next tee, coming inland only to negotiate the giant dunes which obscure the castle from the club-house. The actual golf holes seem straight, but the land follows the broad curve of the bay for about a mile and a half in an arc which must be a quarter of a circle, with lovely sandy beaches between the dunes and the water. The castle itself gets ever closer, and ever more impos-ing, which is impressive considering how little of it there is left.

The 11th and 12th holes zigzag, to leave the 13th closest of all to the castle. It is a par three of only 110 yards played over a quarry, and the members walk up to the green, leaving their bags by the tee, ready to turn back towards the clubhouse. It is as if no-one wants to go any closer for fear of disturbing the Trolls. On the beach at this point, there are lots of even-sized large boulders, which when the tide comes in and the cloud returns, give us yet another colour of sea – black. Inspired by the foam of the gentle waves, we call it Guinness black, and speculate how, if ever there were an EU Guinness lake, it might keep its head. Neff points out something about the strata in the Saddle Rock, the headland on which the castle sits, but as that is the brand of ball I am playing, I retort that the ruins constitute pinnacles. It is time to go home.

Having already given us every colour of sea imaginable, the next morning still manages a surprise; we can't see the sea, but we can hear it. We can't see it because there is a steady downpour which restricts visibility to about a 5 iron. Things are not promising, and although visi-bility improves somewhat as we drive to our next venue at Seahouses, we do not fancy the aftermath of the long journeys we would then face with wet golf equipment, and so on. We would definitely have played if this were not our last day, honest.

The members are playing their Sunday medal, notwithstanding, but goodness knows what their scores are like. It is the sort of rain that soaks golf bags in about two holes. We have actually met some of these members briefly, following the club rule that Sunday tee times are not allocated until half past five on Friday in the clubhouse, or six o'clock by phone. We turned up at 5.30. There was a queue of members exchanging banter in loud, and only semi-intelligible, Geordie as they signed in to play. I was joking when I said Neff could speak the language, but I needed him to interpret. According to the stewards, the same people turn up every week and book the same times. They could pre-print the sheets. We choose a discreet eleven o'clock tee-off, well after the medallists have gone out, playing in fours. This is another reason why we do not want to play in the downpour – the thought of coming up behind fourballs playing medals with wet clubs. As we leave, we can hear a very noisy sea beyond the dunes. Is this what is meant by a sea change in the weather, we wonder?

After booking in for golf, we had spent Friday evening in Seahouses, amongst other things playing a game of crazy golf, and eating at the establishment generally acclaimed to be the best of the choice of six fish and chip shops, known as Pinnacles! (Sadly, we fail to find a pub called The Titleist Arms.) As we are not to play on the Sunday, the position in the contest for Harding's Hipflask needs a play-off. We decide that retrospectively, this should be the crazy golf. I was winning easily, until the 17th where my unfortunate seven lost out to Neff's hole in one. That's crazy golf.

For the record, Neff was playing Stableford with a full allowance of thirty-six shots, and the scoring system was eclectic by stroke index. We were tied after three rounds. He really stuck at it. That's commitment for you, but then, he is a second row forward.

****

Northumberland remained a long way off from my Dorset base, and it was not until I was close to completing my littoral peregrination that I returned. Because of the "westerly tilt" of Great Britain, Berwick-upon-Tweed, in England, is actually further north than both Turnberry and Royal Troon, venues for the Open Championship on the west coast of Scotland. There is actually a golf course, Magdalene Fields, listed in the *R & A Handbook*, in England, but north of the River Tweed. Now, the England–Scotland border follows the Tweed, and only switches northwards to include Berwick in England as a result of some obvious political compromise. Everyone knows that, for sporting purposes,

Berwick is in Scotland, where Berwick Rangers play their football. Also, I had in mind that Berwick is still at war with Germany, and England clearly is not, except at football, of course. In fact, it was the Crimean War in the 1850s which was declared in the name of England, Scotland and Berwick-upon-Tweed, but the Treaty of Paris which settled the peace omitted the last named. So it's still at war with Russia. That's a good enough reason for not going just north of the Tweed.

Eventually I arrived again at Seahouses with all its fish and chip shops, which are gathered there on behalf of the other villages on the coast, which may thus remain unspoilt. Fortunately, *The Good Pub Guide* also listed The Olde Ship, where I stayed ready to play the course the next morning.

SEAHOUSES

When I finally arrived to play at Seahouses Golf Club one Friday morning, I was only the fourth person in evidence, the others being a player from Moortown, his non-playing wife, and the Secretary, who explained the layout of the course. There were originally twelve holes, between the road and the sea, and about thirty years ago another six were added across the road. There is now a brown road sign indicating a right turn to the golf club, in case you cannot spot it as you drive through the middle of it!

I was coming off a case of love at first sight with Wallasey Golf Club which I had played the previous day, and something had to go wrong. It was mainly my driving that went astray, but it was the sort of course where provided you keep the ball on it, and avoid the water hazards which are around, but not obviously designed into play, you will not suffer. There are two odd features of the layout; the 4th and 7th holes cross over each other for no apparent reason that I could see (after I played from the 4th tee to the 7th hole), and the 9th and 18th are close to each other and play in the same direction (as I found when I pulled my second on the 9th onto the 18th green). For some reason they reminded me of two famous pieces of Scalelectrix track, the crossover, and the "coming together" with the tracks too close to share, but not actually crossing. These features must slow up play something rotten. Neff and I had made a good decision back on that rainy morning.

Before the concept of signature holes existed, there were numbers 10 and 15 at Seahouses, both short par threes, the first across water, called Logan's Loch, to a short but wide green playing roughly north-wards, and the second, called The Cove, playing southerly, across a cove to a long thin green, reminiscent in their own modest way of the 12th at Augusta, and the 17th at Pebble Beach. You can afford to be off line on the 10th provided you have the right club for the wind, but you need to find the line for the 15th. I hit both greens, but three-putted the 10th. The holes in between pass back and forth across the cliff top, with the wind a big factor. I struggled on the greens, which were grassy and a little inconsistent, and in need of a cut. It was odd because as well as a tractor mowing the fairways, I saw a ride-on mower cutting the tees. Afterwards, I spotted this machine on a trailer, obviously hired or borrowed from elsewhere. As tomorrow was medal day, perhaps they were saving the greens' weekly scalp for then. This is a low budget club.

For me this was a pity, as the gentle caress which I had cultivated when putting at Wallasey was no use. Mind you, the green fee was a quarter of Wallasey's, and the annual subscription £210, which if you play twice a week, works out to about two quid a round, or just over 10p a hole, and the course is on the very edge of town. You pays yer money and you takes yer choice.

I then made my way to seek the company and hospitality of Mr and Mrs C J, friends from University whom I had scarcely seen since. Thinking of Neff's "hooker" style of play, I expected that C J would be smooth and straight on a golf course because at College I had known him as a very elegant batsman and, particularly, rugby player, a centre three-quarter. Rugby talent is hard to define, but he possessed the quality that suggested a prototype for Jeremy Guscott. Someone like Jason Robinson is an exciting runner, but you can see him work-ing on it, as it were. A generation earlier, whenever there was a break upfield and people like Will Carling and Rob Andrew were straining every sinew, veins bulging, to keep up with the play, there on their shoulder would be Guscott, not breaking sweat, apparently still in third gear, ready to inject a change of pace if it was needed. It was how David Gower would have played rugby, one thinks, and Ernie Els, perhaps? It was how C J played for our College team.

I know this, because for a season I played outside him on the wing. He never seemed to pass; I suppose he did not need to, or perhaps I could not always keep up... He did not only score tries from hand, for the ability to read the game, to anticipate, is a part of excelling. Our fly half that season was great at kicking from hand, so the team decided he should attempt drop goals. It proved a very successful ploy, not that I remember the ball ever going between the posts. The thing was, the Number 10 tended to give to his drop kicks what I can only describe as a shank (sorry to mention the word), and before the defending side could even turn to run back, C J had anticipated and was touching the loose ball down for a try.

Timing is another aspect of great players, and in this respect, C J's – or perhaps that of his parents – was awry. He must have harboured hopes of playing for the University, but when he turned up to Freshman's trials, he found himself marking none other than T G R Davies, already a British Lion and, although he was famed as a winger in the great Welsh side of the early 70s, unfortunately at that time he played in the centre. As the other incumbent University centre was J S Spencer who went on to captain England, this was bad timing. During the vacations, when the rest of us went touring Europe in camper vans or America on Greyhound buses, C J spent a winter in Australia, where he could play rugby. He once found himself on the substitute's bench next to the great French Number 8, Walter Spanghero, who was, unfortunately, playing for the other side. Again, bad timing. Try to be on the field when Spanghero's on the bench, and vice versa.

SEATON CAREW

I was really looking forward to playing at Seaton Carew Golf Club for three reasons: firstly, I was to play with C J and Mrs C J; secondly it was designed by Dr Alister Mackenzie who, if you recall, introduced us at Teignmouth; third, it appeared to have two eighteen-hole courses, The Brabazon at 6855 yards, and the Old at 6613. I was to be disappointed in this last respect.

Seaton Carew does indeed have its Brabazon and Old courses, but they are not distinct. In fact, the course planner indicates four courses: The Old, The Brabazon, The Micklem, and The Bishop. Each is composed of a different eighteen of the total of twenty-two holes available to play. When we reported at the pro shop, we were given a card for – and I quote – the New (3). Now, it is not uncommon for holes to be named, but never before has it been useful. Here, we had to read from the card the name of the hole we were playing and look that up in the planner, not the number. For those of you who know Seaton Carew, the course we played had Gare at Number 11 together with Dog Leg at 17.

It was a Saturday, and busy, and not a good course on which to hit wild drives, we noted, as we watched the group in front in stark silhouette on some rising ground searching for balls. They were silhouetted against Corus Redcar, the steelworks on the opposite bank of the river Tees, which at that moment were belching forth steam, or possibly white smoke. Quite evocative, though not of classic links golf, which otherwise this was. Playing out into the wind towards this and many more signs of industrial mayhem was tough on the eyes in more ways than one. We struggled to get started; on one hole I was first to play my second shot despite being the only one on the fairway, but last to play my third while off it. All of us missed the green, but while C J chipped dead for par, and Mrs C J missed a putt, I messed about for a triple bogey.

As I had expected, Mrs C J gave the ball a very healthy clout, usually straight down the middle. This was a period in my golfing life when I was struggling for length into the wind, and I am not unused to having to play my second shot before a lady companion, but I was impressed when this happened on hole Number 5 – sorry, that should be "Road" – as the yellow tee I used measures 338 yards, compared to her red tee of 329. It was C J who surprised me. Having expected him to play like Nick Faldo, I got Seve Ballesteros. For example, on hole Gare, we thought he was in a bunker, but it was of the grass variety, and he hit a magic iron shot to about 10 feet. We were both in the fairway, with me out-driving Mrs C J who had an 11 yard advantage (not that I was counting), and we both missed the green. Although the greens were big, they seemed eminently missable, being of the "emergent" type – not quite an upturned saucer – but running down at the edges so that anything but a straight ball would tend to bounce or run off. It was classic linksland where ideally on first acquaintance a caddie would have told you which side of the fairway to drive to leave an approach which would stay on the green.

Of course, it would still have been necessary to execute the shot correctly, and C J was having trouble. On hole number Beach, he hit his tee shot very nearly, but not quite, into some solid, spiky, glaucous bushes which ran the length of this hole whereas I found the middle of the fairway. As he chipped out, I hit my second almost, but not quite, into a greenside bunker, but instead lost the ball in the bushes. He came up short, but still almost chipped in with his fourth, while I chipped badly with my second ball and took seven. Mrs C J meanwhile, as she seemed to do most of the afternoon, belted it down the middle, missed the green, chipped badly and three-putted for a six.

This was the seaward area of the course we liked best as it seemed to be in better condition than the inland parts, and offered views of links golf at its classic best, as opposed to industry at its chronic worst, and for good measure the wind was behind as well as we played home. So we enjoyed ourselves, particularly on the last hole where my companions both cleared a large mound in the fairway with their drives to finish close to the green. It was somewhat ironic that while Mrs C J and I were splitting fairways, C J would wander off laterally only to reappear at the green to win the hole. Possibly I had the final satisfaction, though. Cosy Corner, our Number 16 and one of only two short holes, was playing 187 yards into a stiff breeze. I used my driver, and holed the putt for the only birdie between us.

Of the good Doctor designer, famed for his par fives at Teignmouth and elsewhere in the USA, it was difficult to spot his signature – except that this course was, uniquely in my experience, par seventy-five, with five par five holes.

The first sporting love of both Mrs C J and me in our youth was tennis, and we found ourselves wondering idly if there was any connection between this and our initially successful driving of a golf ball. The only part of tennis that resembles golf in any sense is the serve, which is entirely up to the server to hit. We were also trying to define what makes a good golf course; was it the presence of some very good holes, absence of any bad holes, consistency, variety, length, fairness, and so on? The list grew long. Perhaps you could start with a maximum score, like in ice skating or gymnastics, and deduct points for everything not quite right, but we realised that the Old Course at St Andrew's would not do very well if you did. C J did not like a particular hole at Seaton Carew – and claimed that it was not good – because he had nothing at which to aim his second shot. It is true that the green was protected by a large mound, but I had a reasonable view of the target (once I had exited my fairway bunker). As he was my host for the night, I thought it churlish to mention that this might have been because he was off line, again. He had a point though; you do need something to aim at. C J said that he tended not to remember holes well. My guess is he is too focused on the shot he has to play, which is how he maintains a single figure handicap while only playing twice a month or so. Perhaps there is a lesson in that for me. Apart from that, C J learnt something from me – the pips!

BERWICK-UPON-TWEED

Berwick-upon-Tweed Golf Club is at a place called Goswick, five miles south of the town, and appears to be getting confused about its name. The clubhouse calls it Berwick-upon-Tweed with Goswick in brackets, but in the *R & A Handbook* it is plain Berwick-upon-Tweed. On the other hand the card and newly printed course planner, following a recent overhaul of the course, just call it Goswick. I bought a souvenir hat, with the logo of a flying goose. It reads Berwick-upon-Tweed above it, and Goswick below. Perhaps, with more and more Russians taking up the game, they want to make it clear that they are no longer at war. Whatever the course was called, I have been waiting to play it for about 30 years, since the days when Celia used to have regular business in Edinburgh, and travelled by the railway which it separates from the sea. She would come home and tell me how much I would love to play it. She was right.

So, fast trains go past, but not so often, and the good news is, the A1 is a couple of miles away, so the loudest noise is made by the twittering, hovering birds. Anyone who cannot cope with this has a serious problem. The first and last holes are a little odd, the 1st doglegging round a clump of conifers to an elevated green in the sand hills, nearby to which is the 18th tee, from which one plays straight back towards the clubhouse. The other holes play roughly parallel to the shoreline, beyond which there is a magnificent, deserted, sandy beach. We were joined by yet another old University friend, Arvo, who had actually been C J's rugby captain at school, but, in contrast, was a Number 8, and a fast bowler. His golf could have been explosive had he learned as a youth, but in fact he only took it up in his 40s.

We were playing a form of Stableford better ball match play, where the hole was won on the Stableford points, so we could also keep personal tallies. We all started fairly ropily, with only Arvo netting two points on the 1st. The short second is called Crater, because you cannot see the bottom of the flag. Mrs C J and I both got pars, hers worth three points. All square. The 3rd hole is the first of a series of four averaging 459.5 yards off the yellows, each in the opposite direction to the previous. The two northerly ones are both par fives, somewhat unusual I thought, until I learnt that the wind usually blows *across* the course. Today, what wind there was, was beautiful, a gentle zephyr which started from the land, but turned round to blow offshore and help us on the last few holes.

These four holes are all par fives for the ladies, which meant that Mrs C J was a good choice of partner for me. She and her husband halved the 3rd (with a six to a four), and C J and I both took two points on the next, bringing us to our stroke 1, 413 yarder, which played 407 yards from the ladies' tee, par five. Mrs C J did not need that many – boom, down the middle of the valley fairway – crack, front edge of the plateau green – putt to just outside gimme range. Net eagle. Four points. We're one up. It did not last, as we both took eight on the 6th, a superbly designed hole which uses the undulating land brilliantly. In case you wondered, it was originally designed by James Braid, though it may have been improved by Frank Pennick 40 years ago. Unfortunately I could not match C J on the next where the other two hit into deep grass on a high bank which keeps the railway out of sight. A wayward driver would do a lot of reloading on this course. Golfwise, Arvo had been quiet since the 1st, but on the short 9th he holed from off the green for a clean win. This left C J, on the green, with a birdie putt which, he declared, was now a pip. After Mrs C J's, he desperately wanted his own birdie, but it would not really count if he holed it, or matter if he missed. He missed.

This hole was called Cheviot View; we could see the hills, and it was raining on them, but that was where the rain stayed. We could also see three castles – Bamburgh, Lindisfarne, and Haggerston – but no sign whatsoever of a petrochemical plant.

The match improved at this point. Arvo matched my three pointer on 10, but on 11, my partner and I both had three pointers which brought us to one down. For a while they held onto our coat tails, with one or the other matching our score until it all went pear-shaped on Number 16 when we both hit poor drives, and lost to C J's two points to go dormie two down. C J had his third pip for a birdie, and inevitably he missed, after Arvo nailed the winning three points on Number 17. The 18th hole is possibly a little weak, but I did not complain as C J once more failed in his quest for a birdie, and I "pipped" him in the singles' contest by one point. Arvo played his part – and gave C J the pips.

If I have a complaint, it is this. There are two four foot high pre-historic standing stones at the entrance to the 17th green, and they have called the hole "Stonehenge". I frequently pass by Stonehenge, and, well, sorry, you'll have to come and look...

It was great to meet the C Js (and Arvo) this way. The golf gave us something contemporary to talk about, and whenever we felt it was time to give it a rest, we could pick up on the intervening 30-odd years, and vice versa. On the way back from Goswick, we talked about the relative merits of the two trips. Possibly, Seaton Carew was the tougher test of golf, but Goswick had been the more pleasurable total experience, though we admitted that a good round at one and a poor one at the other, and changes in the weather, could have clouded judgment. The answers to the questions "Which one would you go back to to-morrow?" and "Which club would you join?" were not necessarily the same...

5

THE VICTORIAN BOOM

I once went on a guided tour of the Colosseum in Rome. Our English-speaking Italian guide – possibly he had been rejected by the Mafia for being too much of a spiv – told us lots of interesting things about the building which I forget, but when we went inside and he talked about the entertainments which used to take place, two things registered with me. The first is that we now regard these activities – real men and animals fighting each other to the death – as totally barbaric, except that people continue to crave such scenes of mayhem through virtual games and cinema. The guide's point was that, though the images may now be simulated, the desire to observe them still remains.

The second point was that the Romans did not of course have cinemas. The only pictures they had were painted on walls, to which the vast majority had no access, so amongst the reasons they went to the Colosseum was the actual chance to see elephants and lions. Nowadays, we can see Lions at play in the antipodes on television, and through the same medium, we get so close to Tigers that we can see the markings on their balls.

Incidentally, I wonder how long it might have taken a film crew to get a shot of the Tiger chipping his ball to execute a right-angled turn and hole out on the 16th green at Augusta on the last day in 2005?[21] Apart from the context, which was as gladiatorial as one would want without the threat of anyone dying, what was particularly special about

---

[21] Fred Perry, the 1930s tennis player, told a story of how he once set out to be filmed hitting a champagne glass – with a ball, not his racquet – positioned on the corner of the service box. He did it with about his third attempt, but the cameras were not running. Once they were, he spent two further fruitless days trying to emulate the feat.

Tiger's shot was the way the ball stopped on the edge of the hole as if to make sure it had everyone's attention, before executing one final roll and impudently displaying the Nike swoosh. The shot itself was magic, but however did he line the logo up? The Nike executives must have been beside themselves, until they remembered that the TV pictures from The Masters belong to the Augusta National which, in a strangely un-American way, does not approve of commercialism.

Back to the point, which is that in 1864 when the good burghers of Westward Ho! in North Devon[22] decided to lay out a golf course on common land by the estuaries of the Taw and Torridge Rivers, what could they have known about golf? There were no cinemas or television, just paintings, and early photography, but what can one learn of golf from a still photograph? The result, Royal North Devon, is the oldest existing golf course in England, though not the oldest club, which honour goes to Royal Blackheath, founded back in 1608. Now, I am no historian, but I recall that the Gunpowder Plot in 1605 was an attempt to assassinate the newly crowned King James I of England, who had recently come south from doubling up as King James VI of Scotland, so it does not require a great leap of imagination to figure out how that club may have started.

Being no historian, I decided to leave the question of what happened in Westward Ho! – and why its citizens changed its name to that of a Charles Kingsley novel, so becoming the only placename in England and possibly the world to include an exclamation mark – to a future date. I would need additional source material, and at this point I had only my trusted three reference works: *The Royal & Ancient Golfer's Handbook*, the *AA 2002 Easy Read Britain Road Atlas* (obviously not the one I started with, but seemingly the most reliable for blue flags), and the decidedly unreliable *The Good Pub Guide*, on this occasion not required. The listings in the Handbook show information provided by the clubs themselves, including the dates of foundation, and as I identified the clubs I would have to play, it was interesting to note these dates.

It is true that the date is often the foundation of the club, and not necessarily the present course, just as the designer listed may not have been responsible for the original layout, perhaps being called in when the

---

[22] It wasn't actually so named until later.

course was relocated, or extended to eighteen holes.[23] However, I have mentioned that in the case of my literally littoral courses, it is a reasonable assumption that where they started is where they are now located. Coastal land is not generally worth a great deal; until seaside resorts became popular in the latter part of the 19th century, communities were located near the most useful places, where there was access to the sea through estuaries and harbours, so nearby linksland and cliff tops were readily available from the start. Grazing, their only alternative use, could probably continue, as it does to this day at Royal North Devon. So, avail themselves the Victorian Englishmen did: ten years on from the start at Westward Ho!, there were six coastal courses in England; ten years later still, in 1884, there were twelve, but by 1894 the number had risen to forty-four, including Axe Cliff in South Devon.

AXE CLIFF

As you drive along the side of the River Axe through the village of Axmouth towards the sea, there is a heavily wooded slope on the left, and it is not obvious where a golf course will fit it. If you are lucky, you spot the sign to Axe Cliff Golf Club quickly enough to make a first-time manoeuvre onto a lane which slopes upwards at quite an unusual gradient. It goes on long enough to make you think it is heading for the cliff top, but then it comes to a car park, still on a definite slope, with steps up to a clubhouse, and there you are. It is a modest building, because the gully or ravine in which it sits is not wide enough to permit anything more extravagant.

If you consult the map on the back of the scorecard, you will discover that the 1st hole is on the other side of the clubhouse, continuing uphill in the gully. If you do not consult the map, you will be bemused. If like me, figuring that a 245 yard opening hole is tempting for a driver, you take one with you up to the 1st tee (if the clubhouse was to be a face and the entrance to the course its mouth, the 1st tee would be behind its left ear), you find you have the perfect club to reach the bunkers which stretch right across the fairway. If like me you have just registered that your car temperature sensor reported 29 degrees, there is

---

[23] When, they all asked, did 18 holes become standard?

no breeze, it is clear seaside air (no city dust to filter the sun's rays), and it is 1 PM, you don't go back to change it.

The 1st green is long and thin, and when you stand on the 2nd tee behind it and finally figure out which marker post to go for, try and hit to the left of it. It is a vicious dogleg up onto the land to the north of the gully, with a blind landing area. (The change of direction is vicious; I don't know about the original dog.) That way, you may find the blind fairway, from which you can hit down to the blind green. Don't go right and right again as I did, there is a spinney there. You'll find the 3rd tee no problem, but you won't see your ball land, as it is a blind shot. After finishing the 3rd (avoid the left side of the green as the ball may kick off into the rough), the 4th tee is a few yards uphill, but it appears to be facing nowhere in particular. The hole only measures 257 yards, but there is no sign of a flag. So, you do what the map says, drive the wrong way up (or indeed, down) the 5th fairway. You find the hole, walk a distance to the 5th tee, and play back towards the marker post, as the landing area is blind. If you make it, there is an innovation to behold, a warning bell. You may wonder though, is it to tell people on the 5th tee that it is safe to drive, or people on the 4th tee that it is not?

I began to wonder at this point, was this course designed by a family? I've occasionally come across a house where everyone designed a room each. Here, it's like different people each wanted a type of golf hole, so rather than choosing a consistent layout, they stuck them together as best they would fit.

You probably will not be surprised that the uphill 294 yard 6th hole features a blind landing area, but then you find the 7th tee, and suddenly everything becomes apparent. This is a par three, playing directly over the 1st green to the seaward side of the gully, and you can also see the 17th green with its peculiar approach, not to mention the 18th, chiselled out of the hillside. Beyond all that, there appears to be a golf course designed on fairly conventional lines, that is, with a different patch of land being used for each hole. Mind you, the 8th has a blind tee shot, but from the 9th tee you can see where you are going, towards the bay at Seaton with its white cliffs and shingle beach. Only the second shot on this par five is blind.

The second half of the course begins with a par five going back in the opposite direction, which means that it starts with a blind tee shot, but after that, the course is fairly ordinary for a while. Then you get to the 16th tee, and although you can see the fairway, you don't see your tee shot land as land itself appears to be in short supply. It falls away in the most dramatic fashion, quite stimulating, but extremely difficult to judge. As you will probably run through the thin strip of a green, be pleased that there is a hidden bunker beyond. It keeps you in bounds.

This description does not really do justice to the hole, so forgive me if I do not attempt the 17th, which is stranger, being blind at both ends, as it were. To refute my assertion that courses are much as they have been for years, this one was lengthened during the last fifteen from 5111 yards par sixty-seven to 5969 yards par seventy. You will be pleased to know that the "signature holes" are unaffected.

When Queen Victoria died in 1901 – a year in which no further coastal clubs were added, perhaps as a mark of respect – the total stood at 55, eventually rising to 74 before the spread was halted by the Great War. Given the general speed of communication and travel available to the Victorians, I find this coastal development remarkable. It is not geographical either; there is no apparent domino effect where one course nearby leads to another. They sprang up all over the place (if that is the expression), including Clevedon, which has in its time been in the county of Avon, but is now safely back in Somerset.

CLEVEDON

Clevedon Golf Club is probably easy to find when approaching from the north-east, but from the south-west I had to persist in driving through the town and turning away from roads signposted to Bristol. Eventually, you drive up a sharply inclined lane, across a hole or two, and there it is. From the looks of Clevedon, it is probably a bijou sort of place to live when one works in Bristol. There was a touch of the bijou about the golf course – an elegant clubhouse, or perhaps the lushness of the vegetation. The 1st tee is the other side of the car park. You pass a wooden starter's hut on the right, and there is the view of the straight par four 1st hole, 400 yards plus, with clumps of tall trees on the right of the fairway. On the left of the fairway, and running its length, is a hedge such as one might find on many an English golf course. The difference here is that instead of a field, or a lane, or even houses on the other side of the hedge, here there is the Bristol Channel. Well, actually, there is a drop first as we are on elevated ground, but you can't see that. The Mayor of Clevedon believes it is the sea, because there are signs throughout the town pointing to "Sea Front", but I have never heard of the Brown Sea, nor seen a sea which so resembled a ploughed field – except that it was moving about.

As if to underline my point, the 2nd hole, a par five, continues along this "hedge line", and is named The Bridges, in honour of its view of both of the Severn Crossings which are not far away upstream. Clearly, the watercourse is still a river at that point; when, I wonder, does it turn into sea? When it turns grey? Not that it matters, of course, because estuaries count for my purposes. It's just that the course is unusual...

Hole Number 3 is called The Gap, and continues in the same direction, with a slight dogleg, through a gap – between two copses of mature trees. Hole Number 4 is called The Drop, not because it is where Wyatt Earp got the better of Billy the Kid, but because it drops. It measures 175 yards, and it feels as if only 100 of them are in the horizontal plane, with the remainder vertical. It is very difficult to select a club for holes like this, or possibly very easy, since any sort of flick might do. I might have experimented, but I was waved through, so I flicked a slick six. Good guess.

We have reached the end of the course, and leaving the hedge behind, the next hole plays in a reverse direction with a clump of tall mature trees to the left, and a thick wood of them to the right. Seriously tall, and mixed deciduous and evergreen, they must be far older than the course. The hole itself is called Underwood. The next turns back yet again, with the tall copse on the left this time. They make a splendid pair of holes, but one could be anywhere – anywhere that is except on the coast of England! The second shot to the 6th hole is great; downhill over a pond to a two-tier green, and if you hit the target, you have the satisfaction of walking at 90 degrees to the line of play and leaving your bag by the next tee, whereas if you miss, you have to take it with you, and then drag it back uphill. As far as I noted, this is the only green that does not have a series of small white markers bearing the legend "No Trolleys" embedded a few feet apart in a ring around the front and sides of the green, because the pond does the job. Each marker is about half the area of a hole, embedded in a dirt patch roughly the size of a sprinkler head. What happens if your ball pitches on or finishes in one? There is no local rule on the scorecard.

The 8th hole plays back to the clubhouse, and when I saw someone playing the 9th ahead, I initially thought he had cut in. If so, it was a poor drive, but in fact it was, notionally, a drive of some 3100 yards. Going by the card, this player had driven a ball from the 1st tee to the

9th fairway! In reality, it was a monumental slice across three fairways. As this 9th hole plays away from the clubhouse, increasingly inland, so the 10th returns, but being a par five, it deviates left, to a blind green. Up until now, this is a splendid – though not remotely seaside – golf course, notwithstanding the white "No Trolley" markers, but after this point, something happens. There are two paths leading away from the 10th green. They look like they meet, but in fact they diverge, and I ended up on a disused tee for a disused short hole, which puzzled me. I then followed the correct path through more trees to a series of holes, which also have their fairways defined by trees but now much smaller trees than those I have seen so far. For this amongst other reasons – coming up behind other players, feeling slightly under the weather, wondering about the white markers – I rather tired of the course, which seemed to lose its charm. The last four holes are remarkable, as they play around a small, miniature even, inhabited, double-glazed keep and bailey castle. Number 15 is straight and sharply uphill; to say that 16 has an elevated tee is to put things mildly – players in the fairway call you up (or down, as it were), and by the time you have made the descent to your ball through the woods, they have finished the hole. The 17th plays across the entrance road up a rise with a severe side slope to leave a nasty second shot down to a sunken green, and hole Number 18 speaks for itself. It is simply called Blind Rise – and for good measure, it finishes beside the overflow car park. What with the castle and everything, the experience was almost – but not quite – bijou. It might be better to start at the 9th.

The exception to this Victorian proliferation of coastal golf courses is the central south coast, and here the strict insistence within my rules that a course should be literally littoral may be significant. Between Poole in the west and Hastings in the east, the seaboard is fairly urbanised, and probably already was when the golf boom hit. Perhaps for this reason, I have seldom visited places there, as my purposes would have been non-golfing. There are a number of courses which might be "seaside" but are not exactly on the coast. Using my reference material in combination, I identified an additional eleven courses close to the coast in this area, dating from the period 1885 to 1914, so perhaps a little later than elsewhere, because the required linksland was not to be had. In fact, two courses – Gosport & Stokes Bay and Chichester – are littoral but fail to qualify for peregrination, being nine-holers. The former could well be links because nearby Hayling certainly is. I couldn't wait...

HAYLING

Unlike Purbeck and Thanet, Hayling really is an island. Have to cross a bridge. Plenty of flag signs, but where's Hayling Golf Club? At last, a big bank of gorse. Looking hopeful. Is anyone besides a golfer pleased to see gorse? Turn into Links Lane. Car park. Gorse. Scrub. Links. 18th green. 1st tee. Clubhouse. Indescribable clubhouse. Players on tee with irons. Tight hole? No, par three. Number 2, par five, Angled fairway. Love that type of hole. Not a dogleg, what's it called? Number 3, angled fairway, plenty of options. Left, over or right of marker post. All about power, accuracy, and wind. Number 4, reverse direction. Guess what, angled fairway, not too many bunkers though. Number 5, nice par three. Nice par three for my scorecard. Big green. Super putting surface. One over so far. Hole 6 is straight! Wide water course fronting green only trouble. Fooled by course planner showing narrow water course not fronting green. Par five 7th called "Death or Glory". Why? Water hazard to clear was on last hole. Old pill box on left? 8th tee elevated. Views. This is an estuary island, in the Solent. Views not good. Blunt end of Isle of Wight. Rubbish land, useful for nought. Except golf. Give me more.

Reached elevated section. Number 8, called Carter, 352 yards, play as double par three, second over mounds. 9th really great dogleg. When exactly is a "bent" hole a dogleg? 10th driveable par four, with right wind. Playing 11th, mouth waters at sight of curving 12th fairway. Happy to get par on it, index 2. Only three over. Only manage bogey 13. Signature hole? – up and over highest part of course. Going back in now, wind behind, water hazards left. Two big lakes, first tidal, second not? How about hole 14A? Not in use, but definitely there, tees and green. Disappointed with consecutive bogeys. Course deserves better. Angled fairways invite spot-picking with driver. Doing that, but execution failing. Hearing strange noises. Turns out to be wedding party in indescribable clubhouse. Denouement hole Number 17. Quadruple bogey. Gorse. Twice. Last hole is flattest. Terrain not smoothest throughout, but evidence of recent heavy rain nicely drained away. Summary? Brilliant, perfect, dump.

Hayling is in the extraordinary area of the Solent where strange things happen. It is only linked to the mainland by a causeway, and there are three tides a day instead of the usual two. The tide comes in, goes out a bit, panics, comes back in again before it decides it is safe to go back out fully. With this kind of complication, the features of the natural harbours at Christchurch and Poole to the west must have been immensely useful in the days before steam power (Poole is actually the second largest natural harbour in the world), so it is perhaps not surprising that Bournemouth dates only from Victorian times.

Bournemouth has possibly more than its fair share of golf courses including two in public parks in the middle of town, one of which was host to PGA tour events as recently as the late 1970s, but none is literally littoral. Further east of Christchurch is a little area of Hampshire which always seems quite urbanised, yet remote from anywhere. The roads to London pass to the north, and it is bounded by the New Forest to the north and east, the estuary at Christchurch to the west, and the sea to the south. This is where Barton-on-Sea is to be found, proof at least of the modern value of coastal land.

BARTON-ON-SEA

Barton-on-Sea Golf Club is one of only two qualifying courses to comprise three loops of nine holes, the other being Prince's, next door to Royal St George's at Sandwich. Apart from two with thirty-six holes, there are a number of others which also boast a nine-hole course alongside the eighteen. As a rule, I have not played these, because I declared nine-hole courses ineligible, and while I can imagine circumstances where one might like to warm up (or down as the case may be) on the nine hole courses, the impression I form is always that the nine-hole course is somehow inferior.

Consequently, I have never felt short-changed in any way if I have visited a course and not played the nine-holer, rather regarding its existence as a bonus if time and circumstances permitted. But when there are three loops, which must by definition have equal status (otherwise, it would still be an eighteen and a nine), which is the eighteen-hole course? If I only play two loops, I feel dissatisfied not to have played the third, but if I do play the third, am I now able to construct three sets of eighteen-hole scores? I don't think so.

On a different occasion and course, I had an enjoyable round partnering the affable pro from Barton-on-Sea. I asked him about the three loops, and he said it was great because there was always somewhere to start. Maybe this is a clue; some day, I must ask a member. Also, if they use different combinations for competitions, it could do away with that "here we go again" feeling that tends to bother me the moment I switch to competition tees.

Barton has twenty-seven holes because the members voted to sell their clubhouse for development and a vast amount of money, thus resulting in a new entrance to the course which is nearer Lymington than Barton itself, an impressive clubhouse with glass sides and a complex, angular roof. For some reason, it reminds me of an evangelical church. It could be something to do with the bell tower. I do not know why a golf club should require a bell tower; I suppose it could be a water tower, or an incinerator chimney, but if I went around trying to find answers to questions like that, I would never get any golf in.

So, the question I asked in the pro shop was which loop should I start from? The answer was whichever I liked, so long as I then played the next loop in the order they appeared on the card, to whit, Becton, Needles, Stroller, Becton and so on. Sorry to be pedantic, but if it does not matter which loop you start on, why does it make a difference which loop you play after you have finished one? Anyway, I started on the Needles, which followed by the Stroller, gave me a combination unique on the coast of England of perfect symmetry – two lots of nine holes, each having three each of pars three, four and five. Unusually for me, I hit a hook on my 1st hole. After some searching for the ball, I finally walked towards a white blob 30 yards short of the green in the middle of the fairway. It was my ball, a 300 yard plus drive; the hole doglegs left more than I had expected, and the wind was powerful. Sadly it was too powerful for the opportunities that I feel the 6-6-6 layout offers to present themselves.[24] The 197 yard 2nd was downwind, and I went over the back of the green, but the 186 yard 7th was into it, and I only just managed to get up in two. The 9th on the Needles loop is only 102 yards, to an island green surrounded by an artificial lake with a fountain in it. It would have looked fine in Spain, but here, with the Isle of Wight in the background, it seemed incongruous. The wind was doing its best to blow the water out, and the fountain – not pretentious, I believe, but necessary to oxygenate the water – was drowning itself. (In case you're wondering, I got a three.)

---

[24] From the beginning, I always felt it was easier to get par threes and fives than fours. You only need one good shot on a three, and you can afford a mediocre one on a five.

It became subsequently clear that this was the newer part of the course, with the original holes to be found closer to the cliff edge, on the Stroller course, which I played, and the Becton, which I did not. Maybe I am a little hypersensitive, as the best efforts of those involved to extend the course at Sherborne have not worked out too well, but whenever I have visited extended courses you can see the join, as it were. Actually, as I think about this, I suppose that where a course has been extended without my knowledge, if it has bedded in well I would not notice, would I? So, let me rephrase that. I have visited a number of courses where extensions have not integrated well with the original holes.

I would not say I did not enjoy my round at Barton-on-Sea, but I felt it was more a decent blow-out than a proper round of golf, as I struggled to stop my eyes watering. Otherwise, I am sure I would have played the third loop. And yes, while I thought I had hit a good second shot to the Stroller 9th, that same young lake was lurking there to swallow my ball...

Stop press: A member tells me that Becton-Needles is the medal combination, so whatever is happening, you can always get a game on Stroller, named after a famous show jumping horse.

Needless to say, the Needles loop of Barton-on-Sea looks out at the western end of the Isle of Wight, with its series of rocks known as The Needles. I remembered them as tall and pointed as the name suggests, but since then I have visited the Isle of Capri with its Scogli, and the impact of the needles has been blunted. Also it was close to 50 years ago that we went on our family holiday to the Isle, with its Needles that you cannot sew, Freshwater you can't drink, Cowes you can't milk, Ryde where you walk and so on. I think we saw the "Queen Mary", then the second largest ocean liner in the world. Those great ships would have sailed out of Southampton en route for New York via Cherbourg right past Barton-on-Sea golf club. What a sight! Then, I remembered that Celia and my mum and I had spent a week on the Isle of Wight about 12 years ago, and I had played golf while they visited the home of Alfred Lord Tennyson, my mum's favourite. Then I panicked. Did I have to play the littoral courses of the Isle of Wight as well? I looked in the Handbook, where IoW was listed under "England"; I went so far as to check whether there were any qualifying courses (there are) before the following reasoning occurred to me: Q. Where is the Isle of Wight? A. Off the south coast of England. Q. Off the coast of England. I put it to you, if it is as you state *off* the coast of England, how can it also be *on* the coast of England? Perhaps I should have been a barrister.

Axe Cliff has definitely been altered, Clevedon has probably been extended, and information I have about Hayling rather knocks a hole in my theory that seaside golf courses are pretty much where they have always been, and also mostly unchanged. The course planner for Hayling explains that the original course founded in 1883 was to the east, and the move to the present site took place in 1897. There is now a pitch and putt course immediately to the east, so if it started there, it did not move far. J H Taylor advised on the new layout at that time, and it was changed again in 1933 after the club acquired the freehold, under "the watchful eye of J Simpson". In *Classic Golf Links*, Donald Steel states that a certain *Tom* Simpson oversaw the redesign in post-war years, and implies that bulldozers were used. This book first appeared in 1992, so the war in question would be the second world version, wouldn't it? Steel also states that there are no links courses apart from this between Dover and Penzance. This makes a point, but actually, Littlestone and Rye – which have entries in Steel's very work, are west of Dover. I would also include Warren, though it makes an ultimately forlorn attempt to link Dawlish with Exmoor. Whose version should one believe about Hayling? I am glad I am not a historian.

I am also, frankly, glad that there are not more coastal golf courses in central southern England, for this reason: I hate the A27. If you have never driven it, imagine the M25 with roundabouts. Even on the longer stretches, the traffic – at any time of the day, it seems – can just come to a temporary halt. This appears to be because driver A, being unhappy with the progress being made by driver B in the inside line, pulls out to overtake. Driver C, travelling in the outside lane, is happy to travel faster than the speed Driver A considers safe, and is thus obliged to brake. Driver D, following C, also brakes, to the consternation of driver E, who sees no reason for slowing down. Somewhere behind E, driver Q looks up suddenly from the text message asking whether he wants chips or mashed potatoes with his dinner and brakes hard, and the traffic behind is obliged to stop.

If everyone travelled at the same speed – the speed limit – this would be less likely to happen, and presumably this is how the improbably-sounding variable speed limit on the M25 works. I say this with a certain smugness, because I drive at the speed limit, a practice I have pursued since the day when my third speeding fine within six months came through, giving me nine points on my licence. It is remarkable how many drivers appear to believe that speed limits are an infringement of civil liberty, that it is a sacred and undeniable human right to exceed them. In order, the most flagrant breaches are: temporary limits of motorways (you don't know who stays behind, but you can count them come past), the 40 mph zone on the edge of 30 zones in villages (people follow me through the 30, but lose patience at the 40 signs), and open undivided roads where it is apparently fine to overtake someone doing the legal maximum of 60 mph, preferably on a bend.

With the help of my *AA Easy Read Britain* – giant scale 2.34 miles to the inch or 1.48 km to 1 cm (who thought of those numbers?) – and, as you know, self-proclaimed as "Britain's Clearest Mapping" – I moved eastwards. For once, it had me fooled. I went to play Cooden Beach near Bexhill – rather soggy for a beach, I thought – and half way round I realised there was a coast road as well as a railway line separating it from the shore. So I abandoned the round. Rules are rules, particularly when you are soaking wet and have already lost three balls.

Here is a list of courses and dates of foundation:

Royal North Devon	Devon	1864
Royal Liverpool	Cheshire	1869
Alnmouth (Foxton Hall)	Northumberland	1869
Furness	Cumbria	1872
West Lancashire	Lancashire	1873
Seaton Carew	Durham	1874
Felixstowe Ferry	Suffolk	1880
Great Yarmouth & Caister	Norfolk	1882
Minehead & West Somerset	Somerset	1882
Hayling	Hampshire	1883
Formby	Lancashire	1884
Newbiggin	Northumberland	1884
Royal St George's	Kent	1887
Cleveland	Yorkshire	1887
Littlestone	Kent	1888
Royal Cromer	Norfolk	1888
West Cornwall	Cornwall	1889

(continued)

Littlehampton	Sussex	1889
Newquay	Cornwall	1890
St Enodoc Church	Cornwall	1890
St Enodoc Holywell	Cornwall	1890
Churston	Devon	1890
Berwick-upon-Tweed	Northumberland	1890
Burnham & Berrow	Somerset	1890
Leasowe	Cheshire	1891
Wallasey	Cheshire	1891
Bude & N Cornwall	Cornwall	1891
Bridport & W Dorset	Dorset	1891
Hunstanton	Norfolk	1891
Sheringham	Norfolk	1891
Clevedon	Somerset	1891
Silloth-on-Solway	Cumbria	1892
Warren	Devon	1892
Isle of Purbeck	Dorset	1892
Clacton on Sea	Essex	1892
Royal Cinque Ports	Kent	1892
Royal West Norfolk	Norfolk	1892
Weston-super-Mare	Somerset	1892
Whitby	Yorkshire	1892
Seascale	Cumbria	1893
Lyme Regis	Dorset	1893
Falmouth	Cornwall	1894
Axe Cliff	Devon	1894
Rye	Sussex	1894
Mullion	Cornwall	1895
Frinton	Essex	1895
Seacroft	Lincolnshire	1895
Formby Ladies	Lancashire	1896
Saunton East	Devon	1897
Saunton West	Devon	1897
Thurlestone	Devon	1897
Barton-on-Sea	Hampshire	1897
Filey	Yorkshire	1897

| Sandilands | Lincolnshire | 1900 |
| Dunstanburgh Castle | Northumberland | 1900 |

A full list of the courses in my peregrination is given in the index.

Amongst the interesting questions which will in all likelihood remain unanswered by yours truly is the question of why the citizens of Seaford in East Sussex chose in 1887 to build their course inland, when 20 years later, the municipality developed Seaford Head.

SEAFORD HEAD

Seaford Head Golf Club has the distinction of being the best municipal course in my peregrination. It happens to be the only one, but it is not at all bad. It is moderately priced, with no restrictions, and there is a reservation system. I was held up by traffic on the awful "Sussex Turnpike" (aka the dreaded A27) and missed my time, but it did not seem to matter. There were a few people wandering about, muttering about tee times and missing persons, and I noticed that an awful lot of people were carrying their clubs. I suspected a trolley ban, but there was no sign of one.

Someone called Fred was lurking by the 1st tee. I was going to give him another name, but anyone who knows Seaford Head will surely recognise him, and it makes no difference to anyone else. Also, he is over eighty, as he told me several times. He was "trying out" a set of clubs for reasons I forget, but I would guess they were pre-1980 forged blades, so I cannot imagine why. He also told a lot of "one-liner" jokes, most of which I have also forgotten, such as:

Mechanic: 'Your car won't start because it has a flat battery.' Politically incorrect stereotype of a racial or ethnic group popularly supposed to be cerebrally challenged: 'What shape should it be?'

Actually, you cannot "lurk" by the 1st tee at Seaford Head, because it is approximately in the middle of the 18th fairway. (I doubt it would be built now, for safety reasons.) The cliff edge is the top of a fairly steep escarpment, and the course plays up and down the slopes as well as the more common "across" layout. Amongst other things, this meant it might have been slightly difficult to find my way around, but I had Fred who, to his credit, also gave me the line from the tees, because you cannot always see the flag. He did this so successfully on the lengthy opening hole that I chipped in for a birdie from the fringe.

At home I have a "trophy board" to which I affix a small picture of a bird, with details of any hole I birdie. I went through them the other day, and it was interesting (well, I thought it was interesting anyway; you have to remember that there are no trains to spot where I live) to note how many times I had birdied the opening hole of a new course. In the days when I played only occasionally, it would have been enough to ruin the rest of the round, as a consequence of peaking too early, but these days, it's not uncommon.

Seaford Head does not so much undulate as *slope*, which naturally makes for some interesting shots from elevated tees, and out of valleys, and there are a few holes where the tee shot requires a significant carry over the oblivion of gorse and other brush, significant anyway for a public course which anyone can play (and may well run out of balls and patience with the game). My guess is the slopes were the reason why people were carrying clubs. They would be hard work for a traditional pull trolley, and an electric version might not have enough juice. As a public place, non-golfers would appear from nowhere walking dogs and such like, as I discovered when I was suddenly "exposed" relieving myself in some bushes.

Fred's long game was OK (for a man over eighty, you know) but he seemed to sort of stutter as he got nearer the hole each time. I, meanwhile, having set a high standard with consecutive pars to follow my opening birdie, was playing well. On the short downhill 10th hole, I hit my tee shot to about four feet; Fred was twice as far away on about the same line, and he holed, but I missed. That's golf. Hole Number 12 is also short, only 110 yards, but it plays up an incline of about 30 degrees. It's the sort of place where you could spend a while looking for your ball, only to find that you had holed in one. I got a three; Fred was short, and stuttering somewhat, took another five shots before picking up. That, too, is golf.

The par five 13th leads up to the cliff top, from where one can see the coastline in both directions; to the east, the Seven Sisters (seven white cliff peaks, quite impressive) and to the west, Seaford, Brighton and beyond (rather disappointing). As Fred put it, there was the ferry at Newhaven for the Continent, and there was Eastbourne for the incontinent. Once the ascent is made, there is no turning back, and you play along the cliff top, finally reaching the 18th tee, looking down towards the clubhouse. It was one of the most elevated tees I have come across, but Fred's claim that it was one of the most famous holes in golf is, I think, a little exaggerated.[25] Mind you, Fred is over eighty, as he told me.

Unfortunately, I bogeyed the last, but still finished with an 82, apparently good enough for Fred to tell his mates in the bar about. I also caught the tail end of a joke he told them, which went '...sh-t in the carburettor'; 'Oh yes. How often do I have to do that?' When Fred told me the battery joke again, it was time to leave.

Seriously, thanks Fred, I enjoyed it, and leave you with this:

> This is the story of Fred
> A member at old Seaford Head
> He was terribly matey
> And well over eighty
> And his memory fills me with dread.

I suppose another interesting, more general question would now be: was there a similar spread of inland golf courses at the same time as the coastal invasion, or did it take some time for people to realise the game could be played anywhere? Well, if you want the answer to that, get yourself the *R & A Handbook...*

---

[25] Sorry Fred, but it does not feature in the book of *Britain's 100 Extraordinary Golf Holes.*

6

MY LODGER'S CAR IS A PORSCHE

The Lodger and I met as post-graduate students at London Business School. Like most of the class, we took the two year MBA course in our late twenties. It was a great time, reminiscent of carefree under-graduate days, but without the emotional angst that tends to spoil student life for long periods – sometimes even lasting a fortnight. Unlike university, I also enjoyed the course work, did well, and subsequently joined the Faculty. The Lodger, meanwhile, having come to shake off a career in advertising, found himself persuaded back, with promises of a fast track management career. We joked that the difference in our starting salaries was small. Just a figure 1, in fact, on the front of his.[26] In the summer that we graduated, I took The Lodger for his first round of golf, at Highgate, the most central of north London courses, and quite handy if you worked in Regent's Park and enjoyed a kind of academic freedom, as I did. There were compensations for the lesser salary. I remember nothing of my newest – and destined to become incomparable – golfing friend's first round, and I am sure he doesn't either. After their first round of golf, most people cannot remember how to take their shoes off.

In the main, people who went to Business School in the UK in those days did so out of dissatisfaction with their first career choice rather than as part of a long term strategy. The course director called us "heroes", but he also freely admitted that most of us could be classified as "retreads". Perhaps that is why it was fun. In the early 1980s, we still nurtured other aspirations. The Lodger admired Jeffrey Archer for his parallel careers in politics and as a thriller writer. I preferred

---

[26] My salary was £8,000, very much the low end of the range. His £18,000, at the top. We've had a lot of inflation since then.

Douglas Adams, creator of *The Hitch Hiker's Guide to the Galaxy*, who probably made less money but was funnier. To give my friend the benefit of the doubt, we did not know then what we do now of Lord Archer of Weston-super-Mare. (And, let me freely admit that my golfing visit to Weston has no relevance to this narrative. It has to go somewhere. I am sure Jeffrey would approve of the opportunism.)

WESTON-SUPER-MARE

Weston-super-Mare Golf Club advertises its "all the year round greens" in golfing magazines as a reason for a visit, with the proud boast of "no temporaries here" – except on the day I visited, when there were nine. Some serious kind of work was under way. The good news was the green fee was reduced. The bad news is that "temporary" temporary winter greens – as opposed to those the greenkeeper prepares during the autumn – are the worst sort. The good news is that this course is essentially flat; the bad news is that while it is essentially flat, it is not actually flat anywhere suitable for a temporary green.

I remembered little from my first visit apart from this, so I felt I had better return. This time, I went in the right direction, seeking out the blue flag on the road map to the south of the town, not the one to the north to which I found my convoluted way at first. That turned out to be Worlebury, hard to find, at the top of a steepish incline, designed by Harry Vardon, but not littoral. This time I followed the signs through Weston's shopping malls towards South Beach, and there it was, just round the corner. There were two holes coming in, and two going out on the stretch of course beside a lane, with the visitors' car park at the one end, and the clubhouse and members' car park at the other. I thought this was a bit mean, but I just happened to notice the pro shop was in the visitors' car park, adjacent to the 1st tee, which saved me walking to clubhouse and back for nothing.

It was one of those rare English days when saving energy is important, as the temperature was hovering around 30 degrees Celsius. There were no temporary greens, but with the sort of haze that came with the heat, it was not entirely easy to see that there were fairways. The course is flat and, by definition, flat courses lack definition. Inland, it is usually provided by trees, but this was linksland, and there weren't any. There was a bank of dunes with tall scrubby shrubby vegetation covering it, and at one point I nipped up a public footpath to observe that I was at least literally next to the beach.

The flattest course I have ever played is probably at Lannemezan at the foot of the Pyrenees. Every fairway is lined with trees and for the claustrophobic, it is the sort of golf course one would be made to play in Room 101, but at least the trees provide shade. Here there was nothing, and while the seaside usually produces some kind of breeze, any there might have been was stifled by the dunes. It was indeed stiflingly hot. The first four holes play alongside the dunes away from the clubhouse, towards what is either a headland or an island in the Bristol Channel, and I was somewhat surprised to encounter a lane after four holes, which had to be crossed. There were deposits of golden, really fine sand on the roadway, and a matching beach to seaward, beyond which there were what can best be called mud flats (have I mentioned that it is flat round here?) – a vast stretch of brown silt with that wrinkled effect skin assumes when left too long in a bath. There were what looked like further islands just beyond the mud, but the vision was in fact Wales. One might have set off for a swim and reached Wales before finding deep water. If you're thinking of a seaside holiday at Weston-super-Mare, check the tide tables before you book.

People certainly do take their holidays there, because I then had to walk through a caravan park to get to the 5th hole. It was an interesting stroll. I was impressed to see how all the vans now have extensions – just like their owners' homes, no doubt – made of the modern equivalent of canvas, which more than doubles the area of the original. I also noticed a sign which read "Regrettably no ball games are allowed in the park". Well, there was a great big beach nearby, but it seems a bit spoilsport when all these golfers walk through…

There are just two holes on the other side, out and back. There is an incongruously large elevated tee for the hole coming back which creates the effect of a canyon for the green going out. I wonder where the earth came from? From flattening the rest of the course, perhaps? On the inland side of these two holes was a sort of creek (evidenced by masts of sailing boats) which came up beside a vertical cliff face and seemed most odd, for being inland. On top of the cliff, which rose fairly sharply out of nowhere on the landward side, was a church, and around it a graveyard. Had this once been the shoreline, I wondered? I know that the East Anglian coast is receding, so perhaps England is slowly moving west and will eventually join up with Ireland, and we can then set sail for America. It took a third or fourth look at the church before I realised that there was no roof on the nave. I didn't like it.

On this more exposed stretch of the course there had been a gentle breeze, but as I went back through the caravan park, the dunes intervened once more. The next hole was a par three towards some more distinctly man-made flat-topped mounds which housed three sets of tees, and flanked a green. I remembered the latter – the par five 13th hole – it looks like your second shot has a very good chance of ending up close because if it is moderately wrong in direction, it should be thrown back on line by the mounds. Unfortunately, the temporary green had been set up well short on my previous visit.

As I played back towards the clubhouse alongside the holes I had already played to the left and those I was about to play on the right, the heat took further toll. There were bunkers here and there, and good – if rather flat – greens, but in the absence of wind – a consideration which one would normally rate as positive – the course did not offer much in the way of variety. As I played up to the 10th green by the clubhouse, it seemed hotter than ever, and though I started the second loop with the short 11th, the thought of struggling through the haze towards the far end of the course, lining up on the church with no roof, but otherwise apparently intact, complete with graveyard, did not appeal – notwithstanding the chance to have a go at the par five between the mounds. So, I flicked a wedge sideways from the 12th tee onto the 18th fairway and played in. The first recorded instance of "good weather stopped play".

On balance, I would say that Weston-super-Mare would be a good place to visit when plagued by temporary greens at one's home course. To take advantage of the all-the-year-round seaside greens. Or should that be "mudside"? Weston-super-Lutum??

During the 1980s we worked hard. The Lodger's golf became useful as self-styled "corporate hospitality" boomed, and the company golf day was born. Being translated, corporate hospitality means executives spending their shareholders' money rather than working with it. A colleague at Business School and I had left and started our own enterprise training company which was also booming. He too played golf, so we could have our company golf days if we chose. As our own shareholders, we could do so with a clear conscience, though often one of us would want to talk business while the other did not, which was tedious for both parties. However, as noted, it was impossible in those days to join a club without a long wait and a large down payment. Playing with work colleagues was a tolerable substitute.

Consequently, when a conglomerate made an offer for his advertising agency, The Lodger bought a villa in La Manga, a much smaller complex than it is now, and very much a "little bit of Essex beyond Benidorm". On my first visit, I took with me *Teach Yourself Spanish*. The first time I tried it on a local, the reply was, "Pleath, speak Eeenglish. I think ees better." Until I went to Barcelona ten years later, I felt I had never really been to Spain. The Lodger was on an "earn out", that is, he was to receive the majority of the sale proceeds after five years when he would also be free to leave. I was on more of a "burn out". The business partnership in which I was involved grew until it divided like some basic organism, and the protoplasm of which I was nucleus continued to develop, but in the process, I became less able to bring the necessary enthusiasm for the actual delivery of training courses. I preferred the green sort. Fortunately I was blessed with a fine bunch of staff, so I went part-time. In return, I blessed my senior people with a share of the business, though in truth, I forgot to ask them if they wanted it.

I well remember the beginning, and the end, of my first visit to La Manga. On the North Course, I began 6, 3, 15, DNCH.[27] On the 2nd hole, my partner's tee shot stuck in a date palm – the first time, with or without a golf ball, that I had seen one. The end was the par five 18th on the South Course. With a very strong wind behind, I waited an age for the green to clear, to see if I could carry the famous barranca with my second shot. Then I took no time at all to play, and topped it into a lake. Afterwards, I was really disappointed. For all I knew, that was the last chance I would have, so why squander it? I have always tended to play too quickly, though I must admit that my golf in those days was pretty much a random event. If you had asked me which club I had used on say the 14th hole, I would probably have replied, 'Was there a 14th hole?'

Fortunately I was wrong about revisiting La Manga. The following year, I went over four times, and we began our great series of contests for the Cochinillo Cup. Delighted with the success of playing for our own trophy, we then introduced The Two Lifebuoys Trophy, played over Norfolk courses in December, the Belchalwell Bowl, played over

---

[27] Did not complete hole.

courses in Dorset, and on one occasion, the Torbay Tankard, which featured a visit to Churston.

CHURSTON

Churston Golf Club looks like many an English course, with a clubhouse next to a busy road, an expanse of green grass lined with trees, a 1st tee alongside the clubhouse and an 18th green beyond it. It is not at all reminiscent of a seaside course, apart from one incontrovertible fact. You can see the sea. There is a decent view of Torbay and Torquay to the north, and I would venture to suggest that if you cannot see them, it is probably not golfing weather.

The course starts with a modest par three, a mere 231 yards from the yellow tees. We both got fives, but as it was stroke index 11 and we were playing Stableford, that was a point each. In those days, I used to take such scoring for granted, but should one really get rewarded for a double bogey? Anyway, it's not the easiest opening par, and then you leave this part of the course and cross a road and railway to confront another par three. Only 155 yards, but all carry and bunkered in front, across what the course planner describes as the bottom of a low depression. This is not the 2nd hole, which is a 370 yard par four with a drive across this same depression, but the 17th, so there is time to savour the thought of playing it during the round.

The 3rd hole follows the 2nd towards Brixham and plays along the highest part of the course, which affords some excellent views of Torbay, the self-styled English Riviera. It certainly has a Mediterranean look when the sun is shining. Lots of evidence of human interference with nature, and not of the Seaton Carew kind, rather the tourist "industry" at work, or the north-south divide, as it is sometimes known. Earn money in Durham, spend it in Devon. I could not actually remember much more about our match, so I dropped by the club when I happened to be passing the area. Well, not exactly, it was a detour from the A38 Plymouth to Exeter road, in fact. There was however a lot of traffic passing the road next to the clubhouse, so much that I almost gave up on the idea of turning right into it. Such activity is not what I associate with seaside golf. Unfortunately, Churston was staging a charity event on this day, so I was unable to play. Instead, I found a footpath to the beach which crosses by the 4th and 14th greens. At that point, the course is still meandering beside houses and gardens, but then it goes off into what one might call open country, except that it is not "open". The whole area is surrounded by woods, and the early views of Torbay from the top of the central ridge through the course are to be savoured, as they are not repeated.

The South West Coast Path goes along between the course and the beach, at a height of perhaps 80 feet up the wooded cliffs. It is re-markable how far one can walk in a relatively short time if one does not have to stop to search for balls, putt out, etc; it is also remarkable how much space a golf course takes up if one sets out to walk around its perimeter, as I did. From this point, Churston resembles St Andrew's in that it goes out and back, with a kind of loop at the end but, that apart, I have to admit the resemblance is slight. My journey from the 14th backwards round the course to the 4th I estimate to have been two and a half miles. I met walkers on the way, which was an odd experi-ence for me. There is a never-the-twain-shall-meet about walkers and golfers. Each thinks the other strange for wasting time pursuing their own pastime, though I suppose on the coast, they have at least in common that though the sea is there, neither party actually interacts with it. In the glades of Churston, golfers can remain oblivious to the presence of walkers, though not vice versa. Periodically one hears the unmistakeable clink of a metal wood on a ball, followed by the thrashing sound of a ball entering undergrowth, or a shout of 'Fore', or perhaps 'Bollocks'.

I used the course planner and card of my game with The Lodger to navigate, and I ended up walking back alongside a few holes. The greens looked OK, not obviously difficult. As well as the gross scores on the card, there were Stableford points, and another column of num-bers which I took to be the number of putts I required. On four instances, this was 3, and once, 4. We were playing gimmes, so how ever did I take four putts? I also had six singles, so one way or another, I ended up with thirty-six putts. With the 18th hole a fairly routine par four, any denouement in the match would take place on the par three 17th across the depression. On the tee, I had twenty-eight points to my opponent's thirty so, having found the green, this was a good hole for a single putt, birdie two, worth four points. I needed my opponent to falter, but records merely indicate that he scored a three, for as many points. He repeated the three point feat at the last while I three-putted (obviously going for the birdie) and clinched the match. A pleasant course, worth visiting if you happen to be passing, though if approaching along the South West Coast Path, note that you will have some difficulty taking a trolley.

It is hard to believe this, but in 1991, Spanish telecommunications were such that the La Manga complex had one telephone number, and everywhere within it had a four digit extension number, reached via an operator. To call abroad, you had to go to the office, ask for the number, and when the call was connected, take it in a booth. One evening I called Celia, and she asked how the golf was going. I replied that I was frustrated because my ball kept going into greenside bunkers. She replied with the soothing words, 'That's quite good, isn't it?', and I realised that indeed, I was hitting bunkers in regulation! In other words, a tee shot followed by an approach shot. Regularly. Fantastic.

After our first visit that year, The Lodger's earn out came through, and on the advice of his accountant, he repaired to his villa to avoid UK capital gains tax. This may have been good tax advice, but behaviourally, it left something to be desired. The "villa" was not of the class of that inhabited by for example, David Platt, the England midfielder after his transfer to Italy,[28] and the only people to be found there were ex pat Brits who just wanted to play golf. Now, golf may be the perfect complement to other aspects of life – and The Lodger took the opportunity to write a thriller which sadly never reached the shelves – but Life needs more than golf, and The Lodger found himself sneaking back into the UK, where the hospitality he afforded to me in La Manga was reciprocated chez nous. I believe that affairs with the Inland Revenue have long since been settled amicably, but just in case, he remains The Lodger, so-called because his car – a Porsche 911 – spent several months parked on my drive. In those days, old bangers drove around bearing the legend "My other car is a Porsche". We had a sticker made for Celia's Citroen 2CV; it read: "My Lodger's car is a Porsche".

You cannot get two people and two sets of golf clubs into a Porsche, so when we travelled up to Norfolk for the Two Lifebuoys Trophy, it was for me to do the driving. Driving was the operative word at Royal West Norfolk, driving rain.

---

[28] Before his transfer to Sampdoria, Platt played for Aston Villa. When a reporter from the *Birmingham Post* asked 'Don't you miss the Villa?' he replied, 'No, I live in one now.'

ROYAL WEST NORFOLK

Royal West Norfolk Golf Club – an A to Z

Take the **A**149 from Hunstanton to Wells, and turn off at **B**rancaster. Follow the signs for the beach (there are none to the golf club). Beyond the public car parks, there is an anti-quated creaking **C**lubhouse. The course is laid out on a strip of linksland behind high **D**unes, with marshland on the inland side. **E**xpress permission is needed from the secretary to play as a threeball, but never granted to a fourball. The early **F**airways are shared in opposite directions. Maybe there is a connection.

'**G**ood grief,' exclaimed the elderly member The Lodger and I disturbed in the Smoking Room, 'You're not going out to play!'

High spring tides flood the approach road, and render the clubhouse an **I**sland for a number of hours. 'I thought you were playing golf.' 'Sorry darling, I missed the tide.' I suppose it is an excuse worth trying! This is definitely a members' club – no visitors in **J**uly, August, and early September.

The member The Lodger and I disturbed had been having a quiet **K**ip in the smoking room, which connects the men's **L**ocker room to the entrance hall. You must pass through it. He clearly thought we were **M**ad. True, it was **N**ovember, but we had travelled there specifically to play, and at least the wind and rain were behind us on the **O**utward half. Coming back in, my course planner was turned into a piece of **P**apier mache.

Her Majesty the **Q**ueen has a residence nearby at Sandringham. Whether this has anything to do with the Royal prefix, I do not know. I just needed a word beginning with Q.

The bunkers are lined with **R**ailway sleepers. At the far end of the course, there is a fine view of Brancaster **S**taithe, where the folks of Brancaster can set sail for the North Sea, if they so desire. At this end of the course, **T**idal creeks act as water hazards. I know there are not degrees of **U**niqueness, but this course is more unique than most.

The railway sleepers in the bunkers by the way are **V**ertical. **W**rack, also known as tangle – seaweed and dead vegetation left by the tide – is ground under repair. I fancy **X** is a common entry on scorecards. Definitely a course for match play. Par seventy-one and 6428 **Y**ards does not seem so bad, but all five par fours on the outward half are over four hundred yards. Woe betide an east wind. But **Zzzzz** – you can always catch up on some sleep in the smoking room, waiting for the tide to ebb.

Back in those heady days, one September afternoon Celia and I headed out of London on the A40, in search of damsons for jam, or possibly a damson tree, to grow our own. We found a wonderful secret instead: The Buckinghamshire Golf Club. As we drove along the lengthy wooded drive, through the wrought iron gates, passing the 8th green with its lake on the left, the manicured 9th tee on the right, the chipping green the other side of the river flowing beside the drive, and finally arrived in front of the elegant clubhouse, I have to admit that my initial impression was that this was not the sort of place that people like me tended to be found in. It was an aberration even to have got this far. But, there was a sign directing visitors to enquire about membership, so we enquired. 'It does not,' said Celia, reading the details, 'seem expensive.' This was an aberration on her part, reminiscent of the time when we stayed in Nuits St Georges and she remarked that the wine seemed cheap.[29] A few days later, The Lodger and I turned up for a trial round, and we duly became members. It made a big difference to our golf in a number of ways, one of which was winter play. Apart from our occasional expeditions to the seaside, we tended not to go and pay green fees to play in unpredictable, but probably bad weather. Once we belonged to a club, we could always abandon a round if conditions became intolerable, so it was worth trying. Indeed, at the Bucks, it was necessary to get in as many rounds as possible, in order to bring their average cost down to a level one would find acceptable as green fees.

After moving to Dorset, I maintained my membership until I simply did not visit London often enough for it to make sense. In what turned out to be his last conversation with Celia, my friend announced that he had renewed his one more time, but needed my new year's resolution that I would make a point of playing with him as his visitor, in order to get his average cost per round down below a four figure sum. I am not sure if he succeeded. These days, The Lodger's business career means that he cannot play golf often enough to do himself justice, so he does not maintain a membership for the sake of it. There was

---

[29] There were French francs in those days, and doing the calculations, she had misplaced the decimal point.

however something of a silver lining in this otherwise cloudy scenario. In his business's more formative days, he used to visit Barnstaple in Devon, staying at a hotel in Braunton, close to the enticing links of Saunton. Inevitably, we contested the Saunton Salver:

SAUNTON EAST

Geography dictates that most people will approach Saunton Golf Club from the east, but if you have the chance – and particularly if you are taking someone with you for the first time – try the approach from the north-west. It is superb. As the coast road rises below Croyde Bay, the wide stretch of Saunton Sands comes into view, with its magnificent backdrop of sandhills. Is this the golf course? Are those sandy patches really bunkers? No, they are on too grand a scale, but soon there are glimpses through trees of fairways and greens where the land has "calmed down" a little, before the road goes inland and the entrance to the course is reached.

Below the clubhouse terrace, there is the 18th green of the East Course, with the sharp turn of its dogleg fairway very evident. The big sandhills by the beach are to the right, and in every other direction there are sandhills too. Very little else, just the occasional patches of different shades of green hinting at where the golf courses wend their way through the unadulterated links. You walk down by the practice green and back up to the elevated 1st tee. The view of sandhills is re-inforced, as if that were needed, and there are more golf holes to be seen in the distance. The one which matters is in front of you. Par four 470 yards. This is Saunton. If you can find the fairway – it is actually reasonably wide, despite the mounds either side – you will find it is fairly flat, and if you are a long hitter, nicely warmed up, and the wind is not against, you might just reach the green. Otherwise, you play along this green avenue between the dunes, hoping to pitch on and get down in two more for a five. This is Saunton.

There are many people who later in life come to appreciate their parents despite having thought them rather strict in childhood. Severe but fair, demanding but rewarding, in fact; in golf, this is Saunton East. The 2nd hole offers promise because it is a par five, but you must be straight off the tee or a ditch will get you, and the lay up area in front of the elevated, bunker fronted green is quite narrow. On the 3rd you may well drive over the left hand mound into the wide part of the fairway; if so, you have a reasonable chance of reaching the green. This is not so likely on hole Number 4 – 428 yards, stroke index 1 – where from the fairway you can at last glimpse the green through a gap in sandhills up ahead. Raise your head to the heavens, perhaps in despair, and you will see the rounded hills inland, but at eye level everywhere you see sandhills. As you walk along you may spot through the gaps as they emerge other groups of people, near and far, engaged like yourself in classic, possibly perfect, seaside golf. By links standards, the fairways, if you can hit them, give you a level stance, and the greens, if you can get near the pin, offer you a chance. It is fair, but it is severe.

Surely hole Number 5 offers some respite? 'I have done my chores, dad, can I go and play now?' 'Yes, but watch yourself.' Roughly translated, this means it's only a 113 yard par three, but do not miss the green, do not bounce through it, and do not play above the hole! Eventually, if you have survived this far, the course relents. Actually, when all is said and done, it is there for you to play golf, to enjoy yourself. Number 6 is not long, and offers you a choice of how much of a diagonal fairway to attempt to cut off. Hole 7 is longer but straight, and if the wind has also been against so far, it will assist here. This section of the course is furthest from the sea, and the holes are flatter and wider, with the sandhills more dispersed. But, you do not get something for nothing under this regime, so the ultimate targets are tougher. There is a blind drive at Number 8 to a wide fairway, but the green is almost entirely surrounded by mounds. Number 9 is a sweeping dogleg, with an undulating green tucked away in a corner behind another large mound. The start of the back nine is more generous than the front with another elevated tee to a wide fairway playing to an elevated, tiered green. Hole 11 goes to the furthest part of the course, angled round an out of bounds, and if you have the concentration to spare, you can see how the linksland begins to become arable, before you turn back towards the sandhills, hopefully negotiating the sloping 12th green which is about 35 yards in diameter. I hope you had a good time in this section, because it's time to come in and do your homework.

Number 13 is a par three, only 138 yards, plateau tee to elevated green. Sounds easy, perhaps, but why do you think it is called "Saddle"? A few practice shots should tell you. This gentle adjustment in topography tells us we are firmly back in the sandhills, about to play surely one of the great par fours on the coast of England. "Narrows" is its name, and it's straight, and it's "only" 432 yards, but there is something about the way it calls for a long iron to be rifled between the sandhills as they close in to only ten yards apart approaching the green which presents a big challenge. If the ball is in the air, what is happening on the ground should not make any difference, but it definitely seems to here. After this, tough but fair is the watchword, with the course just about letting it show that it does love us really. There follows the par five 15th where a good, well-angled drive will let a good second run up onto the top tier of the green (but a badly-angled drive will find a ditch); the 16th is a sharp dogleg to an eccentric green behind a mound but there is a wide margin for error off the tee; Number 17 is 186 yards down onto a big flattish green; and, in contrast to the opener's 470 yards, the closing hole is only 387 yards. But, don't you get greedy and try to cut off too much of the dogleg. You will regret it. 'So, you made it then. Well done. Good boy.'

The purists might say that Saunton East is not the perfect golf course despite essentially flat fairways which reward well-directed drives and honest greens which call for accurate approaches, because the 8th tee shot is blind, over a big sandhill. I have two comments: one – building a tee in the sandhill would create a charming and definitely purifying 244 yard par three, and two – sod the purists.

With respect to the elderly and really young children, I have not said too much about the wind, or the way that rainstorms can whip in from the sea, but Saunton East also offers a variety of tees. The distances above are from the whites, but there are longer blues, shorter yellows, red for the ladies, and very forward blacks, to suit all games and conditions. I could happily play at Saunton East for the foreseeable future, say every day, except for one thing – the West Course.

SAUNTON WEST

If the East Course is a strict but loving parent, then Saunton West is a favourite uncle; in the same mould, but indulgent, more fun, sometimes silly, but also capable of playing the odd trick on you. We'll start with an elevated tee, of course, but 343 yards is enough, down to a curving valley fairway. Next, let's try another plateau tee, this time to an elevated dogleg fairway, with a big landing area. Now a challenge – hit diagonally down to the fine fairway, then a long haul upwards to a raised green for this first par five. We're firmly up in the sandhills now, close to the mountainous area behind the beach. Time for a par three, 191 yards, but seriously below the tee. If you have time, from this vantage point, you can probably try and count how many people are playing both courses, but it's too much fun to dally. Two par fours follow, over towards the East Course and back, the second of which cannot be entirely bothered with a fairway. Then comes a remarkable hole, which you might play as a 90 degree dogleg, depending on which tee you are using, and how you feel about the ditch running longitudinally through the fairway. Stroke index 1 naturally, 413 yards, but probably plays longer. Just in case, there is a big notice beyond the fairway, pointing towards the green. After this, there is a rarity, a par four hole which does not need a marker post to indicate the driving line, before the outward half ends with a par three, 141 yards, called "Pond" – because there is a pond in front of the green, though it will probably be dry in summer.

Did you enjoy that? – because now the fun really begins. There's golf in them thar sandhills. The back nine sets off into hitherto uncharted territory in the far dunes, literally miles from the clubhouse, and indeed anywhere. If you like this sort of thing – and I do – you will be delighted to find that the remaining holes comprise three par threes, three par fours, and three par fives, though not in that order. Out here, there is just nature, and golf. You have fourteen clubs and a ball with which to enjoy it, though you had better hit it fairly straight if you only have one of them. It is not for me to attempt to tell you more.

The purists would prefer the East Course, as the better examination of golfing prowess. Well, I know, and I say this; sod the purists!

7

SCORING IN ESSEX

It has been observed that Essex is 60% sex, but the inhabitants cannot spell well enough to realise the fact. Now, it is not immediately obvious that there is any connection between golf and sex, at any rate, as physical activities. Indeed, there are quite a few members of my club who appear to use golf as an excuse for getting out of bed early on Sunday mornings, long after the children have grown up. However, if you are aware of anyone for whom physical sex lasts about four hours, does not really involve breaking sweat, and includes "holing out" eighteen times, as it were, do please let me know.

Yet, no less an authority than Tom Watson is reported to have said words to the effect that a links course without wind is like a woman with no clothes – no challenge. Not perhaps the most politically correct choice of simile, but Tom was more noted for his iron play than for his irony. Probably for him, a links course on a still day is dull routine. Personally, I like it; for some incomprehensible reason, if you take away the trees from a golf course, I drive straight. This is one reason why I elected to play my way around the coast rather than take on the famous English venues such as Sunningdale and Woodhall Spa.

But while accepting that when the wind blows, it makes an event to remember (think for example of the Opens at Carnoustie in '99 and Muirfield in '02), I don't think I agree with Tom. You see, it very much depends upon the woman. I would for example find any of the women who modelled for the paintings of Rubens difficult to er, handle, even when I was younger, and definitely now. At the opposite end of the cultural spectrum, the women who talk in that peculiar way in "freeviews" for the Adult Channel (yes, I have watched them) would nauseate me, clothed or not. But imagine if you will that the woman in question was someone you had never met. It might be stimulating in the extreme, but confronted with such shall we say "forthcoming" behaviour, you might well find it a challenge. You might well be "up for it", but it still would be a challenge. After all, what would she be expecting?

On the other hand, suppose it was your mother-in-law...

There are definitely parallels if not with actual sex, then with romance, or – to use an old fashioned term, courting – to be found in golf. One such is the "bad night out". When you have one of those nightmare rounds in the monthly medal, probably using up your handicap before the turn, but you nevertheless stick with it, refusing to "no return", you can almost guarantee that you will get a beautiful par – fairway, green, putt, tap in – on the 18th. It is the exact feeling you got all those years ago when you took a girl out for the evening, struggled throughout to entertain her or engage her in conversation and, taking her home, were just about to rejoice that it was over, good riddance etc, when she gave you the most fantastic goodnight kiss.

On the other hand, there are occasions when you do really well, and everything works out to your advantage, as if the course lets her defences down a little too far. Does she remember, next time you turn up on the 1st tee? You bet she doesn't! Note the use of "her" and "she"; if nouns had gender in English, it is a sure thing that "golf course" would be feminine.[30]

The other common event in monthly medals is the "interruptus" round, where things are going brilliantly until say – well, at my home course, it is the 16th, where it is possible to go out of bounds either side of the fairway. People frequently do, on both sides – first one, then the other. The round is ruined there and then. Does this happen to you? Then think carefully; have you ever wondered why medals occur monthly?

It is when playing a course for the first time that the imagery of courting, or philandering perhaps, is most vivid. Firstly, if it is not

---

[30] Actually, I don't know if it would be. Genders are a mystery. Why is it El Mar in Spain (masculine), Il Mare in Italy (ditto), but La Mer (feminine) in intervening France? It's even the same sea, for goodness sake. Mind you, in French, la queue is a term for the penis, and le con is, well...

something you do often, it can feel like you are being unfaithful to your home course. Some such people basically feel uncomfortable all the way round, unable to adapt to the unfamiliar circumstances. It's as if they don't really understand what's gone wrong, but they are sure it's never happened to them before. It's a particular problem for seniors, though they do find it easier in matches, when their mates are on hand, and it doesn't cost anything.

If on the other hand you are "a regular" at strange courses, it is the same sort of feeling Don Juan or Casanova must have got anticipating another adventure. It is never a case of "I can't face this" but always "here we go, here we go, here we go..." You like the look of the course, you want to delve deeper into her mysteries, you admire every detail; you put on your best behaviour – and, although you can never tell what the outcome will be, you do your best to score.

Some golf magazines try and rate golf venues with a one-to-five star system along several different dimensions. I don't. With me, it's either "thank you very much", "can I have your phone number?" or "what are you doing tomorrow?"

CLACTON-ON-SEA

I had been told by a former Essex man now resident in Dorset not to expect too much of Clacton-on-Sea Golf Club, so I arrived with modest expectations, particularly having played previously at nearby Frinton. Despite the county's lengthy coastline, these are the only two littoral courses Essex can boast, and as Suffolk has only one qualifier, there is probably something about the terrain on the northern side of the Thames estuary which is unsuitable for golf.

Certainly the approach to Clacton-on-Sea GC is unprepossessing; in the *R & A Handbook* entry it claims to be on the seafront, but the road seems to leave the town and head off back to London before signs indicating a golf course appear. The course is better described as "behind the sea wall" with an old coastal gun emplacement (which I understand is called a Martello tower) dominating the flat landscape. There are drainage ditches known as fleets crossing fairways here and there. They probably pre-date the course, and there is a system for regulating how the rainfall is retained to prevent adjacent lower lying areas from flooding. Their high water level for my visit also provided an early warning to expect dampness on the course, as it was late November.

This and much more information was provided by Ron, whom I met on the 1st tee, out on his own because one of his planned opponents for the day had cried off with a bad back (as we shall see, this turned out to be a lucky choice for the opponents). Ron was a member of the Seniors' Committee, which meant (a) he seemed to know everyone else playing, and (b) half of them needed to stop him and ask questions about rulings in competitions, subscriptions for dinners, etc. Ron told me a lot about the course and the club, much of it about the greenkeeping staff, and much of that unrepeatable. The greenkeepers' perspective is probably that they are trying to do a difficult job with not a lot of help from the members. There was a notice advising members that they were "sponsors" of a particular green, according to the letters of their surnames, meaning that they should look to repair pitchmarks on arrival at the nominated hole – a novel idea, but it also implied that the membership could not be relied upon to repair pitchmarks as a matter of routine.

Ron had chosen to join Clacton over the nearer Frinton, which he said was boring, and explained that after the first nine holes, Clacton's parkland gave way to more linksy terrain. I can't say I exactly spotted the difference, though it is true that the sea comes moderately into view around the 8th hole. There were then some distinctly artificial looking mounds disturbing the essential flatness of the land, which Ron said were the consequence of the area having been ploughed up during the Second World War to prevent its use by German glider pilots as a landing strip.

The first half consists of three holes of each par, something I generally like. I wonder where the convention of only four holes each of par threes and fives comes from? Certainly not the Old Course (which is generally thought to have given us eighteen holes), which has only two long and two short holes. There was little wind, so I did not particularly notice the changes of direction, but Ron said the prevailing winds – there are two, offshore and onshore! – tended to blow across the short holes, sometimes necessitating starting shots over patches of impenetrable scrubby bush which alternated with clumps of hawthorn. Together, these features provided some definition for the holes along the flat terrain. Without Ron, it might have been difficult to find my way around.

Ron and I talked quite a bit about other courses. He had learned to play on the solid clay at Canvey Island, and had only discovered "proper golf" on visits to the Scottish Borders. Apparently Ian Woosnam was once embarrassed on a visit to celebrate Canvey Island's conversion to eighteen holes. As he persisted in trying to take a divot from the course's concrete-like foundations, the ball flew all over the place. This was one reason why Ron preferred Clacton. After the turn, I saw another.

The 9th hole plays along the shoreline between the sea wall and a large patch of scrub, and I could see how on a windy day it might be difficult to finish the hole with the same ball one started with. After a challenging 10th (the stroke index having been inexplicably changed recently according to Ron – see elsewhere), there followed a series of shortish par fours, back and forth from the sea wall, with fleets "protecting" the greens. Well, they weren't protecting the greens from Ron, despite some awkward pin placements. After a routine par at 11, he holed from eight feet for a birdie at 12, and his second shot to 13 nearly went in the hole. The chance of three birdies in a row required a longish putt at 14 which he sent charging past, but he courageously saved his par. At the par three 15th his tee shot left about 12 feet which he holed in a by-now-routine manner, and on the par five 16th, after his third shot had unluckily drifted away from the hole, his uphill putt needed one more roll to have made four birdies in five holes.

Ron told me the 16th was the "photograph hole". I think he meant "signature", as they say on the telly. A picturesque, and indeed, eminently photogenic par three with a teeing ground set in a copse, playing over three ponds edged with attractive foliage, to what almost amounts to a switch-back two-tier green. It was quite unlike the rest of the course, in fact.

Ron pushed his tee shot into a bunker, which he said was deep and sandy. One thing that was good at Clacton was the bunker sand. My ball was in four in the first five holes, so I knew, but this proved to be Ron's only sand shot – two bounces and into the hole. This is known in some circles as a "golden ferret", but what we recognised here was Ron's fourth birdie in five holes. After a wait on the tee of the par four 18th, Ron gave me a lengthy rundown on where to position the ball off the tee, and then proceeded to sky his tee shot, as he put it, thinking too much about *where* to hit it, and not enough about *how*. I remarked that he would have his work cut out to get another birdie, whereupon he took his 18 degree utility club and knocked the ball fiercely forward onto the bank of a fleet where it hit a startled gull! Not quite an albatross, but definitely a birdie of a different kind. Finally, after missing the green with his third and then almost chipping in, a five together with the five he had taken on the 10th gave him a back nine of 33 gross, 27 net! I actually went round in 78, keeping a 6 off my card, but scarcely noticed.

It was a bright day and I wanted to look around to see what the area had to offer (very little, I'm afraid), so I declined Ron's offer of a drink. He said there would be no need for my corroboration, people in the bar would believe his round. Does he do that often, I wonder? I went to Frinton, as I had very little recollection of what it was like, but the course was closed. They were spraying to get rid of the leatherjackets. On the way back to my hotel, I looked in at the Clacton Factory Shopping Village. It seemed to be selling the sort of "designer clothing" that had not managed appeal even to Essex folk, including some leather jackets.

Is it true what they say about Essex? That evening I dined in a pleasant pub where the bar staff consisted of three attractive young women. They were all brunettes – but I was already in Suffolk by then. Over dinner, I pondered Ron's issue of stroke indexing.

ABOUT STROKE INDEXES

Tradition has it that the stroke index of a hole indicates its relative degree of difficulty, subject to another tradition, which allocates the odd and even stroke indexes to separate halves of the course. How long these "traditions" go back I do not know, but they appeared to be the case when I first became aware of them in the late 1960s. However, I have a vague memory that when James Bond famously (and of course, fictionally) played Goldfinger around Royal St George's, he "played his handicap" as it suited him so to do. This could of course be because Ian Fleming got it wrong. As a former military intelligence officer, he would not have been overly concerned with facts.

My impression during this peregrination is that the traditions generally hold today. Index Numbers 1 and 2 are commonly the longest par fours, and the par threes tend to have the highest allocations. However, the English Golf Union has a different notion, and has published a set of guidelines. If memory serves, these read:

The degree of difficulty of a hole is not a sole criterion for the
allocation of an index;

Odd numbers should be given to the more difficult half, even
to the other;

Numbers one to six should be in the middle of a half, and not
adjacent to each other;

Index Numbers 9 through 12 should be allocated to holes 1, 9,
10, and 18 in suitable order;

No three of indexes 7 through 10 should be sequential; Consecutive index numbers should be given to different types of
hole, e.g. if index 1 is a long par four, 3 should perhaps be a
par three or five.

When the course at Sherborne was redeveloped a few years ago,
"The Committee" ran a competition to set the new stroke indexes.
Working on the assumption that the two toughest par fours, one on each
half, would remain indexed 1 and 2 and that one half would be odds
and the other evens, there were only two basically different configu-
rations for each half. So, I entered the four permutations in the competition with, I thought, a good chance of getting it right. Of course, I
had reckoned without The Committee, which did not allow the advice
of a mere national governing body to interfere with its deliberations.
The consequence is that if you are conceding someone five strokes in
a match, your opponent gets them all by the 12th hole, and has a very
good chance of building a substantial lead. Conversely, the 12th is an
alternative starting hole, from where it favours the lower handicapper, as three of the five shots are not conceded until the 12th, 15th, and
17th holes to be played, by which time the superior talent should have
prevailed.

What bothered Ron at Clacton over the recent index changes was
their use in Stableford, not match play, where the considerations are
different. For a 12 handicapper, starting at the 12th hole at Sherborne
brings the "shotless" holes into play sooner, and leaves a nicely handi-
capped finish, which may be preferable to getting the shots "front
end loaded". This is indeed a matter of preference, because while
the shot holes have a material effect on match play, is it not mainly a
psychological issue in Stableford? Ron thought it unfair that thanks to
a recent change, single figure players could now drive very close to a
short but low-indexed hole, and stand a good chance of getting a four

point birdie. But, if you talk to single figure players, category one players in particular, they will say that Stableford is tough. That is because the essential difference between Stableford and medal play is that the former is a damage-limitation system of scoring. It insures the high handicappers against the sort of disasters which low handicappers, ipso facto, do not have. The converse is that high handicappers typically receive shots on par threes, and traditionally, two shots on tough, longer par fours. Both these provide significant psychological advantages. It only takes one reasonable shot to make 3 on a par three (for a net 2), and when playing a long par four as a par five, which is usually wise, "success" results in a net birdie. Does the stroke index really matter in Stableford, other than its function in allocating the lump sum stroke play handicap to individual holes? I bet if you asked a group of club members how they would ideally like the indexes, you would get different answers, reflecting the players' differing psychological relationships with different holes. If you asked my winter fourball partner KPMG, he would recommend that we had a different allocation each. He is left-handed, and also very astute.

The stroke index is much more significant in match play, where it decidedly makes a difference to the players' scores on a given hole, and therefore how *they should play the hole*. Forget Ben Hogan's advice to play the course, not the opponent. You are not him, and neither is your opponent. In most situations, only the lower indexed holes matter, as it is rare for scratch players to encounter 28 handicappers.

(Once at the Buckinghamshire, my scratch partner Compo – scratch meaning a random, unpractised pairing – came up against opponents including the scratch player Tim – scratch meaning zero handicap. When Tim holed in one at the 9th, even though it was index 17, Compo still had two for the half, and a shot for the hole! He failed, of course.[31] Why does such confusing terminology exist? The grip is something we use to hold the grip on our clubs when at the club. In cricket, bowlers pitch the ball on the pitch (or wicket) in order to hit the wicket to take a wicket.)

So, the question in match play is should the holes where the strokes are most often given and received be the most difficult? Or should the low index holes be those where the stroke differential has least

---

[31] For those who have been there, he did not clear the water.

overall impact on the state of the match, given possible differences between the players? Index 1 – par four hole Number 7, 413 yards – at the Buckinghamshire has a stream crossing the fairway a tantalising distance from the tee, and another watercourse 50 yards in front of the green. For moderate players, the safest strategy is to play short of the water each time, but the player conceding a stroke will often feel obliged to take the risk, which obligation will make the challenge greater. On the other hand, against a good player, the moderate's extra shot gives either player a fair chance of winning the hole. This hole therefore argues both for and against its indexing.

Putting the stroke holes in the middle of the round where they have a less dramatic impact on the state of the match, and varying the nature of the holes so that they are not all the same type (eg long par fours) seems to make sense, because it brings differing aspects of the game into play. I can certainly see where the EGU is coming from, but dear EGU, do you not realise that most English club golfers most of the time play Stableford? In a game between a scratch player and a 3 handicapper, the focus is on indexes 1, 2 and 3 whether the format is match play or Stableford. Between players of 15 and 18, however, it switches to indexes 16, 17 and 18 for the latter format. The fact is, the same system is attempting to satisfy two distinct purposes.

With clubs now using computers to record scores, it is trivial to produce statistics which define unequivocally the relative difficulty of the holes on the course. There could be no argument under such a system. As for me, in my littoral peregrination, I would like the stroke index to tell me how difficult the hole plays compared to others.

FRINTON

I am afraid that I cannot remember much about Frinton Golf Club. Two things spring to mind about the town itself: it has, or at any rate had, no pubs; that itself ought to be enough to forget the second, which is that it used to host an important grass court tennis tournament, back in the amateur days. Indeed, the tennis club appears on a road sign beside the golf club, and the Parish and Methodist churches. Frinton folk may be teetotal, but they have their religious priorities. The signposted approach leads to the shore, and there is an attractive sward between the road and the beach, but the golf course itself is behind the sea wall, and too flat to provide sea views.

Neff partnered me the day we visited, and I asked him what he recalled, but as he usually struggles to tell me how many strokes he took on the previous hole, I was not surprised when he was not forthcoming. It was actually an unusually hot August day, and the bright sunshine made it difficult to find our way around. Also, I recall that I had just invested in a new driver to keep up with the G-force (to be precise, one KPMG, my winter fourball partner whose new driver had added twenty yards). All mine was doing was causing the ball to fade gently away from the target line like the best David Beckham[32] cross. When Neff nailed his ancient 3 wood, he sailed past me.

There are naturally enough lots of fleets running across the course, but they could not have come much into play. I found my card, and I scored 35 Stableford points when clearly out of sorts with my game. The four longest par fours are stroke indexes 1 to 4. Number 1 is hole 9, and Number 4 hole 10. Don't tell the EGU. Neff managed thirty points; mind you, he was playing off 54, so when he parred the 185 yard 3rd hole (across a fleet) it was worth four points. He went one better on the 109 yard 13th, with a two for five points. I do recall that there is a good chance to salvage a bad round with birdie chances at Numbers 17 and 18, both being par fives down the prevailing wind. I finished 7, 6. Otherwise, that is about it. I should have included "I don't recall much about that party" to my list of "romantic" outcomes.

This attempt at classifying the experience of playing a new course, apart from being politically incorrect, still leaves me pondering the question of comparing courses, unanswered after the visit to Berwick-upon-Tweed. Once again two dimensions appear, for with romantic attraction, personality counts as much as looks. I have certainly heard the expression "I fancied him until he opened his mouth" as well as the version with her as the pronoun.[33] There is a third to add for the first time visit, which is the question of "Does it sort of click?" (to borrow a phrase used by Ian Botham to describe his special achievements). It did not click at Frinton, and I apologise to the members if

---

[32] Or would do if Beckham were left-footed.

[33] A gay designer friend of Celia's had an interesting variation on this. He used to meet men at a Turkish bath, and would say, 'I fancied him until he put his clothes on.'

I have misrepresented their club. I am afraid I am unlikely to return. There are no pubs.

ADVENTURES WITH *THE GOOD PUB GUIDE*

As you know, I never travel without *The Royal & Ancient Golfer's Handbook*, which of course would not dream of passing opinion on courses. I am of the opinion that all other golf course guides are of questionable integrity, as club secretaries have become wary of submitting information, lest they find they have somehow incurred some liability to advertising costs, or promised to accept two-for-one green fees. Communications from the *R & A* on the other hand are serious and important, and I am sure that even the most bombastic, Muirfield-style Secretary would not fail to return information to HQ in St Andrew's, for fear of possible excommunication. Thus, *The R & A Handbook* is reliable. One might even say *definitively reliable.*

The concept of being *definitively unreliable* was created by Douglas Adams, an epithet belonging to *The Hitch Hiker's Guide to the Galaxy*, and fully deserving of the description, but it is run a close second by another tome I am never without when at large in England, *The Good Pub Guide*. Now, I have a lot to thank the Guide for, it had a significant role to play in my decision to move to Dorset from London, but it is seriously unreliable. I have long been of the opinion that this is because the editor insists on personally visiting every referenced entry every year and, as the front cover proudly boasts, there are over 5,000.

Nevertheless, I always start with the Guide to try and find accommodation when peregrinating, because there are useful maps showing the locations of all the main entries which offer accommodation. I like to stay in pubs rather than hotels, because in a good pub there are usually locals rather than the tourists and business people one finds in hotels, and one learns more about the place, if only by accidentally eavesdropping. Plus, it's great being able to drink good real ale without having to walk home.

On this occasion, I needed to be near to Felixstowe, and there was nothing indicated on the map, so I turned to the "Lucky Dip" section for Suffolk. I suppose you might say I had been warned. As a result, I booked into the Bull Hotel in Woodbridge. Later, when approaching the town, I realised I did not have an address, so I needed to watch out for pubs. On the edge of the town, there was The Seal, and then I passed The Cherry Tree. At the second attempt, I found my way to the town centre, passing The Crown, and opposite it, The Cross. (The nearby Captain's Table, I noted later, looked as if it had been a pub, but was now a restaurant.) Soon afterwards, I found the Bull, but I had to go round a one way system, which brought me to the Kings Head.

With the Bull located, I was at journey's end, and not a little thirsty, so I popped into the Kings Head for a pint of Adnams Fisherman. It was a delightful place with old tables, ramshackle furniture and a stone floor. (I don't like to go straight to the bar when arriving to stay at a pub; it creates an undesirable, though probably entirely accurate, impression. Hence, I went to one I was not staying at.) Later that evening, I went out for a stroll, en route to an Indian restaurant I had spotted, and called in at Ye Olde Bell and Steelyard, just round the corner from the Bull, for an excellent pint of Greene King IPA. Then, on my way to eat, realising I should have visited the gents, I popped into the Old Mariner. A swift half of Adnams was obligatory.

The following night, undertaking a more systematic survey of the town, I came across the Thomas Seckford, which looked a really homely place, and served excellent Tolly Cobbold. I don't know if those were all the pubs in Woodbridge – somewhere I saw a painting of the Ship Inn, facing Ferry Quay – but it was enough, and the towns-folk were doing their pubs, and their three local brewers – Adnams, Greene King, and Tolly – proud everywhere. Everywhere, that is, except the Bull, which was cavernous and empty to the point of making my footsteps echo. It needed a kind of treasure hunt to find a member of staff, until one announced herself by using a vacuum cleaner at nine o'clock at night (well, there weren't any customers, were there?).

Having said that, I will concede that one single visit to a pub may be inconclusive, which is why the Guide ultimately depends upon vol-untary reports, and does eventually manage to remove entries which no longer deserve the accolade. For example, on my first visit to Ye Olde Bull and Steelyard, I was served by a delightful, buxom barmaid. The following night, in her place was an imbecilic-looking man of about 30 with a tee shirt which read "IF U CAN READ THIS U NEED ANOTHER BEER". He managed to stare blankly through me from about four feet for what felt like ten minutes, until I walked out in silent protest, frustratingly unable to slam the wind-damped door behind me, so leaving the barman to his oblivion.

I popped into The Cross instead. It was a very pleasant local pub. The Crown on the other hand was definitely a hotel, with a small bar area, and not really a pub at all. Frankly, so was the Bull. I checked *The Good Pub Guide* again. Along with the undeserving Bull, it listed the Kings Head, which was fine – and also somewhere called the Anchor. I wonder what that was like?

******

Because no land projects out into the North Sea, it is not obvious that Felixstowe lies on a peninsula, but in fact its particular corner of Suffolk is bounded by the Rivers Orwell to the south, and Deben to the north, and it is only via the eight miles or so between the two crossings at Ipswich and Woodbridge that it is joined to the rest of England.

As I drove down from Woodbridge I wondered if the terrain would be pancake-flat like the Essex of Clacton, or show some changes of elevation like Suffolk to the north. Woodbridge actually slopes down to the river. I don't think you could say it's on a hill, but there is certainly enough variation in altitude for golfing purposes. As I headed away from Felixstowe Docks towards Felixstowe Ferry (don't mistake the two), the land looked ominously flat. When I reached the seashore I sighted a group of brightly painted beach huts, drawn up to higher ground as protection against the ravages of winter tides, and looking as if they were huddled together for warmth. I wonder what the collective noun for beach huts in winter is? In summer, it's a parade, or perhaps in the classier resorts, a promenade, but in winter? A refuge maybe, or a retreat?

Then the clubhouse appeared on the horizon, and it was elevated, and there behind it and between it and the sea, was a links golf course. I've never been entirely sure about exactly what defines links – when asked by for example, Americans, I reply, 'You'll know it when you see it'. Here, I saw it. Undulating, scrubby, semi-wasteland, not at all beautiful – except to the eyes of a golfer. I could hardly wait.

FELIXSTOWE FERRY

The 1st tee at Felixstowe Ferry Golf Club is elevated, with views of the sea, and a nicely defined fairway to the right of the small road – "public highway" according to official disclaimer notices – that runs through the course. After a reasonable tee shot, I couldn't see a green, until some greenkeeping staff replaced the flag in the hole, away to the right. They showed no signs of moving either themselves or their vehicles away, so I rather nervously hit a 5 wood, which bounced a couple of times and found a bunker at what turned out to be the front left of the green. As I approached, one of the vehicles departed, leaving just one man, tinkering with a mowing machine. Of course, literally as I drew my sand wedge from the bag, he started it up! No matter, I splashed out of well-maintained, good quality sand to about eight feet, and holed the putt.

The 2nd tee, to a par five, is also elevated, and the drive to the fairway is on a diagonal – one of several holes where you have a choice of how much distance to try and cut off, backing yourself to hit straight, while also judging the effect of the wind. In such circumstances, first-time visitors tend to be at a disadvantage, as I discovered when I found the water on the 7th. On the 2nd, there were cross bunkers about 50 yards short of the green, so choosing a 5 wood rather than a 3, I duly hit my second beautifully into the furthest...

But enough of me. Felixstowe Ferry is a treat. The fairways are all well-defined, the teeing grounds smartly maintained with edged paths around them, and winter tees where they were needed, at the side of rather than in front of their big brothers. The greens "emerge" from their surroundings in the classic links manner that affirms they have not been put there by bulldozers. They are big, with subtle slopes, and even in November, very true. I would imagine they can be seriously fast in summer.

The front nine plays back and forth mostly inland from the road, and if it is a little flatter than it might be, there is a serious challenge from a meandering watercourse which separates the two par fives, Numbers 7 and 8, and passes in front of the greens on the short 5th and 9th. The stroke index 1, 6th hole meanwhile probably plays in a crosswind on most days.

There was a course planner on the scorecard, which indicated on one hole a style (sic) – presumably an elegant device for crossing a hedge, rather than the usual rugged, rustic offering. I thought the watercourse might be a creek, linking with the estuary, but the card identified it as a ditch. Well, if it was merely a ditch, it was one of the biggest I've seen. Back and forth par fives often don't work, but these were great, with the road on the right and the ditch on the left of the downwind 7th, and ditches on both sides of the 8th. This is not a course for slicers; indeed, the club asks for handicap certificates, as there is also a nine-hole course for beginners to use. There was rather more traffic on the road than I might have expected, given that according to the map, it does not go anywhere, but at length I realised that it goes to a hamlet called Felixstowe *Ferry*, which probably explained why none of the traffic seemed to come back again, despite the road being a dead end.

Holes 10 and 11 lead back to the clubhouse, and the 12th is only 144 yards, played uphill (and across the road) to a green where those who have finished or are waiting to play can watch their fellow golfers make a mess of things. One then walks over the seaward side of the course to play a series of three shortish but seriously undulating – both the fairways and the greens – par fours. There is a strange metal object to the left of the 13th fairway, looking rather like a giant candlestick, or a lamp post without a lamp. I guessed it might be a marker for the 18th fairway. Holes 13, 14 and 15 were downwind for me, and I should have done better on them, for the finish is splendidly difficult with a 200 yard par three into the wind, and a classic 17th, a quarter of a mile, straight, but upwind, uphill, and on this occasion, into the sun. A big bunker crosses the fairway about 100 yards from the green, which I thought a little odd – but the two guys in front of me both had to play shots out of it, so it appeared to know why it was there.

The 18th offers a challenging uphill approach shot over a heavily bunkered green, and probably produces some interesting match play results. The candlestick was not a marker (though judging by the fairway, it might have been once upon a time); in fact, there are no blind shots, and you always know where you're going. Unlike say Royal St George's which can be confusing, Felixstowe Ferry is on a very human scale. Indeed, the staff were very human too. I had phoned earlier, and established that it would cost me £25 to play after 1 PM (and presumably more before that), but that I could buy a "winter special" for £20, which included lunch, provided I completed the round while the kitchen was open. I thought I had made a tee reservation for 10 AM, but there is no such system. Nevertheless, I did get a lunch ticket, and when I explained that I wasn't terribly hungry, the steward was quite upset that I didn't want fish and chips (or ham, egg and chips, as a variation). He offered me a drink instead, and eventually we agreed I would take a pot of tea and a cheese and tomato baguette. These were brought in turn by a smiling waitress who, despite a busy time in an obviously very friendly clubhouse, did not need to ask if they were for me. In the event, there were two baguettes, both stuffed so full of cheese that the tomatoes had to be perched on top. I ate them both, of course; who says there's no such thing as a free lunch?

8

LINKSLAND

ABOUT LINKSLAND

As noted, the way to identify linksland is to recognise it when you see it. However, my spellchecker does not recognise the word, but I am confident it exists. I used to own an interesting book, *To The Linksland*; I lent it to someone some time ago, thinking that he too would enjoy it. Obviously, he did. I cannot remember whether the author explains what linksland is, but unfortunately, nor can I remember to whom I lent the book. So, I reckoned it was about time to find out for myself.

It is pretty obvious that when the golf boom came to England, the English assumed that when Scots talked of "the links", they meant the golf course. There are streets leading to the courses at Sheringham in Norfolk, and Budleigh Salterton in Devon, named *Links Road*, and there are probably lots more. But these two fine courses are on cliff tops, played on excellent undulating but not bumpy turf, and I do not believe either could be called linksland. Perhaps the English thought that a "links" was a coastal golf course...

However, in P G Wodehouse's stories of the Oldest Member, he refers to "the links", but there is a lake hole – and surely a coastal course would not have a lake. A pond maybe, but not a lake. This is of course a golfing rather than a linguistic argument. A more obvious proof of the assertion that "links" meant "golf course" in English came to me when I recalled a street in West London called Links Road, so I looked in an A to Z of London.

There are – ready? – 2 each of Links Avenues, Links Drives, The Links, Links Views, Links View Roads, plus a Links View Close, 3 Linksides plus a Linkside Close and a Linkside Gardens, 4 Linksways, and 7 Links Roads (forgive me if I have missed a few). Judging by their present locations, an awful lot of golfing territory in London has been lost over the years, but the Links Views appear to overlook respectively Finchley and Dartford Golf Courses, which is all the confirmation we need of the erroneous Sassenach use of the sacred term.

Well, actually, I am not sure that even the Scots can claim that "linksland" is sacred, or even royal – though it is ancient. There are areas of land called "The Links" which have nothing to do with golf, to be found in towns along the coast of Fife, for example, and there is actually a town called Lundin Links. Oddly, its golf club is known as Lundin. On the other hand, the neighbouring town of Leven has a golf course, known inevitably as Leven Links. I think they are actually adjacent – on the shore, of course.

So, to get back to the point – what is linksland? – and why, you may wonder, do I not just look the word up in a dictionary? Well, I tried; I have two favourites, *The Chambers Dictionary*, and *Collins Concise 21st Century Edition*. These publishers are (or were) based respectively in Edinburgh, and Glasgow, yet the word linksland does not appear in either lexicon. What is worse, the latter defines "links" as "*short for* golf links" and cross-refers readers to an entry "golf course or links" as if to imply that the terms are interchangeable. I am sorry, *Messrs Collins & Son*, but I have never heard a single scorecard-carrying golfer, nor a commentator since Henry Longhurst's time, refer to a course as "the links" (unless it was – if that is grammatically correct – and even then, I haven't). *Chambers*, meanwhile, actually lists the word in the singular only, and refers to "a stretch of flat or gently undulating ground along a seashore; hence a golf course, *originally one by the sea*" (my italics). Er, no. See above.

Actually, the first part of that definition is getting close, isn't it? *Collins* adds "undulating ground near the shore" in corroboration – but I don't believe that is enough. Surely there should be reference to the nature of the land, the spiky grass, unsuitable for ploughing, with grassier areas grazed by sheep and rabbits (thus providing fairways) which sheltered from the wind behind rises in the ground, and wore away the grass, so creating bunkers – or is this account of the origins of the game just romantic balderdash? Anxious, I consulted a Scottish Dialect Dictionary, which described links as "sandy knolls, a stretch of sandy, grass-covered ground near the seashore". More corroboration – but remarkably no mention of the word linksland.

Finally, I turned to what should be an unimpeachable source –
Classic Golf Links of Great Britain & Ireland by Donald Steel, the
doyen of British Golf writers. It has an introduction by Peter Thomson,
five times Open Champion, who should know a thing or two about
links courses, upon which the Open is always played. He uses the word
linksland, and talks about it a bit, but mostly launches an attack on
modern golf course designers, as noted elsewhere. So does Steel – both
use the word, and attack modern designers. He however also describes
at some length the how, where, and what of linksland and the origins
of golf.

I have always thought of linksland as being low lying, close to sea
level, but on the front cover of this book, there is a photograph of
the Ailsa Course at Turnberry with the lighthouse and Ailsa Craig in the
background. The course is clearly many metres above sea level – but it
looks like a links course, and what's more, it is an Open Championship
Venue, so it *must* be a links course. The Open is always played at links
courses, and the *R & A* is never wrong.

As for what Donald Steel has to say about linksland well, it is too
detailed to summarise here, but don't worry. You'll recognise linksland
when you see it.

******

For a man with a literally littoral peregrination to perform, where
better to go in search of linksland than Lincolnshire?

SEACROFT

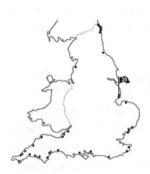

Seacroft Golf Club is to be found by passing through the streets to the south of Skegness, with their strange mixture of hotels, ca-
fes, charity shops, pawnbrokers and so on.
The first question most people are likely to
ask is "where's the car park?" because there
is none in sight. That is because there is not
one at the clubhouse, but it is not true to say
that the club is without car parks; there are two – one mile, and a mile
and a half away respectively – at the alternate starting points of the 6th
and 10th tees. The reason there is no car park at the clubhouse is that
the land is too precious. It is needed for golf, to provide the 1st tee and

fairway, and the 18th fairway and green. To look at, you would recognise this land as linksland yet, beyond the clubhouse, and clearly between the golf course and the sea, is a row of houses. Not, I hasten to add, a "row" as in "terrace" of houses, but rather the sort of "row" which might expect to have the word "millionaires" immediately preceding it. This fact raises doubts: can this be linksland, in fact; and is the course literally littoral?

The answer to the first question is "yes". I have stated my case (of which I am certain) that one recognises linksland when one sees it. I see it here, but if there is doubt, Donald Ross includes Seacroft in his book. In answer to the second question, I ventured along millionaires' row until I came to the point where the road expired and a "Site of Special Scientific Interest" was announced. No vehicles or other man-made things allowed. This land is between Seacroft GC and the shore, so clearly, it qualifies. In fact, the course itself, or parts of it, are an SSSI too, I believe.

It is a splendid course, if you don't mind the houses (and find somewhere to park). Considering how the surrounding fenland is pancake-flat, there are surprising, and entertaining, changes in elevation to come later on in the round. St Andrew's-style, the opening and closing holes have each other on the left, with a gentle ridge of rough running between them. The holes are named. Number 3 is Punchbowl, something to do with the nature of the green, and number 6 Reverse, because the previous five have all been played in the same general direction away from the clubhouse. Number 8 is called Sandpit, not a bad name for a golf hole which has a shallow mound fronted by a large bunker in the middle of its fairway, about 100 yards from the green. So, you might ask, when this is one of the flattest places on earth, give or take the odd sandhill, why is Number 9 called Gibraltar? The explanation is Gibraltar Point, the name of nature reserve, etc, of which we are now officially part.

Number 9 is the first par five, and the beginning of fun, the start of three consecutive pairs of par fives and par threes, each changing direction, and getting the best out of the land, which is used most generously. Harrison, who was with me, speculated on how many football pitches you could make from hole 11 (with a little help from a bulldozer). At least five, and there was no-one else in sight. What a luxurious sport golf is!

The final par five is called Sea View, lest there was any ultimate doubt about the course's littoral nature, but Number 15 bears the name

North Pole. No, you can't see it, not even on a clear day! All in all, these names are rather trivial, but the golf isn't. There is only one thing that bothers me about Seacroft – where on earth did I leave the car?

Harrison found our "hotel", in Skegness, and we couldn't possibly have visited Skeggy and stayed anywhere different. It was not in the Inn category, so there was no reference in *The Good Pub Guide*, though it did have a bar of sorts, from which the proprietor emptied tins of warm lager into pint glasses if you asked him nicely. Whether it would have had a mention in the Good Places to Stay in Skegness Guide is anybody's guess. Probably yes, because one of the greatest copy-writing feats of all times must surely go to the person who came up with the slogan *Skegness is so bracing*. How else do you attract people to a resort where the sea disappears over the horizon at low tide, and the east wind blows "fit to cut you through" as they say in Leicester-shire? Well, one answer is funfairs and amusements and stick-of-rock shops and, Harrison and I noted, chip "stations" every 100 metres. This was consistent with the theory, developed over a series of occasional summer visits to Weymouth, that one class of English people who still go on holiday in England are those who are a little on the large side to fit into aircraft seats for the journey to the Costa del Fish and Chips. We thought there were plenty of such people around, and the chip stations were doing a brisk trade, even though it was not high season. Up the coast at Sandilands, it was definitely bracing:

SANDILANDS

The nearby Sandilands Links & Grange Hotel advertises special packages at Sandi-lands Golf Club with the description "challeng-ing links golf". This is not an erroneous us-age of "links" for "course", but I feel it may be nevertheless erroneous. Sandilands seems to fail as a links on at least two criteria: one, it is flat, plain or plane, indeed, and two, the grass is reminiscent of the sort that grows in a meadow. In fact, if times got tough, I reckon you could turn it over to brassicas and produce a handsome crop, judging by the nearby fenland. I did not recognise true links, but I might well be wrong, and anyway, what really matters is that it is fun. There was a strong north-easterly blowing when Harrison and I turned up to play one September morning. 'Is this the prevailing wind?' I asked. 'We're not proud around here. The wind can come from anywhere,' was the steward's response.

Harrison was in training for the St David's Open,[34] of which he was defending champion, and offered to play me at match play, off 18. Given how he had easily beaten me previously from a more generous mark, I let him. The 1st and 18th holes are set in a plain bounded by a scrubby grassy bank next to the elevated sea wall and a scrubby grassy bank next to an elevated lane which runs along the inland length of the course. By instinct, I set up to play towards the yellow flag in the distance, but Harrison pointed out that the 1st hole is played diagonally across the 18th, to a red flag. Am I right in thinking that the usual flag sequence, when there is one, is yellow out, red back? Downwind, I easily find the green in two. Harrison is on the green in three, and rolls in a nice putt from about 20 feet. I follow suit from about 15. One up. Hole 2 is a par three, and there is no way of knowing what club to use in this wind. I find a greenside bunker. Harrison warms up with a few chips for a seven. I hole another 15 footer for par. I like these greens; they are fairly paced, true and approximately flat. If some links greens are like poppadums or potato crisps, these are scotch pancakes.

At this point, the course is interrupted by a deep ditch. There is an odd house built in a corner of the course, a ramshackle collection of greenkeeping sheds and equipment, and across the lane, a building which to us non-fenlanders looks as if it serves some function for a railway. It is actually a drainage station for a drain – that being the fenland term for a certain type of open watercourse – but all along the course, the elevated lane, which perhaps should be called a causeway, hints at being a railway embankment. The next section of the course serves just two holes, numbers 3 and 16, which again cross over. Number 3 is a par five, and the green is in front of another strange house (built within the confines of the course) which has no windows facing towards it, and looks younger than the course itself. Harrison hits a second shot which travels a prodigious distance thanks to bouncing on the asphalt of the lane. As it curves slightly, there is an outside chance it may bounce back into play, but no luck. That leaves me three up, and I offer my opponent a self-adjusting handicap system, but he states he will review affairs after six holes. Hole Number 6 is a reminder of what is in

---

[34] Not St David's in Wales, but his local church's annual golf event. Amongst the competitors, I believe he is unique in once upon a time having held an official handicap.

store later. Turning back into the wind, it plays about the same length as Number 5, though the respective yardages are 484 and 365. My double bogey is enough to put me five up, and I suggest we adopt a rugby league approach, and play in sets of six. First set to me.

After the straight 7th and the dogleg 8th, both of which Harrison wins courtesy of strokes, it is apparent that we are a long way from the clubhouse. I fight back on the 9th, into the wind but a short par four, and then win the par three 10th, the first hole to play crosswind. At this far end, the course is relatively free of strange buildings, except for the sublime and the ridiculous. To the side of the 10th tee there is a smart new pavilion with cooking facilities, outside toilets, verandah, and terrace with a picket fence and tables and chairs. Not far away, there is an edifice built on a concrete base, made of loose-fitting larch lap panels with a corrugated tin roof. I leave you to decide which is which. The 11th hole, played from an elevated tee on the sea wall, is definitely the last to be wind-assisted, but we both go well through the back of the green in two. It is not necessarily easy playing downwind, though it is surely easier than it is about to become as we turn for home. With Harrison down for five, I have a 12 footer for a four and a moral dilemma. After all, he is my nephew, he was with my father when he suffered a fatal heart attack on his home course, he was a special favourite of my late wife, and he is my godson, someone whose moral well-being I have sworn to care for. If I hole this putt, I will be dormie one for this set of six, leaving him to win the next hole and the third and final set just to square the match. It doesn't take much thought; that's just the tough sort of situation he needs to learn to handle, but as it happens, my putt slides by. Still all square for this set. The situation is neatly reversed on the next, a crosswind par four. This time, I am down for five when Harrison casually asks if this is the 12th hole, before equally casually sliding in a 12 footer for a four. 'I thought I'd make a match of it.' And indeed, it is now all square for the match. There are six holes to play, all into the wind, and my young opponent gets a shot on three of them.

He has been honing his game (in the wind, one could not talk of warming up) and suddenly, he is driving the ball beautifully into the wind and following up with reasonable approach shots, so he wins the next two without the need for the shots he was allowed. The 15th tee, like most of the closing holes, is on the elevated level by the lane, and there is a diagram showing an out of sight pond in front of us. The secret of Harrison's driving is a slight in-to-out swing which imparts topspin onto the ball, helping it to bore its way through the air. Overdo this a little, and it adds right to left draw spin, with fatal results. He overdoes it, and fortunately, there are no cars coming as the ball clears the lane. The cars are biding their time, waiting to come past in steady convoy as I attempt to play, even though the lane appears to go nowhere, and my frustration results in a skier, into the pond. My opponent's second ball is good, and after my penalty shot and weak third, he can still win the hole with a good fairway wood, but again the draw spin is too much, and again the ball flies off the course. Like the wind round here, I am not proud. I will take a win with an 8 whenever I am two down with four to play. I was in fact relieved to hole my second putt; it was downwind, and appeared to be accelerating as it hit the back of the hole.

With Harrison one up, we play stroke index 1, Number 16, the longest of the closing holes, sharing its private plain with Number three, and teeing off adjacent to the strange house with no windows. My tee shot is OK, his good. My 3 wood second is good, and once again, my opponent's draw spin comes into play. His ball flies straight for about 80 yards, and then turns sharp left, into the fens. A punched third from me leaves me 12 feet away, and he is on the back of the green in 5, and takes three more. For good measure, I hole my putt for a nice par. All square. How would you feel if you were Harrison? These are not severe hooks, it is the wind which is causing the damage, and if the course were laid out with fairways on the other side like St Andrew's, he would still be in play. Well, he is game for it, because after my tee shot to the 188 yard 17th comes up well short, he has a choice of iron for safety, or wood for glory. He opts for the latter, but striving for that little extra induces a pull – into the fens. And so finally to Number 18, 332 yards, playing much longer, with me dormie for this six, and with it, the match. Two good drives, and a weak second of mine, and I am left thinking that I would not mind halving this final hole for a fair result of one up. The special thing about golf is that you cannot do anything about the shot your opponent hits. Unfortunately, Harrison hits a diabolical semi-shank, and then plays a weak third to the front edge, races it past the hole, and takes two more for a six. I am about 12 feet away, and it would not be good for my godson's moral welfare to see me three-putt from that distance, so I am obliged to win the hole and the set, two up. I won the first four and the last four holes, but in the intervening section, Harrison murdered me. Watch out, St David's players!

On our night in Skegness, Harrison and I visited a snooker hall. He was rather good, which is a sign of a misspent youth, or in his case a degree in sports science. He could make breaks, but curiously he tended to miss easy-looking pots. I pointed this out, and he commented that when they were fairly easy, he felt a pressure to end up with a good position for the cue ball, whereas he concentrated on just potting a harder chance. I thought I recognised the well-known symptoms of a "pip", and we talked about it. Harrison said that when he was practising, he would employ a "toofer" – after a miss, have two further attempts and, if succeeding with both, continue with the break (with some difficulty, it has to be said, depending on the configuration of the rest of the balls). He suggested I try this on the course – after a missed pip, take two more and hole them both. I tried this for a while, but it was inconclusive. If you holed only one, did the second, missed shot nevertheless count as a pip itself?

Where I did employ the "toofer" – an expression which derives from the retailing offer "buy two for the price of one", now generally supplanted by "bogof" – "buy one get one free" – was with chips. Another undesirable habit I have when playing alone is to play the occasional "cusp" shot. Cusp is an acronym for Concentrate U Stupid Prat, describing my response to circumstances when, standing over a chip, some part of me will suddenly hit the ball before the rest of my being is ready. My mind may well be thinking about what to have for dinner or, strangely, some girl I went out with when I was nineteen. Toofer, or bogof, is a good game to play after a cusp, particularly if it is busy up ahead and I need to kill time. I play two chip shots, and I have to hole both putts to be able to claim an up-and-down for the hole. I think it is quite good practice too and, if you hole only one, you can keep playing until you either miss both or hole them.

Harrison has two sisters, both of whom work in television. One turned down an assignment on the show *The Weakest Link*, because she did not care for the humiliation of the contestants. Possibly the weakest link in this book is about to follow; what "links" Lincolnshire and Cumbria, or perhaps that should be Cumberland? One answer is, they are both famous for sausages, though those from Cumberland do not come in links, of course. Talking of courses, they do both have links for golf.

SILLOTH-ON-SOLWAY

Silloth-on-Solway Golf Club is the most northerly course on the West Coast of England, and not much more than a John Daly drive from Southerness, a fabulous links course on the Northern and there-

fore Scottish side of the Solway Firth. (South-erness is one of only two courses where my father and I ever abandoned a round, this af-ter I had lost ten balls in nine holes. And I still love it.) At Silloth, the approach to the course is odd, as one seems to have to climb up a steep flight of steps and walk right through the clubhouse carrying golf bag, shoes and cloth-ing changes etc to get from the car park to the locker room. There must have been a route for trolleys that I did not see. The immediate prospect is a one-out, one-in view of holes, St Andrew's-style, but with a very nicely defined open-ing fairway. Before playing it, however, I discovered that I was without a waterproof jacket. The only one of my size in the pro shop was not the one I would have chosen, but once I had bought it, some kind of natural law dictated that I didn't have to wear it anyway. The threaten-ing clouds cleared, giving way to blue skies and splendid views of the mountains of Dumfriesshire.

The tees are quite forward in places, and this seems to be standard practice to compensate for the lack of run summer conditions would provide. I cannot recall the precise extent of the generosity of the tee position on the 7th hole at Silloth, but it was here, playing into a bright low sun, that I was waved through by a fourball. As you know, Rules for playing through have been outlined earlier. There now comes an interpretation thereof, a "decision of the rules committee" as it might be known. From the tee, one should aim to walk past as many members of the group ahead as possible to get to one's ball. This should be at least one, if they are searching. Although I missed the fairway, I walked past all four. But, this was stroke index 1, and I still had a long iron, a blind shot over a bank down to what I hoped would be a receptive green. I must say that I am a lot less convinced of the efficacy of blind greens than of blind fairways, but anyway, I hit this beautifully. I found the ball on the sunken green, left my bag visible to the boys behind, and osten-tatiously removed just my putter. Unfortunately for me, what they could not see was the way I holed the fifteen footer for a birdie. Perhaps they guessed from my body language. Anyway, I resisted the temptation to flap my arms and moved on to the 8th hole.

A year or so previously I had kept a record of all the birdies I had scored, far fewer perhaps than it should be, for I am pretty sure I don't honesty believe I have "the right" to score birdies. They score me, as it were. Across all the courses played I had birdied a hole of every number except 7, and by stroke index, I was deficient only on number 1. So, I had completed the set at a stroke – well, three strokes, anyway. This put me in a very good mood, but I have to say I can remember little more about the course.

Just as the visit to Silloth started with thoughts of getting wet, so too it ended. With a low and therefore warm sun but a stiff cool breeze, I had worked up quite a sweat, so I decided to take a shower in the locker room. I now make a point of investigating the facilities thoroughly before removing my clothes, probably as a consequence of this occasion, when I did the reverse. There was a notice in the showers which read "because of the long pipe run from the boiler, please allow several minutes for hot water". Perhaps The Committee had got fed up with people turning on the showers and forgetting them, for they had installed "push for thirty seconds' worth" taps on them. Rigor mortis would have set in before I had got any hot water!

One sometimes encounters golf courses which show an abrupt change of character midway round, most obviously when a nine-hole course has been extended to eighteen. This is not the case with Silloth-on-Solway, but it is true of this narrative. It is disappointing that I do not have more to say about such an obviously fine course, but I am aware of the reason, and I hope you will understand. I played it in the immediate aftermath of my wife's funeral.

I have explained that the decision to extend my coastal golfing tour of the West of England to the whole country came during the period immediately following Celia's death. Silloth may well have been the start, in fact, and I would be giving a thoroughly false impression if you were left thinking that was simple or remotely adequate compensation for my bereavement. I have to go back to September 30th, 1999, when Janet, the elder of my two sisters, suffered a fatal heart attack. She had recently undergone a surgical procedure on her cardiac artery, and seemed to be recovering well. Although things were clearly not perfect, we thought she was "getting better" – that's how we all tend to see health issues; you get ill, then you get better – and her death was a great shock. Her husband David and I are good friends – when we were younger I was the little brother he never had – and he and Janet had three grown-up children. They all helped each other, but he told me later that everything that happened between the event and the subsequent funeral remained a big blur.

In February 2000 the first signs of what turned out to be Celia's terminal illness – a rare degradation of part of the digestive system – appeared, and after a series of crises and hospital visits between periods of relative stability, she finally died peacefully in the arms of her sister, her best friend, and me on February 8th, 2001. I can remember everything that happened afterwards. We had no children, but there is a need for someone to be around, and thankfully David was able to stay with me for a few days. As the news spread, I received one particular phone call from someone we had only met twice many years ago, which at first surprised me, and then made me realise that my wife had also been an important person in other people's lives, and they too needed comforting, so that is what I set out to do. This was fine with David around, but after seventy-two hours he went back home, and I was alone. What did I do? I am surprised you ask. I went to the golf course.

Sherborne Golf Club is a fairly magic place. I frequently find myself giving thanks for being there and not in some office somewhere. It is not perhaps in the top echelons of excellent golf venues, but as a place to be alone with white spherical objects and nature, it is difficult to beat. The sky is enormous, as indeed it tends to appear in most of Dorset to people who have lived for twenty-five years in London. Tension not actually caused by golf itself disappears upwards into the ether in no time. On this day, I was relieved to make good contact with the first ball I hit. Perhaps there was a chill wind, because there was water in my eyes which made seeing the ball awkward both before and after the stroke, but after three or four holes, my mental perspective became very clear. I thought back to our decision some years previously to move from London to Dorset. This was a decision which, had we had children as most people do, we might not have taken, but we were not so fettered, and we had the most wonderful time. It enabled us to relive all the pleasures of making a home together without the sometimes painful experiences of getting to know each other and, as we moved to a less expensive house, we had all the money we needed, and for the time being did not need to worry too much about working.

So I realised that we had been immensely lucky. I thought of other circumstances, including those of my sister who was in her first month of retirement, where premature death denies couples the chance to enjoy such wonderful times together, and I felt most privileged. I simply had to regard the time left for me as some kind of bonus, rather than a form of prison sentence. I came home from the golf club determined to make Celia's funeral a celebration of her life, and with the hope that everyone who attended would feel privileged to have known her. I shunned the word funeral, preferring to call it a Service of Thanksgiving for her Life. On the day, we were blessed with beautiful weather, and I believe that my desire was fulfilled and that Celia would have approved.

But, after the Lord Mayor's Show comes the dustcart, and after the thanksgiving and burial, everyone would go home, and I was about to be on my own again, for good. So, I planned to stay in a friend's cottage in Cumbria for a while, which is where we joined this narrative. I started writing about the visit a few months later, and while there was rather more than this on the subject of bereavement, of golf I penned just about what there is above and below. I was very very tired, and I relaxed sufficiently during the stay to remain just very tired. I must have been in some kind of a trance, because according to the scorecard, I went round in 74, two over par, for 47 Stableford points. Looking at the scorecard, there is a hint of a pip on hole Number 2, but that apart, it looks genuine. I even recorded fairways hit and greens in regulation. Well, they do say that if you can just play and think of nothing, you will score well. I must have been feeling pretty numb.

At that time, I wrote that I fully intended to return to Silloth. The exact words were, 'If Silloth had been a girl, I would not have just asked for her phone number, I would have made a date for tomorrow' but now, I just don't want to remind myself about how I felt at that time. I have been back to the cottage a few times, but made no effort to revisit Silloth. Back then, I may have been able to accentuate the positive as the song has it, but I fancy I did not also really eliminate the negative, so I won't risk it. You'll just have to take my word for it about Silloth – and while you're there, make sure you also go to Seascale.

SEASCALE

'The best fourteen pounds' worth of green fee I have ever spent,' was how I greeted the Professional at Seascale Golf Club who happened to pass by as I walked off the 18th green, having carded a pip-free 77 for 43 Stableford points (though I didn't mention that fact to him) – but then, as we agreed, they tended not to get many visitors at the best of times, and it would be hard to charge them a lot more. 'But,' said the pro, 'look at the facilities we've got thanks to IT being there. This is the finest clubhouse for miles'; and indeed, it was the best on the coast of Cumbria. In my opinion, so was the course. There are some downland holes inland, with bumpy linksy holes near the sea, including changes of elevation and direction, and a railway line actually running between the course and the beach. I was pleased about this because I had made special provision in the rules for such a contingency, and this was the first time it had been invoked. I was also pleased with my play on the par fives, as I birdied all three – a "first" according to the annals of my memory. Golf is a very special game; there are surely few others where one can continue to achieve personal bests over the age of fifty. It was February, the tees were forward, but I must have been playing well, for holes Numbers 6 and 7 measure 467 yards and 555 yards respectively from the yellows but play in opposite directions, so it wasn't just the wind.

It is not difficult to work out why the course does not get many visitors: it is in just about the most inaccessible place in Cumbria, if one is starting from the M6; most people who visit Cumbria are walkers, not golfers; and there is the magnificent landscape...

There is just one blot on the landscape, and IT does rather dominate the far end of the course, even though there is a small river on the boundary preventing immediate access, always assuming it was desirable. I have to admit that when I was eating an apple at this far end of the course, I thought very carefully about putting it down on the turf between shots and perched it on my bag. Originally, IT was called Windscale, but it really gained fame when the name was changed to Sellafield, with the notion that everyone would forget about Windscale. Everyone seems to know what I mean when I just identify the course by its proper name of Seascale, so nothing more need be said.

Although if ever there was a place for licking one's Titleists, this is definitely not it; if you get the chance, I urge you to play Seascale.

Notwithstanding the better-rated Silloth-on-Solway and the fine South-erness, you have to go far north along the coast – and that includes a 100 mile detour round the Mull of Galloway – until you get to Turnberry to find a better links, and the green fee at Turnberry is just a little more than £14. I might go back myself one day, when I feel so inclined.

There is something else I would urge. I have explained that I was able to regard myself as fortunate to have been blessed with the time and opportunities that Celia and I were able to spend together, rather than desperate in having been denied things to come. I would prefer not to be widowed of course, but I feel especially saddened when I come across stories of someone dying whose adventures are still dreams of what will be one day, but not yet – and so never to be turned into reality. If you and your wife or husband or partner have plans to do something different "when the time comes", name the time! Preferably, go out for a meal or a drink, sit down together tonight and name it tomorrow, and make sure it is not the sort of tomorrow that never comes. If you have children who are under 18, perhaps you can't, but if they are older, don't worry about them. They would much rather you spent your money fulfilling yourselves than leaving it to them. As the slogan goes – I forget whether it has any links with golf – just do it!

9

ORIGINS OF THE SPECIES

Like St Andrew's, the courses at Carnoustie are public. There are three: the Buddon Links, which is not a bad course for the less capable (I've heard it said that it is dull, but as I once scored 75 there, I am not having it); the Burnside, which is great; and the Championship which, as anyone who remembers the 1999 Open Championship knows, is awesome. It tends to be remembered for Jean Van de Velde's unfortunate demise, but it destroyed most of the field. The leader after the first round was the Aussie, Rod Pampling. He missed the cut!

When I visited in 2002, a day ticket for the Championship plus another course was £85. Alternatively, if I remember this correctly, as a resident of Carnoustie you can buy a season ticket for £200. It lasts a year – but there is a ten year waiting list. Across the road from the course, there are some Clubs, housing the various affiliations that have been formed over the years to play on the public links. Before and after playing, members can meet there, and affiliate. Visitors are also welcome to refresh themselves. Looking casually at the name plaque on the outside of one of these clubs, I thought to myself, '1943. That's an odd time to form a club, in the depths of war.' I first confirmed with myself that this was Scotland not Ireland, and therefore definitely at war in '43, before I realised that the date on the plaque was 1843.

Where would you guess the oldest course outside Scotland to be? The answer is Pau, in south-west France (not a million kilometres from Mont de Marsan, home of J V de V, in fact). I know that it was laid out by a garrison of Scots soldiers in 1856, and to this day it is known not as *Club de Golf de Pau*, but Pau Golf Club. Notices in the ancient clubhouse are in English.

As mentioned, the first club, or affiliation of golfers, in England was Royal Blackheath, but the oldest *course* is Royal North Devon at Westward Ho! which dates from 1864.[35] It makes use of a strip of flattish land which sticks out at a river mouth in a similar fashion to the links at St Andrew's, from which it differs in respect of being some 400 miles south (though strangely, only 30–40 miles west, because of the western slant of Britain). Despite being fairly inaccessible even today, never mind in 1864, the locals nevertheless brought down Old Tom Morris, Open champion and greenkeeper, to lay out a course similar to his own at St Andrew's.

ROYAL NORTH DEVON

Royal North Devon Golf Club, I am told, really resembles St Andrew's, which I have only visited as a spectator at The Open. On an ordinary day, they say that all you can see from the tees there is a series of flags. The day I visited Royal North Devon was scarcely ordinary; it was November, but so warm that I was actually obliged to play in shirt sleeves. The sun was powerful, but at an unusually low angle, and I noticed that every centimetre of grass appeared to host a spider's web. I imagine that they are always there, but usually invisible.

If the sun gave excellent close-up vision, it seriously interfered with long range reconnaissance, and if I had not met up with a member called Alan on the 1st tee, I really think that I would not have been able to find my way around unassisted. Unlike the Old Course, this one seemed to take a number of unexpected twists and turns, within and between holes. Not that Alan's advice was entirely straightforward either. He kept talking about the gorse, and how it was hard to play out of. Now, this was early in my career as a peregrinating golfer, but I have always been fairly confident that gorse is a dense, spiky shrub that grows in clumps up to about 8 feet high, and has yellow flowers.[36]

---

[35] For the record, the place was called Northam at the time. It did not become Westward Ho! until later.

[36] According to my mum, the answer to the question, 'What's always in flower when it's the kissing season?' is 'gorse'. It never stops flowering, and kissing never goes out of season.

There was no evidence of any such vegetation, but Alan kept saying that the gorse was a major feature of what was frankly a fairly feature-less course. Eventually, it dawned on me – reminiscent of the Monty Python sketch in which the timid accountant wants to become a lion tamer, but he has mistaken armadillos for lions – that Alan was referring to clumps of spiky, tough, glossy, dark green, grass-like growth. My botanical knowledge is sketchy, but I believe it may be described as glaucous, and could be known in other parts of the UK as reeds. Alan was right about one thing; it is murder to get out of. You do not lose your ball so often, or have so obvious an unplayable lie as with gorse, but it absorbs energy from a moving club head, wraps itself around the shaft, and brings tears to the eye. Alan was right about another thing; it is a feature of the course. Unfortunately, it is by no means easy to see where it is, and the sunlight of this November day made it virtually impossible.

The second thing Alan said which puzzled me was this: 'I don't mind the turds. Some people complain about them, but I don't mind them.' For a second time, my mind flashed back to my youth. Did he mean *The Turds*, the fictitious rebellious rock group which featured regularly in *Private Eye*? Surely not. No, he meant the turds dropped by the grazing animals on the common land which is part of the golf course (or vice versa). Tucked away on the back of the scorecard at the end of local rule number 3 is the sentence "Dung itself is a loose impediment". Abnormal ground conditions caused by dung, on the other hand, are classified as mere ground under repair. The mind boggles somewhat, and whatever it is, I do not want it on either hand. I agree with Alan though. If you are going to be a member at Royal North Devon, it is preferable to learn to tolerate the turds. Otherwise, why not join Saunton? It is less than 3 miles as the crow flies, but probably 20 via car through Barnstaple, which can be something of a traffic bottleneck. You could always move house...

I am sorry I cannot tell you more about the oldest golf course in England. Do its charms, like St Andrew's, take their time to emerge, until it becomes one of the great golf courses? Opinion amongst the professional golf community in south-west England is divided. There are some who swear by it. Others swear at it. I suppose I should revisit it one day. But to get there, I have to go via Barnstaple with its traffic problems. And, you see, if you turn right before, rather than after Barnstable centre, you get to Saunton. Maybe one day when I tire of visiting Saunton I will go back to Westward Ho!, perhaps on a day when the gorse stops flowering...

I thought perhaps I ought to gather more information on how and perhaps why the townspeople of this Devonshire backwater came to found a golf course, so I typed Westward Ho! into my internet search engine. After a slight pause, it came up with about 221,000 entries. Top of the list was neither a Devonshire town nor a Charles Kingsley novel but a Las Vegas casino. I added "golf", and this reduced the list to a mere 57,000. Number 2 was the Westward Ho Country Club, somewhere unimaginable, announcing that it had recently added a nine-hole golf course. However, number 3 was Royal North Devon's own site. It calls the "gorse" spiky rushes, so perhaps they are not reeds, and mentions its museum. Of golf. I know, I know; I should have paid attention when I had the chance.

In fact KPMG, my winter fourball partner, has a strong counter argument in favour of Royal North Devon's charms, pointing out that because its land is a conservation area governed by so many Trusts, it is almost impossible for any changes to be made to the course. It is therefore much as it has ever been, and playing there is to experience golf in its "native state". Also, the course grows on you, as it were. Perhaps. I am prepared to accept the second point, but I will take his word for it. As for the former, I have never been able to see the point of getting an orchestra to play Mozart on instruments like those contemporary to the late 1700s, and then making a CD of the performance which I can upload onto my computer, download onto my iPod and listen to while flying over the North Pole on a great circular route to Vladivostok. Give me a hickory shafted cleek, a featherie ball, and *a knowledgeable local caddie* to help me find it, and maybe I'll play there again.

RELIGIOUS NOTE

If there were ever any doubts that golf is a religion, the winter fourball at Sherborne dispels them. Sherborne has a fine Abbey, and though I have never visited it at eight o'clock on a Sunday morning, I will wager that you will not find as many people there as you will up on the golf course. There, on alternate Sunday mornings during the winter months, you will find 96 men, playing each other in pairs at better ball Stableford in a complicated league system, starting at several different tees and so returning to the clubhouse in great droves at lunchtime. In terms of both the ritual involved, and the devotion required – you simply must turn up, whatever the weather, and it will probably be still dark when you set off – this is definitely a religious activity. Perhaps there is no divine being involved, certainly not a benign one. KPMG definitely believes that if it were not for his bad luck, he would not have any luck at all.

******

Tied for second place in the seniors' littoral golf course competition are Royal Liverpool, Alnmouth, and Alnmouth Village. It seems a little odd that two courses should be founded in the same Northumbrian village in 1869. Did the members fall out before they even started? The village course is only nine holes, so it is ruled out for my purposes. In fact, it transpires that this *course* was founded in 1869, but the members moved some time later to adjacent land at Foxton Hall, which they use as an alternative name for their *club*, Alnmouth. So, just to make it as clear as mud, Alnmouth *Club* dates from 1869, as does Alnmouth Village *Course*. For the record, it is pronounced Allenmouth, just down the river Aln, pronounced Aln, from Alnwick, pronounced Annick.[37]

As luck would have it, I was searching for something completely different when I came across a book called *A History of Golf* by one *Robert Browning* (not the poet, but the editor of the magazine *Golfing*, from 1910–1955). Written and first published upon his retirement, this was a paperback reprint from 1990 which I probably acquired at a second-hand bookshop. I have certainly never read it, otherwise I would have been able to tell you that it was the visit of General Moncrieff of St Andrew's to stay with the Reverend J H Gossett, vicar of Northam (Westward Ho! was itself only a single farmhouse at this time) which brought golf to the English. The general pointed out the golfing possibilities of the land, and the reverend did the rest.[38] Manifestation indeed of golf's religious origins, and for good measure, the reverend bequeathed his initials to Royal North Devon's most famous son, J H Taylor.

I mention above golf *coming to the English* as there is evidence of earlier golfing activity not only in Blackheath, but also in Wimbledon and Manchester, but in each case, this was expatriate Scottish activity, and the courses they played on have long since disappeared. Sadly,

---

[37] Or so I am told. It depends who you speak to.

[38] There is no mention of Old Tom Morris, but the club lists him as architect in *The R & A Handbook*.

Browning makes no mention of Alnmouth. I already have, of course, on a visit with Neff.

Browning's account certainly mentions Royal Liverpool, mainly for its role in developing amateur championship golf. It also suggests that Scots based in West Kirby may have been the first to play golf on The Wirral. What he does not explain is why Royal Liverpool is so named, when it is indeed on The Wirral, and not in Liverpool at all. There were certainly no tunnels in 1869 when it was founded, but there was a race-course which Liverpudlians used to frequent on what is now the golf course, so people must have been used to taking a ferry across the Mersey. In those days, it may have seemed like a form of rapid transit.

Royal Liverpool, often known as Hoylake in the same way that Royal St George's is referred to as Sandwich, has hosted The Open Championship ten times, but the last was in 1967, when it was won by Roberto De Vicenzo, the only South American to win it or any other major. Now it is set to return in 2006, around the time this book is due to appear, so as you have no doubt rushed out and bought this copy hot from the presses, it might be diplomatic for me to make non-contentious comments about the visit.

ROYAL LIVERPOOL

I telephoned well ahead to make our reservation at Royal Liverpool Golf Club, for the weekend before the clocks change in late March. Harrison was joining me for a "birthday treat". Quite why we don't go on his birthday – June 1st – escapes me;[39] I have generally enjoyed my March renewal each year – that is exactly how it feels, a new year to look forward to, with a new spring and long days, and when I was a boy, Easter holidays just round the corner, but March is not the ideal time for golfing expeditions. They say it comes in like a lion and goes out like a lamb, but this year it was taking its exit like Hannibal Lecter.

The Club confirmed our reservation by letter, and sent a two page list of instructions for our information. The green fee included lunch, which we ate in the monumental clubhouse. Assuming it is original, it

---

[39] Not really; he has a very nice family.

very much typifies the affluence of Liverpool as the principal western seaport in mid-Victorian times. The fact that the people at the next table to us left hurriedly on receiving the news that their house had been burgled sadly signifies Liverpool's circumstances today.

There was no-one much to be seen in the way of players, nor much of a golf course on the 1st tee, which looks predominantly out towards the flat practice ground. As noted, there was a wind blowing, and – had it not been for the remainder of the weekend that followed – I would have described it as strong. Our visit to Knott End was to follow. Thick black rain clouds kept being blown up, but they were all carried over to Snowdonia, and we spent most of the time in half-sunlight.[40] This, combined with watering eyes, meant we took a time to become acclimatised. The 1st hole is a dogleg, playing across the wind initially, before turning more into it, around an out of bounds. I won with a five to Harrison's seven, but he countered with a five to my six on the downwind 2nd (it was as hard to know what to expect with the wind behind as it was with it against). We then turned into the wind for the long 3rd hole, which Harrison easily won with a six, four strokes better than me. Then, we settled down, and with the wind in all directions, we reached the turn with me one up – but I had played the last six holes in level par. Harrison, playing off 24, had done well to live with me, by virtue of having some excellent holes. We both got birdie 4s on the long 8th, following our par fours on the stroke index 1, 5th.

This corner of the course seemed to have more definition than the later holes which were over flatter ground, and I would say that we felt intrigued rather than charmed by the course. It will look quite different for The Open, with all the stands around, of course. All we had for an audience was a group of lads who called us up from the green of the short 13th. I hit to a severe downslope behind a greenside bunker, and there is only one thing that happens with an audience looking on from that "nitby" position.[41] I duly played my third from the sand, and with immense good fortune, the ball hit the flagstick and stopped close by. The match continued close with Harrison contributing six net pars and a net birdie in the last eight holes. He won the upwind 17th, and only just missed a putt on the 18th to halve the match. I had gone round the par seventy-two course in 88 which, as mentioned, included a quintuple bogey 10. I do not recall whether this is the only time I have broken 90

---

[40] I am told by people who know The Wirral that this is superior to spending time in Port Sunlight.

[41] For the benefit of novices, nitby stands for "not in the bunker yet".

with a single score in double figures, but I am certain that it is the first time I have done it at an Open Championship venue!

Did I really, you ask? Well, we played the yellow card, which is SSS 71, and totals 6240 yards, quite enough in the wind in March. In competition the members play the green card, SSS 74 and 6921 yards. Rather too much, I would have thought, but still a good way short of the white card, which comes in at 7228, incorporating modifications made for the return of The Open. Someone I met later told me that when De Vicenzo won in 1967, there was a flat calm. Let's hope for some wind in 2006, because looking at a map of the layout, if the prevailing wind is at 12 on the face of a clock, there is a hole playing to every hour of the clock except 3. This variety, rather than the more physical threats posed by some of the other venues, must be Hoylake's chief defence.

In sole fifth place in the seniority rankings is Furness Golf Club, founded in 1872. I grew up learning the names of the many Lancashire towns because of their football clubs, including in those days Barrow, short for Barrow-in-Furness. At university, I knew someone who came from Barrow, who used to complain that, though it was part of Lancashire, rather than try to get by road to Liverpool, in the same county, it was sometimes quicker to take ferries to and from the Isle of Man. Well, now Barrow is part of Cumbria, but still as difficult a place to get to, particularly if like me, you start in Penrith, in the top right hand corner of the Lake District, and head for the bottom left.

Arriving therefore some time later than expected, I found a gaggle of men milling around the 1st tee, so I went elsewhere for a while. This turned out to be a mistake, because what I had failed to realise was that while they were milling around, they weren't actually planning to tee off until everybody had pitched up. This was one of those informal turn-up-and-play afternoons like we have at Sherborne, but our convention is to meet in the clubhouse, and only move to the tee when ready to play. Are you listening, lads?

I was looking for a new driver, so I wandered off and found a driving range. The Professional in the shop showed me his latest acquisition, a Taylor Made driver with a head capacity bigger than most motor cycles, the first of the new generation which is about to be declared illegal in 2008. 'Look,' he said, 'the whole club face is the sweet spot. I love it.' If it was his shop, he probably loved the price too – a mere snip at £399. I bought a second-hand, intermediate sized driver for £20. Well, you never know.

FURNESS

Barrow-in-Furness, a town with its own air-field, home to the mighty Vickers who made such a contribution to national defence, now casts a forlorn aspect of decline and decay. Not that it was ever pretty, one supposes. However, it boasts two very nice golf courses, the other of which, Barrow, offers sea views, I believe, but is not coastal itself. There is a strange strip of land parallel to Barrow itself called Isle of Walney, and Furness Golf Club is located there, adjacent to a place actually called Vickerstown, between housing and the beach. Technically, it is probably not linksland because the whole island has the same undulating topography, but this is to split hairs. It is classic golfing terrain, but of the scrubby rather than grassy variety, and the houses that line the landward side of the course are not at all reminiscent of those on the Monterey Peninsula. It probably does not get many visitors, being seriously difficult to reach from most places.

The driver I bought was purchased with an open mind and, just as a friend argues that it is worth buying a cook book if one gets just one good meal from it, I very rapidly earned value for the outlay. I scored a rather miserable six on the opening par five, then lipped out for a two on the par three 2nd to begin a sequence which went par, birdie, eagle, birdie, par, par, par, bogey. OK, the eagle was on a 290 yard par four downhill and downwind, probably from a forward tee, and I holed a running chip, but I was two under par for the front nine, and I'd lipped out on the 2nd and left a putt 5mm short on the 8th. Two under par, thanks to a £20, second-hand driver!

Sadly, I then caught up with the gaggle of members who were playing in fourballs, and lost concentration. I also lost my tee shot on the 11th, and decided that I probably would not be able to complete the round before darkness fell. After the 12th, I cut through to the 16th, where I played two balls, and scored birdies with both! I have the score-card in front of me, which shows that I parred 17 and 18, but now as I write, something does not quite ring true. Would I really have stopped the round just because I was held up if I'd really scored two under for the first nine, or had I dreamt the whole thing? I still have the driver, though it never again performed with any success, and was replaced a few weeks later.

This happened during my second stay in Cumbria as a newly-widowed man. Perhaps I just didn't think golf was so important, not a matter of life and death, anyway. It's enough to be alive and playing; never mind the score.

So much for the sublime old courses of England. Now to consider the origins of my littoral peregrination. There is no doubt about where it all started; at Sheringham in Norfolk, in 1971. My parents (who for obscure reasons were affectionately known to their grown-up children as Nellie and Mank) used to stay regularly in a cottage owned by friends in this seaside resort traditionally popular with people from Leicestershire, and I had joined them. I had taught myself to play golf after a fashion in what can be referred to retrospectively as my gap year. Mank never had; but he was a good sportsman, and significantly, he had been finding golf balls on walks along the cliff path bordering the golf course.

So, armed with enthusiasm, but without golf shoes, we reported to the professional's shop, paid (I think I recall) £2 between us for green fees, and hired sets of clubs for thirty-eight pence each (the decimal equivalent of seven shillings and sixpence). I wonder if there is anywhere left to do that? I teed off, hitting a very moderate drive, then Mank tried. I can only recall that Nellie was in hysterics at his attempts to hit the ball, while I was desperate to leave the vicinity of the clubhouse. Mank displayed an immediate grasp of the fundamental principle of golf – to play the ball as it lies – by seeking to hit his next shot from the practice putting green, immediately outside the clubhouse lounge, but I managed to get us all away before we were spotted. I quickly and casually played my second shot with a wood onto the 1st green and duly holed out for a par. I was both pleased and strangely disappointed. Pars were rare events in those days, and to get one on the 1st meant there was likely to be little to look forward to for the rest of the round.

I remember nothing more of this expedition, until we were back at the cottage, having finished dinner. Nellie and I decided to go down to the pub called The Two Lifeboats for a drink; Mank just sat in an armchair. When we said, 'Aren't you coming?' he replied, 'I'd love to, but I just can't move.' He was 61 at the time, about to take early retirement, and still recovering from a hernia operation, and well, he *was* temporarily unable to move. In the years that followed, we would carry our bags for thirty-six holes, getting our money's worth from day tickets. It's worth remembering just how tiring the first ever game of golf can be.

The following Christmas, I bought Mank a 5 iron, and a book by Arnold Palmer called something like "My game and yours", which started his golfing life. Using balls "recovered" from Sheringham and Arnold's wisdom, he honed his swing on the same cricket field where at the age of 47 he had once taken eight for 40 and scored 99 not out in the same match. Provided the body is willing, it's never too late to take up golf. Twenty years later, Mank was still playing three times a week when he died of a heart attack on his home course.

SHERINGHAM

Unsurprisingly, Sheringham Golf Club holds a special place in my affections and memories, but I do not think I am alone in that respect. It enjoys a spectacular setting on top of sandstone cliffs which the wind is little by little depositing on the course, and there have been enforced changes to the layout over time, mainly to prevent greens falling into the sea. The 2nd hole doubles back past the clubhouse, and the 3rd reverses direction again, hugging the cliff edge. People walking the cliff path don't realise what danger they are in, particularly from golfers who are prone to slice the ball. Like most of the self-taught, Mank and I were prone to slice the ball.

At the 4th tee, the footpath and course diverge. Mank had a favourite non-golfing spot, a bench where one could watch golfers slice into the gorse. Most would reload, not even bothering to search. (I am told that a man with a walking stick sitting on a bench is considered harmless. I am also told that a walking stick is an excellent device for lifting the branches of gorse bushes, revealing anything that might be lying beneath. Gorseberries, we called them.) From the saddle-shaped 4th fairway, one plays up to a plateau green. On reaching it in person, one is confronted with the panorama of the rest of the course stretching out into the distance, complemented behind by a great view of the town and its strange mound beyond known as Beeston Stump. It is not bobbly linksland, the changes in elevation are sweeping, and pronounced. The 5th hole is played from a terrific elevated tee, and so is the 6th, though the cliffs are still too high to contemplate scaling even at the lowest point of the course. From its furthest point, the course comes back in towards the plateau 11th green, goes back out again, and turns for its homeward stretch along the side of the railway line.

The coast of north Norfolk actually has the sea to the north, and the beaches at Sheringham are known as the East and West. In my experience, this is also the case with the winds. I have played there in every month except February, and never known a calm day. I have also lain in bed working out how exactly I would play in the westerly wind, only to get up to find it blowing hard from the east. The locals claim that this part of Norfolk is hit by the north wind which sweeps down from the Arctic, encountering no other land on the way, but my memory is that only the short 8th hole is ever played crosswind at Sheringham. The wind is either against going out, helping the slice over the cliff, or it forces balls onto the railway line on holes 16, 17, and 18. Medals must be heartbreaking.

Some time during my golfing lifetime, the holes were given slate tombstones and names. The 17th is known as "What train?" supposedly commemorating an occasion when the famous lady amateur of the 1930s, Joyce Wethered, holed an awkward putt to win some critical amateur event, without apparently noticing the steam train which went past as she did. When asked afterwards if the train had not put her off, she replied, 'What train?' It has to be noted that there are various other versions of this story, at other courses, involving other players. A small plane flew over Jack Nicklaus once, and when asked about it afterwards, the great man replied, 'Obviously it wasn't a jet. I would have noticed a jet.'[42]

The wind direction on Miss Wethered's occasion is not recorded, but I recall a time when it was behind me on the 2nd, playing alone, one November. The winter card shows the hole as a par five, measuring 538 yards; there are plenty of bunkers, and a brace of old quarry pits (or bomb craters) to negotiate. The first hazard, however, is the clubhouse car park, into which, and out of bounds, I sliced. (The wind doesn't have

---

[42] In his heyday, when Jack was in contention - and he usually was – TV producers would never seem to learn that after he stood over his putt, there would be at least twenty seconds before he hit it. Twenty seconds with nothing happening is death on television.

to be against for a slice to be troublesome.) Generously, I offered myself a mulligan, and caught it just right. It finished on a gentle upslope, and my Macgregor fairway wood launched the ball high downwind for the second bounce to leave the ball on the green, 15 feet from the hole. I must have been quite stunned, for I calmly holed the putt. I didn't have the nerve to claim the mulligan, for this would then have been an eagle – but it remains the best par five I have ever scored.

Like most people, I played very little golf through my twenties, and I have cause to thank Mank for what opportunities I did have. It is, I suppose, a case of one good turn deserving another. He took the game up in his retirement and became a member of a local club, and when his beloved allotment was acquired for other purposes, golf became his principal outdoor activity. All cloned from the chance discovery of golf balls on Sheringham Golf Course. Nellie and Mank used to stay in their friend's cottage at the beginning and end of the season, and would depend on us for transport if the long distance bus service was not available. We took to spending a week with them at the end of September. When we got back, we would declare the autumn upon us, and start using the electric blanket. After the Sheringham cottage was sold, we took to going to Portpatrick in south-west Scotland, at the end of May. When we got back, we declared that summer had started. That was a much better arrangement.

Mank and Celia got on very well. Both were essentially optimists. For Mank, the holiday we were on was invariably the best we had ever spent. He liked to get full value as well. When my sister Jill, Harrison's mother, phoned to tell me of his death, I discovered afterwards that I had involuntarily written down the word "seventeenth". It was only a nine-hole course, but they were playing eighteen holes.

The parent-child relationship had easily changed to a basis of friendship with the arrival of Celia in the family, though Nellie and I could still contrive to rub each other up the wrong way from time to time. With Celia keeping a low profile, Mank was ever the soothing influence, his favourite question being, 'What's spoiling?'

10

A GOOD WALK SPOILED?

You may recognise this phrase as the title of an excellent book by John Feinstein on Life on the PGA Tour, but it was Mark Twain who first employed the expression to level a foul accusation at the Royal and Ancient game. Understandably, I cannot bring myself to repeat his exact words here. Now, Twain also described a bank manager as someone who lends you an umbrella when the sun is shining and asks for it back when it starts raining, so he was obviously a decent sort of bloke with a fine sense of humour. One can only surmise that he was joking when he thus described golf – though if he was, it was in seriously bad taste.

GOLFING AND WALKING COMPARED

Fortunately, when it comes to making comparisons, golfers have an advantage over walkers. Most golfers have been obliged to go on walks (when unavoidably staying with non-golfing family, or recovering from a hand injury, for example), but few walkers can have real experience of true golf. One does not need heavy boots, an emetic-green kagoul and an ordnance survey map in a plastic cover to experience a walk, but a round of golf does require some essential capability which anyone, picking up a bag of clubs for the first time, does not possess. If you should be fortunate enough to have met someone who proved even vaguely competent first time out, your new career as his or her agent starts now. Let's face it, one's first round of golf bears as much resemblance to the real thing as a furtive first cigarette does to smoking forty a day.

142

So, having established that the golfer is in a superior position to judge, let us ask the question 'Is there such a thing as a *good walk*?' Clearly, there is. It is great to walk to the pub, in the knowledge that one will not in any circumstances be tempted to drive back – but is this what Mr Twain meant? Surely he was referring to some more substantial expedition. Well, there is a popular series of published walks in the West of England, based on the idea of driving to a pub car park and setting off on a circular perambulation which returns one to the pub a couple of hours later presumably with a decent thirst and appetite to match, but the routes tend to involve the following: walking along roads without footpaths; crossing stiles, ditches, hedges and barbed wire fences; striving to avoid twisted ankles on uneven surfaces, commonly either stony or muddy; struggling with undergrowth on unfrequented paths, or standing to one side as lots of people pass in the opposite direction on thoroughfares; being barked at randomly by dogs, and emerging into a field with no sign of where the path continues or whether the large grazing animals are walker-friendly.

As you can gather, I have tried some of these walks, and I eventually discovered it far easier just to get to the pub about ninety minutes later, say after watching the lunchtime football. I admit that the "circular" aspect is clever, but it is surely borrowed from golf, where it is obvious that one wishes to return at the end of the round to the clubhouse with all its facilities and rituals. Most traditional walks end in the disappointing recognition that, having achieved the target however modest (the pub at the other end of the village) or ambitious (say, the summit of Everest), one then faces the plainly anticlimactic requirement of *returning whence one started*. A round of golf is seldom anticlimactic, and I do not need to tell you that there are no roads to walk along, few physical barriers to cross (unless having a nightmare round and running out of balls), smooth, even "manicured", turf on which to walk, few if any people passing in the opposite direction, and unless the course is on common land, no barking dogs or grazing animals.

These days, I try and anticipate this anticlimax on behalf of everyone, so that when staying with friends in the Lake District I offer to drop them off one side of Cat Bells, for example, and pick them up on the other a few hours later.[43] Compared to golf, walks do possibly

---

[43] In case you wonder, Cat Bells is the name of a "fell", being a topographical feature which like a "down", sticks up.

offer advantages of changing scenery – and no doubt, if one puts in the effort, spectacular vistas – and people who walk tend not to do the same one every week. I am fortunate to be a member at a scenic course, and have a penchant for "collecting" interesting golf courses, but even in the days when I lived in West London, there were few places to walk as safe from mugging (or importuning) as West Middlesex Golf Club.

The lure of the sea is at the heart of my peregrination, although as a golfer one does not go on or in it but just "knows it's there", and I have to acknowledge that, were it not for all the valuable golfing time it would waste, I might be tempted into walking the South West Coast Path – IF someone arranged for my belongings to be moved along so that it became a continuing journey. There are some close to "good" walks along the World Heritage Jurassic Coast in Dorset, and if ever I have seen "a good walk spoiled" it happened at Seatown on the Sunday before August Bank Holiday, in 1976. It had not rained in the South of England since the Saturday of the Lord's Test (June 19th – and one week before my wedding day, which is how I remember. It seemed a really bad omen at the time). Celia and I had been refreshing ourselves at The Anchor, one of the few literally littoral English pubs, but like everyone else we were turfed out at 2 PM (a legal requirement in those days). For no particular reason, we got into the car, as we watched a bunch of middle-aged hikers preparing to set off along the roller-coaster cliff path. This being the hottest, driest summer on record, they had long since spurned their coloured kagouls, and wore only shorts and singlets above their heavy boots. Even their OS maps were unprotected (not that they needed them, since the cliff edge fairly determines where the path goes). The next thing we knew, we were woken by a heavy drumming on the roof of the car. The soporific effects of the lunchtime beer had taken effect, so we had slept through the arrival of the storm which ended the great drought, but we were in time to witness the return of the hikers, straggling in like the last few horses in a particularly severe Grand National. I can tell you – even at this distance – that atop a Jurassic cliff at 500 feet is no place to be caught without a kagoul.[44]

******

Golfographically speaking – or do I mean geogolfically? – The Anchor is found between Lyme Regis and Bridport & West Dorset

---

[44] I checked this on an OS map! The walk is actually up somewhere called Doghouse Hill, and it rises to a height of 155 metres, 510 feet.

Golf Clubs, which during the years I have lived within range of them have become favourite places to visit, though with rather different feelings. Playing alone, I feel as relaxed at Bridport as I feel insecure at Lyme Regis, because this is the only course where the Lodger and I – we who once played the first nine of the Campo Norte at La Manga in seventy-five minutes, competitively – have been accused of slow play. And it has happened twice.

LYME REGIS

Unlike most courses in recent years, Lyme Regis Golf Club has become smaller. I am not sure if the present course is shorter than it used to be, but it has certainly become more compact, thanks to the land's ongoing habit of slipping into the sea. It remains a very pleasant place, but one of the consequences of recent re-design is that the views – and these are what turn a tolerably good golf course into a superb golf experience – are no longer "stage managed". Starting on the old 1st hole (now the 10th) you could be excused for thinking you had arrived at a decent but fairly average English parkland course, when you are in fact about 500 feet above, and in places only 500 feet north of the English Channel. After the first three holes, the trees thin out and you begin to see inland across the spectacular Marshwood Vale in the west of Dorset. Moving from north-east to south-west, Dorset's undulations seem to get more pronounced, rather like the crumpling of a piece of paper stuck in a Xerox machine. Here they are superb. Then, rotations in the direction of play bring the Dorset Heritage Coast into view, with Golden Cap, the highest point on the south coast of England, dominating the panoramic view stretching beyond to Chesil Beach and Portland Bill. As you play in that direction, somehow you seem to be looking down on Golden Cap, which is not the reality. After a return to the clubhouse, there is a reprise of this experience, then an extended run along the cliff top, followed by a final turn to reveal a spectacular view of the town itself with its famous Cobb.[45]

---

[45] I have never been entirely sure what exactly the "Cobb" is, but as it is clearly a non-golfing thing, work it out for yourself.

Well, that's how it used to be. These days, the Heritage Coast heaves straight into view as you cross the ridge on the 1st fairway – perhaps typical of today's "in-yer-face" approach to things – and while it's still as good, the whole thing is a bit short on foreplay, as it were. Talk of "fore" play brings me to the Incident on the 3rd hole, now the 14th. Acting as instructed in the pro shop, The Lodger and I waited an age to tee off, and to play subsequent shots. At the 3rd hole, the vanguard of a ladies' match which had teed off behind us invited themselves to play through, so when we finally found ourselves on the green of this par five hole, the second group of ladies was close behind, only a wedge shot away as we putted. It was all too much for one of the home team, who strode forward declaring the situation ridiculous. She was of an appearance which, had she in some farce been given the line 'I have never been so insulted in my life', would have induced someone to have responded, 'Oh surely now, you must have been!' In this somewhat surreal situation, it was left to The Lodger to announce, 'Madam, that is the rudest behaviour I have ever encountered'. There was nothing anyone could do and fortunately, as sometimes happens, the tempos of the various groups settled down and we played on sandwiched within this match, but not before we had expressed our displeasure to the vanguard group whom we passed again on the 4th as they played the 5th hole (still the 5th hole today). As we sat outside the clubhouse with a welcome drink after the round, rather impressively, our assailant actually walked over and offered us an apology.

On another occasion, we were playing the 5th hole when a man appeared out of nowhere, said, 'I know you're visitors here, but you could at least move quickly between shots!' and disappeared whence he came. I mentioned him when playing a match at Sherborne against the serving Secretary of Lyme Regis. He knew of whom I talked, and also the lady player. I don't know if it's me or this Club, but recently I hit a second shot on this former 3rd hole, and on reaching the green, was simultaneously delighted and appalled to find my ball pin high off the right side of the green. Fifty yards away, on the next tee, were the two players who had been on the green as I hit. Would they speak? One played his tee shot, and at length the other proclaimed, 'Kindly refrain from playing until the green ahead has cleared!' There were a number of things I might have said and, 'Sorry, but that ball travelled 260 yards, which I did not expect' came out of my mouth. There was not much they could say in reply, but in truth, they would not have been able to see me as my ball landed, so it would have been apparent that the shot was a freak. They could have been more charming, or I would have settled for sarcasm: 'Bet you're pleased with that. Don't think your insurance company would've been if it had hit us.'

"Freak" is no word to use in the description of the course at Lyme Regis. Given its position, it can be prone to what they call fog (but surely what people living at sea level would call cloud) and the pro told me it does not do much for the greens, but I have always found them, and the fairways, in excellent condition. It can be subject to bad weather, and my winter fourball partner KPMG, in pursuit of his regular bad luck, has played there five times without ever seeing the sea, but it is a superb place to play. As a "test of golf", you would have to admit that it falls down a little as both halves end with very short par fours. With the lane restricting space on the other side of the car park and clubhouse, it's hard to see what could be done to improve the situation. What they really need is more land...

Possibly because there are "strong feelings" about the pace of play, Lyme Regis has just about the most complicated set of starting instructions I have come across, with play alternating during the day from the available 1st and 10th tees. In order to work out which tee to start from, you need to establish the following: are you a twoball or foursome, or a threeball or fourball? Or a greensome, perhaps, they are specifically mentioned. Is it GMT or BST? Is your preferred starting time one when the designated tee will be closed to all starters? If you start when you want to, what will be happening on the other tee when you get round to it? Have the starting regulations been in any case suspended on the day in question? Wherever you start, are you likely to get a ladies' match up your arse?

I suppose it is a fact that golf courses are more crowded these days than is perhaps good for them, but I have never been a great fan of these alternations, basically because the rhythm of the round can often be disrupted half way round, and despite the best efforts of Lyme Regis, if you go out at the beginning of a designated twoball period, you will either come up behind fourballs who started during the later part of their session, or you will proceed smoothly to arrive at the alternate tee while fourballs are still teeing off from it. There are a number of coastal clubs that only allow twoball play, but that is perhaps a luxury, and some would say, a little antisocial. For peregrinating purposes, I like places where they have reserved starting times, as I can phone and choose when things are relatively quiet, which suits me playing alone or with the people who have accompanied me on my peregrination, but

KPMG for one argues strongly against them, on the grounds that they ruin prospects for a genuine "club environment", when you can turn up at most times of the day and week and know you will get a game. As usual, he has a point.

This happens a lot at Sherborne; there are various times of each day of the week when different groups of people turn up to play, not necessarily everyone every week, without prior planning. I must admit that, while there are some individuals who for deep dark reasons will never play with each other, Sherborne is a very friendly club, perhaps because of this facility and, once you know about these groups, you can join one or, if you want a quick game of singles, you avoid them.

If you can choose a time for one visit to Lyme Regis, try and make it so that you start on the 10th tee, as the views unfold better this way. Talking of unfolding views, at the western edge of the World Heritage Site Jurassic Coast is Budleigh Salterton.

EAST DEVON

Seaside golf courses are usually fairly obvious, and where they are not, they tend to be well signposted. Not so East Devon Golf Club. Although I have visited it a few times, I still have to make several passes through sleepy Budleigh Salterton, looking for the telltale cul-de-sac named Links Road. It is well worth a visit, though.

The course is heathland, on the cliff top, with generous fairways and big greens, and some inviting downhill drives (inevitably compensated for by some testing uphill ones). Of necessity the 1st hole plays away from the clubhouse, but then the 2nd hole is directed straight back towards it. I have come across this design feature elsewhere, notably at Thurlestone and Isle of Purbeck, and also Highgate in North London, which I used to visit regularly. If I started a round there say something like 8, 7, I used to take the opportunity of writing it off, and returning to the 1st tee. It seems unlikely that a course would be laid out to provide players with an early opportunity to abandon a medal round. In the days when the courses were built, the common form of the game was match play, and of course it does make sense to be able to play up to three extra holes as necessary without straying too far from the warmth of the clubhouse, so perhaps this is the reason.

After the 3rd hole, East Devon goes inland, and it seems a shame that there are not better views. The par five 6th hole is known as Heart's Delight, but I find it rather gloomy. It plays downhill, isolated from the rest of the course, into an ever-narrowing funnel of trees. Eventually one arrives – with some difficulty – at the uphill, upwind 206 yard 8th green, from where it is possible to see as far as Portland Bill to the east, and Start Point to the west, a span of about eighty miles of glorious coastline. Thereafter, the eastern view remains, and there are further glimpses to the west around 15th/16th. The 9th hole is a great downhill par four, and the 10th an apparently short par three, played to a three-tier green and therefore difficult both to judge, and subsequently to putt. After a slightly eccentric 11th, the 12th hole is a scimitar-shaped uphill par five, but if ever there was a "signature hole" it is Number 17. Played downwind, the tee shot is a lay-up to the end of a fairway which literally falls away into a decidedly no-go area, leaving a second shot which is for me a 3 wood across a valley. Even if you hit the green, it is a tricky surface with no certainty of a two putt. This is one of the great 17th holes.

It is quite prominent from the clubhouse and, seen from the wrong end, as it were, it looks really weird. It's hard to explain. You'll have to go there.

I mentioned that I have played it more than once. I simply had to go back, because on my first visit I was scoring really well until I encountered a bunch of – well, insert your own favourite word for people who do not quite seem to have grasped the fundamental principles of getting round a golf course in daylight – who should take full responsibility for my failure to complete the 17th hole successfully. Playing alone, I often have time to observe the patterns of others; and on one heather-lined course I kept seeing groups of men wandering around like free range hens, which set me thinking about the causes of slow play.

SLOW PLAY

We all have our preferences for play, and mine is for the intimacy of one partner. Threes are OK, but can be rather odd, if two form a sort of pair and leave the other out on a limb, but if you like mucking in and having a laugh, you probably prefer fourballs. The trouble is, they are slow. Consider this: hitting ten fairways out of fourteen is pretty good, OK? Well, that's about 70% so, on a course where missing the fairway means finding heather, four players drive, each with a 70% chance of finding the fairway. How often do you think they will have to search for a ball?

The probability they will not have to search is that they all hit the fairway, which is 70% × 70% × 70% × 70%; this comes to less than a quarter![46] This makes the game slower, but it is a fact of golfing life. Most people seem to look up at a group ahead on a green and think that is where play could be speeded up, but I believe that is simply a perception that comes from standing and watching. What happens afterwards is they walk off, you all play and walk up to the green, but the group ahead has not even teed off by the time you get there. If anything, people do not spend *enough* time before putting. When it is their turn, they walk up to the marker, put the ball down, stand briefly behind it, take a stance and hit, and exclaim, 'Oh, it never moved an inch.' I always try to look at a putt from the other side of the hole (you can often do this when walking onto the green to mark the ball), and walking from the hole to the ball helps with a feel for the distance. I might not be brilliant at holing out, but I do not have many three putts.

Contrast the slapdash way a lot of people putt with their procedure on the tee: a couple of swishes, then carefully select a spot for the tee peg and place the ball; stand behind and look at it; swish again; take a stance; check alignment; freeze for a number of seconds; hit. Sometimes, a number of adjustments and repetitions are included in the routine. Sometimes, I fear rigor mortis will set in. A few degrees of inaccurate alignment are not critical from the tee (provided the stance is square); on the green they are vital.

But not even this is the true curse[47] of slow play. In a singles game, when you get to the next tee, you know whether or not it is your honour, and you act accordingly, by playing first if it is your turn and doing your fiddling around afterwards. If it is not your honour, you pay attention while your opponent plays. In the study of logic, there is some-

---

[46] Express 70% as .7; then .7 × .7 is .49; call that .5; .5 × .5 is .25 – a quarter.

[47] This is the word my autocorrecting spellchecker came up with. I fancy I might have intended "cause" but this is fine.

thing called the principle of excluded middle, which states that something either is ×, or is not ×, where × is some proposition, such as "a
true statement", "a black crow", or "it is my turn to play". In fourball
play, this principle does not apply. The principle which applies in fourball play is roughly this: at least one player at any one time does not
know what the score was on the last hole; another may know the score,
but has temporarily forgotten who his partner is (and therefore that it
is his turn as lead-off player for the side); a third (having a poor day on
the greens) will suddenly recall that he might just have a Gleneagles
ball marker which could change his luck, and begin searching for it in
the nether regions of his golf bag – before walking to the next tee. The
probability that it will be his honour is normally 70%.

******

Talking of changes of luck, I have never seen anyone's game dis-
integrate more dramatically for such a slight reason as happened to
Heathcliff when I was partnering him at the Bucks. He caught sight
of the Isle of Purbeck green fee tag on my bag. That was all it took. 'I
drove down there one Saturday,' he said. 'Eleven bloody points. Seven
going out. Four coming back. Isle of Purgatory, I call it.'

ISLE OF PURBECK

Isle of Purbeck Golf Club qualifies as a
coastal golf course by a roundabout route.
The road from Corfe Castle to Studland which
runs past the clubhouse goes all the way to
Shell Bay where it serves the chain link ferry to
Sandbanks, but the land on the "inland" side of
this is unspoilt National Trust territory, joining
the golf course to the waters of Poole Harbour.
This is fortunate, as it means that I am able to relate the following incident.

The 2ⁿᵈ hole comes back to the clubhouse – a design feature mentioned elsewhere – and one which contributed to a day of rich entertainment when Celia and Nellie, then aged about 85, came with me
to watch me play and carry my clubs – in a buggy. There was only
one left for hire, and the person in the pro shop said, somewhat mys-
teriously, 'It isn't the best. Take it for the first two holes and see how
you get on.' Well, it seemed a little underpowered, but we persevered,
and Celia and Nellie subsequently had a hilarious time. It transpired

that the buggy's brakes were similarly underpowered – or perhaps the word should be non-existent. The first two holes merely undulate; many of the rest involve seriously steep slopes, and the only method of navigating them in this buggy was to take the longest possible run at them and hope to reach the top. Failure to do so left only the option of coming back down, in reverse. Nellie said she couldn't remember such a good time since she last went to a funfair – in 1958.

Everyone agrees that the views at Isle of Purbeck are magnificent, but from the golfing perspective, opinions are mixed. The 5th tee exemplifies both perspectives. You can see Poole Harbour and the coast of Poole and Bournemouth to the left, the Isle of Wight ahead, and Old Harry Rocks, which give the following hole its name, to the right. (Old Harry is of course a name for the devil.) What you cannot see from this tee is a fairway. You have to walk forward to the front, and then something approaching the landing area of a ski jump comes into view. With scrub either side, it gets narrower as it gets further away, and it is important to be long, because the hole measures 404 yards, and the second shot is to a long thin green on a sort of inland promontory. Miss it left or right, or be too long, and it is probably a lost ball. Nature is all around, but it can intrude too much into the golf if one's ball disappears into a rabbit hole in the fairway, which can be a possibility. The hole is tough enough already.

The following hole is an uphill curving par five which I like but pros don't, because it is laid out in such a way as to be unreachable in two shots. Now they know how the rest of us feel. The 8th hole is also a par five, and at 594 yards, possibly the longest on the coast of England. The pros can't reach that, either. The par three 11th hole is 194 yards long, with a kind of mini escarpment for a green. If the flag is on the left, it is not far from a sharp drop into a deep bunker, but any ball hitting the green is likely to run to the right and down the slope and leave a lengthy putt. After a drive at the 12th hole reminiscent of Bruce's Castle, the famous lighthouse hole at Turnberry, you are left with a long second to a green which slopes nastily from back to front. I have seen pin positions where the only chance of keeping the ball on the green from above the hole is to hole it.

Not all the holes are as demanding as this, but even on some of the shorter par fours, precision striking of second shots is called for at Isle of Purbeck. Depending on your perspective, it is either golfing perfection, or purgatory.

Unless you take the chain ferry from Sandbanks, to get to Isle of Purbeck you need to pass through Corfe Castle, which has its charming place in history as the venue for the murder of King Edward the Martyr by his stepmother. More central to English history is Bosworth Field, outside the town of Market Bosworth, where in 1485 Richard of York gave battle in vain. As this is generally reckoned to be the point at which the English stopped fighting amongst themselves and took on the world instead, the date has a centrality, and many history books end or start there. The other respect in which Bosworth is central is that it is just about as far away as you can get from the sea in England.

Of less historical interest is the fact that I was born in Market Bosworth, but it makes it interesting to ask myself where the lure of the sea comes from, because it is definitely there, even though through golf there is no actual communion with the water. It is true that Market Bosworth is less than 100 miles from The Wash, a fact which embarrassed me a little when I had to claim to some work colleagues that though I came from an island, I did not "know" the sea. The colleagues were Russian, and we were in Tomsk, Western Siberia. The nearest sea is the Kala, an inlet of the Arctic Ocean, 1300 miles north. But, the fact remains that when I was growing up, the only time I ever saw the sea, apart from a very occasional day trip to Skegness, was on our summer holiday. And, apart from an occasional cross-channel ferry trip to Europe, the first time I saw the sea in winter was very probably when I visited Sheringham one November, as a "treat" for having successfully delivered a lecture course. I played in daylight, and marked the students' papers during the dark hours.

I cannot define the attraction the sea has for me – perhaps I will discover it fully when I finish my peregrination – but there have been some very important occasions when I have needed to go to it. I usually choose Bridport.

BRIDPORT & WEST DORSET

While neighbouring Lyme Regis have been losing land, Bridport & West Dorset Golf Club have been selling theirs. You used to drive to the rickety old clubhouse outside West Bay, more like a typical cricket pavilion, change, get back into the car and drive up the cliff to the car park by the 1st tee. The back nine in those days comprised three holes of each parity, which I used to like, but as that is no longer the case, there is little point in my describing it. The front nine, too, was the first first half of a golf course I ever played in level par. As it began as it ended with a par five, it was unique amongst English coastal golf courses, but no matter. It now has a splendid new clubhouse, as the land around the old one was sold for development, and it is still a splendid place to be.

It still boasts its signature hole, now Number 6, which features on the front of the scorecard, and also in *Britain's 100 Extraordinary Golf Holes*,[48] where it is actually ranked sixth most extraordinary. Quite how one thing can be more extraordinary than another escapes me, but there we are. According to this reference, the tee is 200 feet above sea level on the cliff top, with the "fairway" 120 feet below. Well, there is no fairway, it's a par three measuring 133 yards, most of which do seem to be vertical when you stand on the tee. According to my Ordnance Survey map, the tee is just over 40 metres above sea level – about 140 feet – with the green about 20 metres – 70 feet below.[49] As you can imagine, the wind blows. The fact is, the purists hate it. Whatever club do you use?

I think my favourite hole is the 3rd, called Chesil. After the tough opening hole, doglegging right around the practice ground, the 2nd plays up the slope of the escarpment, and then there is a fine par five along the edge, sloping downwards, wind usually behind, with views along the Heritage coast to Chesil Beach and Portland Bill. If ever there was a par five hole where you believe you can reach with a driver and wedge, this is it. You don't, of course, because you try and welly it. This hole is followed by a tricky par three – in fact, none of them is easy – after which another par five doglegs its way up the escarpment to the high point of the 6th tee. The tee for the 12th hole is close by, although you don't play it yet, obviously. The short hole is created by a fold or dent in the cliff edge, and the 12th hole plays across to land of a similar height on the other side. The 7th hole plays up the slope created by this dent, as a par

---

48 Aesculus Press 2003.

49 This is not a happy entry for Aesculus Press. They list the yardage wrongly, refer to a course called Lyon's Gate which has closed, and confuse the Dorset dialect word "grockle" for tourist, when it means incoming resident. My stating these facts is in the interests of clarity. It is nothing to do with the fact that when I wrote asking if they would be interested in publishing this book, they did not manage the courtesy of a reply.

four, although it is only 242 yards. Numbers 8 and 9 return fairly close to the clubhouse – a bad weather luxury that certainly was not there before the re-design – and a slice off the 9th ends out of bounds in the practice ground. This is one of the few driving ranges that registers a net gain in balls over time.

The latter part of the course plays over the western side of the dent, with views towards Lyme Bay, and on a good day, Start Point. Number 12 is called Golden Cap, on which you may need to line up for your second shot, as the view of the fairway ahead is obscured by a dry stone wall which crosses the course. This really comes into its own on the next, which plays back towards it. It is a 371 yard par four – called Stonewall – with the wall passing about 40 yards in front of the green. Down the prevailing wind this should not present any problem for a second shot, yet you would be amazed at how often someone will top a shot and have it come to rest, unplayable, at the foot of the wall. It defies the laws of probability, though not of course, the laws of golf. After a tricky par three back over the wall again, the two holes which used to start and end the course come into play. For a time, Number 16 was reduced to a par four, as which it was roughly impossible, but now that has been returned to par five status, and 15 is an impossible par four. Numbers 17 and 18 are relatively modest finishing holes, and the clubhouse is splendid. But, I like being out on the course best.

I really do find it hard to put into words what a difference the sea makes. The Christmas before she died, Celia was taken into hospital, and I went to play at Bridport on 27th or 28th December. The sun was low over the English Channel in the afternoon, at an angle almost parallel with the slope of the cliff, and all the golfers were casting shadows about 100 yards long. Somehow, it made me feel very safe, but perhaps that was because it was my wife, and not me, who was in hospital. Part of me wanted to watch the sun go down into the sea (something it does not do in the summer months when it sets over the land) but I felt that was tempting fate. Maybe I was just made more than usually aware.

Possibly in playing seaside golf there is some kind of communion with the ancient elements: earth and air are always there of course, but somehow the presence of the sea introduces water in a way that a typical water hazard does not. It has to be moving about to count. The fourth element, fire, is present metaphysically: the fire that rages inside after a silly three putt, or the fire with which one will drive downhill downwind on the long 3rd hole at Bridport almost onto the green. Or, perhaps the fourth element for golf is not fire, but fore.

The other possibility is that the presence of the sea really has a soothing effect on me. In winter, unless the weather is really bad, the sea often seems quite tranquil, gently lapping at the shore – and calming the inner man? It is there, but I do not have to do anything about it, and it is not intending to do anything about me. As I have said, on the south coast of England in winter, the sun sets over the sea and as it goes down, so it reflects on the water and generates a surprising warmth. I have seen toddlers paddling without clothes in December, though this may say more about their parents than about how warm it really was.

There is always a warm welcome for visitors at Bridport & West Dorset Golf Club, no doubt thanks to Dave Parsons, the Head Professional. Dave is a stalwart member of the Wessex Alliance, a group of amateur and club professionals who meet monthly at a different course on or near the Dorset coast, and I have appreciated his enthusiasm for the idea of this book. As he put it, there are plenty of books about golf courses, but few about ordinary golfers playing them. Well, I hope it does not disappoint, Dave.

One occasion after play in the Alliance, we were sitting round waiting for the ball draw, the high spot of the evening for anyone who will not feature in the prize-givings. Usually the fourball who have played together in the afternoon chip in two quid each for a strip of raffle tickets and pool them. The kitty is exchanged for balls acquired from the host Professional at, I guess, retail price, so at two pounds a time, everyone should on average end up with a ball each, which is harmless fun for all concerned, including the host Pro.

Dave was relating tales of averages learnt on a recent visit to a putting clinic, part of the PGA's provision of continuing professional development for its members. The delegates on this occasion had generally supposed that putting would make a dull subject, but it had turned out interesting enough to overrun by two hours. Statistics are not generally available about the play of club golfers, but copious amounts of data exist for professional play. One such statistic had a special resonance for me. It seems that, faced with a three foot putt, a touring professional will hole it ninety-six times out of a hundred, or if you prefer, out of 100 professionals with a three foot putt, ninety-six will hole it. The actual fact – the data – is that, on the European Tour, 96% of three foot putts are holed. So, what do you think the figure is when the distance is increased to six feet?

The answer is a surprising drop in the success rate to 50%. Only one in two six foot putts on the Tour gets holed. Now, one can think of reasons why: difficult pin positions; players struggling to get up and down; those on worst form not getting their approach putt close; and so on, but it still seems an unexpectedly low figure. I suppose that when we watch golf on TV, we tend to get coverage of the best players on their best form, with this statistic accounting for some of the also-rans.

Have you worked out why there should be a "resonance" for me? Six feet, viewed as one walks toward a green, is classic pip length. Just the sort of distance that I believe should be conceded because I should get it, except that I won't. Well, exactly. Now the fact is supported with evidence from the European Tour. If the pros won't get it regularly, neither will I. Dave Parsons has unknowingly given me a cure for the pips! Well, not a cure perhaps. There is no "cure", but a palliative any-way. Now, when I miss the putt, it's OK. I'm allowed to. Pros do it.

Naturally enough, I set off for somewhere where I might encounter six foot putts.

HIGHCLIFFE CASTLE

Highcliffe Castle Golf Club is extraordi-nary. Given the knowledge that it has a 245 yard par three in the first half, and a hole only 3 yards shorter coming back, you might begin to conjure images of some windswept monster of a golf course atop a high cliff overlooked by an evil gothic castle, with some equally mon-strous being inside manically playing an organ, or shouting "fore" in a blood curdling voice...

You would be wrong, in every respect. Arriving from the west, there are signs to Highcliffe Castle itself, and to Highcliffe-on-Sea, but at the golf club, there are signs of neither. The land is, by golf course stand-ards, entirely flat, the two longest holes are consecutive, measuring a combined total of 794 yards, there are a further six par threes besides the two mentioned. In total it stretches to 4778 yards, par sixty-four. There are lots of mature trees, all around the edge, and also inside the course. As someone said – he is to remain nameless in case he ever needs to play there again – 'Shout fore here, and everybody ducks'.

Only an Ordnance Survey map confirms its proximity to the sea. I fancied I might be able to smell it as well, but I think it was fertilizer on the greens, the sort that leaves footprints when you walk on it. Then I thought perhaps I could hear the sea, but I realised that the noise was traffic. It was coming from the north, the one direction in which you cannot find the sea, not on the south coast of England. It is not reminiscent of a seaside course at all. If it reminds me of anywhere, it is like Pau in south-west France, the oldest course in continental Europe.

The tees are extremely near to the preceding greens, and several times play on one hole crosses over or very close to another. The greens, when they are at the end of narrow fairways, are very narrow, which makes them look quite long. It must be a murderous place to play a fully loaded shotgun start.[50] The 17th green is unusual; only 119 yards from the tee, it is more or less circular, with a sharp grassy ridge which rises to about three feet high out of nowhere and encircles it apart from a four foot gap left for access. I thinned my tee shot, so I played another – the game was over by then, I had beaten the course at match play and lost at stroke play – but neither ball found the green. As the 18th led me back past the tee again, I decided to have another go, which this time looked quite good. I walked back with my putter, but the ball was a few yards outside the ridge (which I think it must have hit on the outside bank), so I hit it, hard, with the putter. It flew along the ground, up the ridge, and took flight, and easily cleared the ridge opposite. I collected the ball, and paced the green – 15 deep, 14 wide, with footprints in the fertilizer to show that these were the diameters.

The dual match results are best explained by my arrogance. Like Goliath, I had supposed that this diminutive opponent would present no trouble. I would score well. Now, it was entirely reasonable to suppose that if I played to my handicap on this par sixty-four course, I would easily break 80, which is always welcome, but there is no logic to the supposition that because it was a par sixty-four course, I would be certain to play to my handicap. I began the round hitting straight, but once a slice developed, sevens and eights started appearing on my card. Hence my win-loss record. And I didn't have a single six foot putt.

---

[50] A shotgun start involves one group on each tee. When fully-loaded, additional groups wait behind the starters where the course layout permits. This can also be known as a double-barrelled shotgun start. I like these names. As far as I know, I made them up.

Playing here must be the golfing equivalent of training at altitude – you become acclimatised to hitting so straight that when you are shown the wide open spaces of a typical seaside course, hitting down the perfect line is a stroll. What would not be a stroll for the member here would be the extra 2,000 yards up and down the undulations of somewhere like Seascale or Sheringham. They really would need to train at altitude to develop their stamina. The members are a game lot, though. It looked and felt a lively, busy club. On the way out, I looked at the events board: Saturday 23rd April, Captain's Inaugural – Shotgun Start.

While it may be true that 50% of six foot putts on the tour are holed, it would not be true to say that each Touring Pro holes 50% of six foot putts. There would be variations. Dave mentioned that statistics on the play of amateurs are scarce, but reported one experiment when 5000 players of all types, by age, gender, and handicap were asked to record the number of putts taken per round, and the total score. Analysis of the data revealed that, independently of all the various sub-groups, 41% of total shots in a round were putts. Someone scoring 100 would have 41 putts, a score of 90 would be close to 37 (36.9), a round in 80 would have about 32 putts, but someone scoring 70 would do so partly by virtue of taking only 28 or so strokes on the green.

It is fascinating that the average for putts in the round remains the same across different scoring levels, but it would also be interesting to learn what the variance was within groups. Amongst any handicap group, there are relatively good and bad putters. How close are they all to this average? The scope for variation is not great. Most of the time, most people take two putts on most greens. It would not be hard to establish one's own average, for control purposes, but if you cannot be bothered, then the next time you feel that your putting has let you down, express the total number of putts you took in a round as a percentage of the score. If you are not making excuses, it needs to be bigger than 41%.

I I

WIRRAL WHIMSY

I am intrigued by peculiar concepts, like vegetarian haggis, for example. Everyone knows that haggis is mainly offal contained in a sheep's stomach, so what can a vegetarian version be? I looked up a traditional recipe, and the only non-meat ingredient was oatmeal. So, is vegetarian haggis porridge, in fact? Once, browsing in a remaindered bookshop, I spotted a title which appeared to be *The Kiss Guide to the Kama Sutra*. Now, I am no authority on the subject, but isn't anyone who needs a kiss explaining likely to find the *Kama Sutra* rather advanced material? I looked again; kiss was K.I.S.S., an acronym for "keep it simple stupid". Well, if you want to keep it simple, you won't need the *Kama Sutra*.

On BBC Radio 2, Richard Baker once introduced the march called Colonel Bogey, explaining that it was inspired by a lyrical shout of fore heard as the composer strolled across a golf course. After the piece, he mentioned that it was named after a mythical character who took exactly one stroke over par on each hole. Nope. It appears to be pure coincidence that while on this side of the Atlantic, "Bogey" was indeed some mythical figure who took what we now know as par on each hole, in the USA a "bogey" was bad news, as in "bogey man". A score of one over par, indeed, "par" itself deriving from the value at which a bond was equal to its nominal value on the stock market. It is not a brilliant use of the word, because one wants stocks to be valued above par, and golf scores to be below. The original usage remains today in a Bogey competition, a hole by hole match against the par – originally the bogey – of the course.

When I first heard the expression "Wallasey whine", I heard it without the 'h' and wondered if there was some microclimate which produced ripe grapes in this north-western part of England. I soon discovered it was a variant on the standard Scouse accent, of which of course there is no such thing. The local variations are subtle and can tell you a great deal about someone's origins. The most subtle are possibly those who come from Liverpool but don't have any sort of accent. As for The Wirral, things are probably very different now that this unusual peninsula formed by the estuaries of the Dee and the Mersey has a motorway up its middle. In the old days, apart from offering access to a privileged few via Flintshire and the Cheshire plain, the Wirral was a sort of off-shore Liverpool. You lived there if you were too rich to live in Liverpool itself, or maybe you lived there if you were too poor to live in the Pool. I've never been sure...

CALDY

Caldy Golf Club has a spanking new club-house and a massive car park with marked spaces for all the usual dignitaries plus "ex captain" and "ex lady captain". How many do they have, I wonder? Do they have a space each, or fight over who gets there first? I park well away from reserved territory, and get out of the car to encounter a wind which even by seaside standards is alarmingly strong. I am also a little alarmed at the green fee. At first glance, Caldy is an attractive enough parkland course sloping gently down to the banks of the river Dee, but it is not obviously special, unlike say Saunton, which charges the same price for a day ticket. Perhaps The Committee are seeking to fund the new clubhouse through green fees.

Alternatively, it might be a stratagem to deter visitors. Apart from a lone player just finishing the 18th, I have the place to myself. Admittedly it is 4.30 PM, but at this time of the day and year at Sherborne, there would be plenty of people about. I play the 1st hole OK; the green is hollow-tined, as are many in early April; in fact, all the courses I seem to have played on for the last month have been hollow-tined, and I am getting a little fed up. I am also distinctly unimpressed when, thanks to the wind, my 5 wood shot finishes 20 yards short of the 150 yard 2nd. After I have twice thinned wedges to finish with a seven, I decide that this is an occasion for taking on the course at match play. This turns out to be roughly equivalent to playing the wind, as the course settles down to play up and down parallel to the river, in what I take to be a north-westerly direction.

I am having something of a bad day chipping. Pitch and run shots (which I always opt for if there is a choice) are prone to land unpredictably on hollow-tined greens, particularly if you thin them, which is what I seem to be doing. On the other hand, I have discovered a low punch shot for finding upwind greens from 80–100 yards. Where has that been all my life? Encountering a couple of temporary greens does not improve my general feelings about the green fee, but when I manage a net birdie on the difficult par three 10th hole, I am at least one up. Then the wind blows my fading drive miles right on the dogleg par five 11th, which is not good. Firstly, I am blocked out by trees, but even if there is a way through, I have not cut off the corner. After curving decidedly right, the hole then bends back the other way. It should be called a crooked stick. Any dog with legs shaped like this would need a stick – not for fetching, just to be able stand up. I am forced to chip onto the fairway and then hit two more hard shots to get near the green, but I escape with a half.

There now follows another wind-for-or-against section, and I do surprisingly well upwind, and equivalently poorly downwind. I do not think this is entirely my fault. At the 13th hole, the flag is directly behind a bunker, and it seems sensible to play for the middle of the green. Thanks to the wind (and a poor strike), the middle becomes the back left, and the flag is front right, practically in the bunker. And, this green is not hollow-tined, which in other circumstances I might have appreciated, but not after losing all feel with the putter on the roller coaster, punctured greens. I manage to keep the first putt out of the bunker, but two more are inevitable. Still, I reach the 15th tee two up. With three downwind and two shot holes to come, I need only one par and three bogeys to beat the course, which I consider to be plain sailing. This is a mistake. In this wind, it takes three to get down from the edge of the 15th green, and five from 10 yards short of the 16th green. All square, facing the 17th hole, with the upwind, uphill, dogleg par five to follow. I get a shot there but none here, which is 145 yards downhill to a two-tier sloping green with a deep ditch running in front of it. What should I do? The hole is close to the front; should I try to get close, guaranteeing the half and giving a chance of a win, or play safe and risk a three putt loss? I elect to go for it, but whoever manages my body disagrees and causes me to half thin the shot, well over the ditch, but off the green, and 15 yards from the hole. I have a downhill chip on a spiked green. If I thin it, it will be in the ditch. Indeed, I do not even need to thin it, I can easily send a decent chip into this ditch. The green is 34 paces deep, so how many paces onto the green would you call a good number to position a forward pin? The greenkeeper thought three would be fun. It would certainly do for Tiger Woods; if he tried to get close, his ball would spin back into the ditch. Really, what is the greenkeeper trying to do? I do not think I am a bad loser, but this is all rather ridiculous (as Peter Alliss might say). Armed with some of these thoughts, I duff the chip. Dormie one down.

Now I have to par the 18th to halve the match. I hit a reasonable drive into the wind, and discover that this hole is not really a dogleg either, not for a working dog. It is more the shape of my cat Holly's tail when she arches it. I play a 3 wood, hoping the wind will drift the ball back into the ever-curving fairway. It goes straight, into the rough on the other side; it finds a reasonable lie but there are still 160 yards or so to go. The time is approaching 7 PM BST when the sun is directly west, so I am able to confirm that the wind is in the north-west, and will be across my next shot. If it were a little more westerly, there would actually be the unusual situation where my first two shots into the wind would be followed by a wind-assisted third. And, as they say in these parts, if my granny had a beard, she would be my granddad.[51] I play – a good shot, but it floats on the crosswind and finishes 5 yards short of the green which is not spiked, and 37 paces deep. This time, the hole is 3 paces from the back. I am not a bad loser, but...

I am not a bad loser, because my chip, on line for the hole, stops three paces and three inches from the back of the green. A par to halve the match, and a good feeling. All is forgiven (except possibly the greenkeeper).

I had difficulty finding somewhere to stay that evening, firstly because there did not appear to be many options, and secondly, because I was overly wrapped up in my own affairs. To use *The Good Pub Guide*, you first turn to the appropriate map for the area you are visiting. Places with entries are marked with a black spot, and if they have accommodation, there is a box round the spot. There were two entries on the Wirral, but I had trouble finding them as they were listed under Lancashire, which I don't think can be quite right. Neither had

---

[51] This is the polite version. There is a more graphic equivalent in which the anatomical reference – still beginning with b – is unequivocally male. After all, it is not unknown for grannies to have beards, of a sort.

a box, but I checked anyway. No bedrooms. So, instead I stared at my *AA Easy Read Britain* for a while until I thought I remembered that Celia and I had once stayed somewhere pleasant in a place called Parkgate, and I booked into a hotel the name of which escapes me. I used the internet, which I have found to be even less reliable than the *Guide*. At least if you phone an entry from the *Guide*, you speak to someone who confirms the booking. On the internet, there seem to be some jokers who confirm the booking, but forget to inform the hotel you are coming.

The hotel had no single rooms left, because this was the day after Liverpool had, historically, played Juventus for the first time since Heysel, a tie they famously went on to win, and the first night of the three day Aintree race meeting which culminates in the Grand National, all of which had failed to register with me. There is a modern tradition at this meeting that the women compete amongst themselves as to how they dress, and an official prize of a Jaguar car went to the winner this year. For some, they take the expression "less is more" to heart and compete to wear as little as possible. In some respects, this is a northern adaptation of events at Royal Ascot. Someone should tell them that Ascot takes place in June, not early April.

Parkgate was odd. There was a black and white photograph from 50 years ago showing a kind of promenade and beach, but now the water's edge has retreated several hundred yards, separated from the land by a stretch of marshy vegetation. The hotel was in similar decline. Did we really stay here, I wondered? It did not serve dinner, so I went to a nearby seafood restaurant. It was packed, mainly with women seemingly trying out their Aintree costumes. Maybe the gooseflesh would improve their appearance in the morning. Apart from this, it was great, run by two females, a vivacious, beautiful 19 year old, and possibly her granny. Trying to be charming, I acted as if they were sisters. I was probably nauseating.

Breakfast the next morning was not quite so good, being "continental", or the Wirral's version thereof. I had crumpets, with cheese, not the best preparation for my round at nearby Heswall.

HESWALL

Heswall Golf Club is further upstream from Caldy, which seems a slightly odd statement, given that it appears below it on the map – but the river is flowing northwards. From Caldy one could look out to sea; not so here, so its qualification as a literally littoral course is perhaps marginal. But, on the principle of equity, I want to try it. The green fee is half that at Caldy, so will it be twice as bad, as it were? Or do I mean only half as good?

Like Caldy, it slopes down gently towards the Dee, but there is more vegetation to be seen. In fact, Heswall reminds me of a mature version of the sort of course one sees with sapling plantations along the sides of fairways. There are also a number of ponds. From just driving around the area, the Wirral seems to have lots of ponds. Perhaps as global warming advances, it will become England's answer to Florida.

The pond protecting the 3rd green is well-positioned – or rather, the 3rd green is well-positioned behind a pond which, I am sure, was there first. I have plenty of time to appreciate its position, as play is rather slow. I turned up as instructed at 9.30 when the tee opens to visitors, to find a party of ladies waiting to play. Two threes precede a twoball, and while the waiting might frustrate some in this situation, they seem to relish it, as it leaves plenty of time for chatting. (For obvious reasons, I have never played ladies' golf, but I have played ladies' doubles tennis – i.e. three ladies and me – and politically incorrect as it may be of me to make this observation, it is a fact that my partners would sometimes break into conversation about something not remotely connected to the game we were playing. It would tend to happen on my serve, when they were closest.)

The waiting at Heswall is frustrating me. Unusually, I have a business meeting some distance away in the afternoon and, perhaps more to the point, it is desperately cold. The wind is as bad as the previous day at Caldy, but at least I was able to get round there quickly – two and a half hours, in fact – but here we are on schedule for four hours. After the 3rd hole, we have to traverse the Wirral Way, a former railway line converted to a modern bridle path, and there are lots of notices to be aware of and respect walkers and cyclists etc. Indeed, there are lots of warning or disclaiming notices all over the place. Perhaps one of The Committee Members is an insurance loss adjuster. The 4th hole is a par three measuring 209 yards from the white tee, down towards the water's edge and directly across the wind. I am playing from the blue tees (I had to go back into the pro shop to ask), the whites and yellows not appearing until the end of winter rules. This seems quite a good idea, because they are proper tees, and there is a proper card for the blue tees, meaning handicap adjustments can continue during the winter. It is fairly uncommon.

The 4th hole measures 179 yards from the blues, and with the flag at the back, I hit a 3 wood which bores its way through the wind without any deviation, pitches four feet short of the flag and finishes two feet past it, without actually going in. I wish I knew how I did it. I hold a vague and forlorn hope that the ladies in front might notice and let me through, but they are engrossed. To be fair, there is little point in their letting me through when there are two groups of three ahead. Still, something must be done. The next three holes play forth, back, and forth parallel to the estuary, and are reminiscent of Caldy, and indeed, of each other, so after a couple of shots, I walk over to the vacant 8th tee, a short hole. There is yet another pair of ladies playing the hole near the green, taking their time. At one point they stand some distance from the green, and when one of them waves an arm, I think first it is to invite me to play, but then I realise it is a gesticulation emphasising a conversation point. I fear I have jumped out of the frying pan into the fire (not the best metaphor for such a cold day) as the group I have leapfrogged appear to be coming up fast to my rear, but fortunately the ladies ahead are playing a shortened course, because they walk to the 14th tee, and this is the 8th hole.

Thus relieved, I have a clear course ahead, and the option to play two balls on some holes to make up for those I missed out. Oddly, the way I am playing declines. I was doing much better with the wait. I must discuss this with my psychologist, whoever that is. The 11th hole I enjoy, because I hit a 5 wood almost as close as at the 4th for another two, and the upwind 13th green is protected by a pond even more challenging than the 3rd. There is a nice finish too, with an uphill, crosswind par four, a downhill par three (I hit the green but miss the putt for a third two), a dogleg par five 17th, and a good if short finishing par four. This is a fine course. Comparisons are invidious, but compared to neighbouring Caldy, Heswall is certainly "cheap at half the price".

To the best of my knowledge and belief, as they say, that is the first time I have ever seen the expression "cheap at half the price" when it actually meant anything. If you analyse it, it is puzzling. So is the phrase "value for money". Is there any other sort of value?

ABOUT PRICES AND VOLUMES

One of the central themes in my business teaching work was the issue of price and value. The perception of value, or cheapness, is subjective, and entirely in the eye of the customer. In contrast, price is totally objective, and usually set by the seller, who should aim to offer the customer value, but not cheapness, because the latter implies the customer would willingly pay more, and if there is any spare going, the seller needs it, sometimes just to be able to stay in business. It is possible to be reasonably scientific about prices, for example gathering information on what competitors charge, but many people who work for themselves are impulsive, even superstitious about their pricing policy. It is not uncommon to hear the following hole-in-my-bucket type of reasoning:

'I hate working for this client, I don't make any money out of it.'
'Why don't you put the price up?'
'The client wouldn't stand for it.'
'Would that matter?'
'Yes, I'd lose the business.'
'But I thought you didn't like it.'
'I don't, but I need the work.'
'Oh. Do you make any money out of it, then?'

In one extreme, I met someone whose price was such that, even if he sold its entire production capacity, his business still lost money. When challenged to raise prices, he nevertheless insisted that he would lose his customers if he did. I call that a lose-lose scenario. Sometimes, one feels that self-employed people should be issued with handicap certificates.

In case there are any Committee Members reading this, here are a couple of thoughts on pricing policy. Remember that it is not The Committee's opinion about whether your green fee is cheap or not that counts, it is the visitors' perception – but you can at least check what nearby clubs are charging. You are still left with a choice. After allowance for any commission or VAT involved, there is no real cost associated with a single green fee, so all the money paid by the visitor goes to the club's coffers. Say that you normally have 1,000 visitors a year paying £35 each. That equates to a contribution of £35,000. Might you get that by charging £50? You would only need 700 visitors. To express this another way, you could afford to lose 30% of visitors before you began to lose revenue, so if you lost only 20%, you would have more income *and* fewer visitors, which would no doubt please the members. We call this a win-win scenario.

Quite why, as an inveterate green fee payer, I should be advocating this policy is not clear. Old habits die hard, I suppose. This is a point at which someone usually chips in with another ill-thought comment, 'Ah, but as an author, surely your green fees are tax deductible'. They may be, but there has to be something to deduct them from, and they still have to be deducted.

The scenario above does not work the same way for catering revenues. Say a pint of beer sells for £2.35. The 35 pence is VAT, so the "real money" is £2.00, out of which there is probably a margin of around 30%, or 60p. In other words, the beer costs the steward £1.40. So, 1,000 pints of beer generates a contribution for the steward of £600. Now, raising the price by 20p (plus VAT) would generate 80p per pint, and the steward could make £600 by selling 750 pints. There could be a 25% decline in sales before the steward started to lose money. Is that likely at your club?

Many Committees think the other way round; lower prices will be good for members and encourage social interaction. Well, they may do, but lowering the price of a pint by 20p plus VAT means that the steward now makes only 40p a pint, and must now sell 1,500 pints to generate the same contribution. That is a 50% increase in custom. Again, is that likely? If the club runs the bar, this is for The Committee to decide, but if the steward is self-employed, such a policy is a disaster. Remember this when pricing society packages. Discount the green fees, and not the catering.

Also remember the motto of Joe Cohen, founder of Tesco, which was "pile it high, sell it cheap". Volume business is all about bulk buying at lower costs, some of which – but definitely not all – may be passed onto the customer. What Joe really meant was "pile it high, buy it cheap".

******

Such talk of monetary subjects leads awkwardly to another Wirral course, which sounds like a place you rent but never pay for.

LEASOWE

Leasowe Golf Club is in the middle of the seaward end of the Wirral Peninsula, flanked by its more illustrious neighbours Hoylake to the west and Wallasey to the east. The 1st hole is a short par four, at 249 yards possibly the shortest there is. There are plenty of bunkers, some in front of, but before the edge of the green. This interesting arrangement turns out to be a principal feature of the course. To get to the 2nd tee, you pass through an archway in a crenellated wall – a kind of mercenary battlement looking for somewhere to defend. Beyond it is the awful Leasowe Castle, which comes close to defying description. It looks as if John Betjeman, in some dream, had commissioned a northern rival to the Headland Hotel in Newquay, and appointed Dr Frankenstein as architect.

The land is rather scrubby, and it is hard to say whether you would call it linksland. Apart from some unnatural-looking elevated tees, the sea wall and the afore-mentioned bunkers, it is flat. The 4th hole is extraordinarily long – 483 yards from the whites – a par four with a bank of bunkers about 100 yards from the green. It is downwind, but a bad second shot finds one of them. The sand is good, but there is no rake. I guess that some of the people who apparently bring their litter for walks along the sea wall would steal any rake left there. It is surprising they have not stolen the sand. Perhaps there is plenty on the beach.

Passing back through the fortifications we leave the public domain. The short 5th (333 yards) is a dogleg with a probably driveable green. From the elevated tee, I observe that someone has actually stolen the sand from the beach! Years ago, I came across an estate agent's blurb which used the phrase "concrete style garden". Here, the sloping coastal defence makes a concrete-style beach. There is a mysterious notice on the 6th tee stating "hole closed or tee moved forward to protect contractors working on fence". The two players in front of me are walking along uncertainly, searching for an alternative tee. I catch them up, and they invite me to "not play through", something of a pity because at 548 yards from the yellows, the hole is nevertheless directly downwind, and might be interesting. I walk on – 548 yards is a long way when you are not playing.

The 7th is another dogleg, and there I meet up with Len. Having had a hip replacement a while ago, he has not been playing, so he is just getting what hinted at being a decent game back together. He is also the only member of his regular fourball left, although he still works as a bricklayer, and it is this trade which has basically worn his hips out. The new one is causing the second original to weaken. He is wearing a very smart pair of claret cords with a well-matched woollen slipover. As someone who once used to change out of office clothes to play golf, I find the idea of "dressing up" from his working clothes, as Len has done, quite novel.

He asks how long I have been a member, and seems surprised that I am visiting. 'You should have gone next door to Wallasey, it's a links course.' So, this is not, then. I ask if there is a big price difference. The answer is not really – the expensive one is Royal Liverpool at Hoylake, to which The Open will return next year. Len continues that Leasowe was founded by John Ball, twice a winner of The Open, who left Royal Liverpool in disgust at that club's decision to admit lady members. This was in 1891. I remark about Open venues these days being criticised for *not* admitting ladies. 'This club doesn't,' says Len. 'You see, there's the Wirral Ladies Club (pause). Mind you, it has a men's section.' All the time, I am wondering whether to ask why Len does not play at the much better-looking Wallasey, but I decide not to. He tells me that they are a decent bunch of lads at Leasowe, so this may be one reason, and he has been a member for twenty-five years. Maybe this was the only club available to join at that time.

But it is certainly not the littoral charm of Leasowe that attracts as we move inland to play alongside the dual carriageway, where The Committee have been forced to introduce out of bounds' areas to discourage people from slicing balls into the windscreens of passing vehicles. Len also explains how The Committee decided to put in a back tee to lengthen the 4th hole into a par five, and the course to par seventy-two. This was shortly before hosting the Cheshire Open, whose competitors registered so many birdies and eagles on the new hole, that they immediately changed the par back, but left the new tee. It could well be the longest par four in my list. As we turn back to play into the wind again, I remark to Len that it is necessary to score one's Stableford points on the downwind holes. He tells me that in a medal held in a flat calm, he once scored 62 (net, I assume) – and failed to finish in the first six. 'Are there flat calms often?' I ask. 'Oh yes. About as often as Olympic Games.'

I mention that the wind does not seem so bad at Sherborne because of all the trees. 'Trees won't grow here,' says Len. 'They've tried. Had scientists in to sample the soil and so on, but it's the wind.' More or less as he says this, we come across the nearest thing to trees the course possesses – gnarled, twisted, stunted, indeterminate vegetable growth, such as Dr Frankenstein might have produced if Betjeman had given him opium and asked for a bonsai garden. One aspect of them was really interesting though – they were all aligned in the same north-westerly direction. I realised this fact had three implications: firstly, the wind in which we were playing was westerly, not north-westerly, so unlike at Caldy and Heswall, this course had been laid out to play mainly crosswind; secondly, assuming this wind was blowing at Caldy, then the 18th hole *really would* feature two wind-against shots followed by a wind-assisted third.

The third realisation was that after years of speculating about prevailing winds, I had finally found a reliable indicator. This is only my 65th coastal English golf course!

I drove home from Leasowe, finding myself as I always have been, confused about why it is apparently acceptable for women to go out wearing what I can only describe as insufficient or inadequate clothing, but totally out of order for middle-aged men to stare at them. I am also confused about why I do it. It's nothing to do with being widowed. I think I've always done it, although I don't remember doing it before I was married. In the restaurant the previous night, I had at one stage had some difficulty knowing where to look. But we can be certain of one thing, this would not have been Victorian John Ball's objection to female members at Hoylake. It is perhaps dangerous in a book like this to address the issue of *equality* in golf, but as the full phrase should read *equality of opportunity*, and I have this opportunity, I will take it.

ISSUES OF EQUALITY

Competitive sporting events are about *anything but* equality. They seek to identify the precise inequalities between competitors, going to extraordinary lengths in measuring the distinctions of one one thousandth of a second in athletics or who is able to hole a putt on the 76th green of The Open Championship. Now, I am not allowed to enter

The Open, because I am not good enough to take part, never mind win, but in 2006, the wording on the entry forms will be changed to allow women to enter, provided they possess the necessary golfing prowess. In an interview in early 2005, The Secretary of the R & A explained that the wording originally nominated men because it was supposed that no woman would ever want to take part. Such decision-making on behalf of others is as old as life itself, and not gender-specific. There is a fine character in an Oscar Wilde play whose stock phrase, 'Allow me to be the judge of that,' extends to permit her to determine whether her husband is respectively hungry, tired, or too hot. But, as for women taking part in The Open, chance would have been a fine thing, would it not?

Nevertheless, there remains a dilemma: is The Open really "open" if entry to it is restricted? As we all know, the original modern Olympic ideal holds that what counts is not winning, but taking drug tests. (Sorry, the opportunity was irresistible.) In practice, the egalitarian practice of merely taking part in the Olympics has had to be sacrificed on the altar of some other god, probably money. If someone takes two hours to complete the 10,000 metres, it interferes with the post-modern Olympic ideal that what counts is not the winning but the taking pictures. Upset the television schedules and you upset the future financial viability of the Games, which is precarious enough anyway. But, from a sporting perspective, one could just about justify the imposition of qualifying standards so that the ability of other competitors to compete fairly is not compromised by someone else's incompetence.

So Annika Sorenstam and Michelle Wie can enter The Open, but I cannot, even though I have been playing for longer than they have combined. But who exactly lobbies for female competitors to be allowed to compete alongside men? There are no calls for women to compete alongside men in Olympic events such as javelin throwing or weight lifting, so why golf? Most Olympic sports have separate competitions for men and women. An exception is equestrian events, where women and men compete on level terms – to the extent that a horseback is level. The differences are primarily in the physiological features of their mounts. Indeed, the horse-loving fraternity has had this problem solved for years. As long ago as 1779, the Earl of Derby and Sir Charles Bunbury created The Oaks, a race over one-and-a-half miles, for fillies –

---

[52] The world's most famous race could easily have been called The Bunbury. The rival owners tossed for the right to name the race.

female horses. No colts would be allowed to compete; they could run in an equivalent race – called The Derby[52] – but any self-respecting filly could also enter that race if her owner felt so inclined. The same rules apply to the one mile classics, the 1000 and 2000 Guineas, where fillies may run alongside colts on level terms. In all other races open to all genders, fillies would carry less weight than colts.[53]

This fairly establishes the rules of equality: females will be permitted to compete alongside males in their own right; they will also have their status as "the weaker sex" acknowledged through an automatic, compensating system of handicapping; and they will have their own events which males will not disturb. Very fair. I for one am glad that the omission of the first of these equal opportunities in the world's oldest golf tournament is about to be rectified.

My tongue is only partly in my cheek. I have little time for those bleating touring pros who voiced objections to Annika Sorenstam playing in a men's tournament. One complaint was that "it takes away a chance for a genuine player to make a living". So does a sponsor's invitation to Jack Nicklaus or Seve Ballesteros – but it also adds interest to the tournament which adds revenue which goes into the prize fund which pays them their exalted incomes which they receive for doing something which they would do anyway. And anyway, the PGA Tour is not exactly a workers' cooperative with each member taking his turn to win. (While I am about it, do you not loathe tournament pros who refer to "another day at the office"? There is absolutely no criterion on which a day spent competing at a golf course compares to a day working in an office. For all but a very small minority, everything about an office *is the same every day* – exactly the last thing a pro wants, given that most of the time, he is actually losing, and desperately needs to change things tomorrow.)

I will also for good measure throw in my contempt for those clergymen of the Church Of England who defected to Rome in response to the decision to permit the ordination of women, claiming something called "the hurt". What on earth is hurtful about someone else being allowed to do what you do? Is this not the response of a toddler who is quite happy not playing with a toy – until another toddler starts playing

---

[53] In racing, there is an added complication of the gelding. We do not have geldings in my golf club, although there are plenty of seniors.

with it? These defectors should have been only too aware that it was not Jesus who discouraged the participation of women, but St Paul, who came along well after the event. The question of what this has to do with golf is obvious; we are talking about religion.

Inextricably linked to the question of equality is the issue of discrimination. There is no doubt that sporting women have been discriminated against in the past. Ann Packer, the first British woman to win the Olympic 800 metres title (and almost give David Coleman a burst blood vessel in the process) was also the first woman to win the Olympic 800 metres title. In these marathon days of Paula Radcliffe, it seems remarkable that women were allowed to run no further than 400 metres until 1964, no doubt at the whim of the male-dominated IOC. There is no doubt too that discrimination still exists, but in the context of golf, is it a big issue that institutions such as Royal St George's and Royal Troon should have their status as Open venues threatened because their policy as private members' clubs is not to admit women members? Women are certainly welcome to play the former as visitors, but there are no ladies' changing rooms, or ladies' tees. (They may play from the men's tees. I am not aware of the protocol for using the changing rooms.)

Firstly, the host club does not run The Open; it merely provides the facilities (in which respect it differs from the Augusta National, which runs The Masters) and its own rules are subordinated to those of the R & A. Does it – and by extension, Golf itself – nevertheless represent a bastion of conservative male chauvinism which must be overthrown?

I would say not, given that Royal Liverpool began admitting ladies in 1891, causing John Ball to skulk away and play a decidedly inferior course of his own. Most golf clubs are mixed gender, and have been for years; can we not tolerate a few that are not, including Sunningdale Ladies'?

Secondly, is it not a matter of choice, a club's right, in fact? Consider the following: by definition, all private members' clubs discriminate; otherwise, they cease to be private members' clubs. Unless they exercise the power of veto over who may join, they become *public* members' clubs. Even then, they may still discriminate, through their pricing policy. With no restrictions on who may join, and no fees, any such grouping of people is generally known as Society, or Life, and many of the best things thus provided are free – but not the recreational use of several hundred acres of real estate. Society – in the form of a local authority – may choose to subsidise the use of a golf facility by operating a municipal course. People may choose to spend their money on playing it.[54]

The clubs that deserve criticism are those which admit lady members, charge them the same fees as men, and effectively provide them with inferior benefits by restricting the times when they may play. "Ladies' day" is something of a tradition in English members' clubs, and though at first glance it appears a positive action in favour of the female membership, it is invariably a sop, an attempt at compensation for the fact that most weekends, the tees are closed for men-only competitions. This common practice also encourages segregation, which (speaking as an eligible widower who might like to meet a female golfing companion) is a shame. Modern English clubs and, to my knowledge, all those in France, do not do this. Competitions are open to all, even if prizes are awarded for different sections. Men and women play alongside each other; ladies play from forward tees, of course, and everyone has a personal handicap.

This might be a modern ideal but, faced with the alternative of having to undertake a considerable amount of modification to both clubhouse and course in order to conform, Royal St George's chooses instead not to invite ladies to become members. Is this the exercise of a right, or a social crime?

According to the "militant feminist" and erstwhile minister of sport, Richard Caborn, who chose to speak out on the subject on the eve of The 2004 Open, it might well be the latter. Women should be free to do anything men do, and such institutions which stand in the way of this ideal should not be allowed to exist. Women are in every respect the same as men, but it should also be respected that they are physiologically different from men. Society should provide them with services which respect this difference, such as Well Woman Clinics. Well, I have no objection to that, so long as women do not object to my occasional consumption of "adult literature" as part of my self-administered Well

---

[54] About 20 years ago, in an inspired attempt to encourage sport for all, the Royal Borough of Kensington & Chelsea offered 50% discount to OAPs and visually impaired people at a new sporting facility. It was a squash club.

Widower Clinic. The female anatomy does not exist in isolation. In addition to its own biochemical phenomena, it generates effects through the eye of the male beholder which are just as real and consequential. Men who wish to gaze upon the unclothed female form are not socially aberrant. Some women would do well to respect this when they choose their clothes.

My wife and I used to dine out on the fact that she proposed marriage to me – on 29th December, 1975, the day that the first Equal Opportunities Act became law. At our wedding, it was she who made the speech. Times have indeed moved on, and much equality of opportunity previously denied to women has been achieved. There is further progress to be made, particularly in the workplace, but can we please have things in perspective?

How desirable would it be if an 18 year old man could walk along the street and face exactly the same prospect of being stopped by the police whether the colour of his skin was black, white, red or blue, and whether the street was in Brixton, South London, or Brixham, South Devon? And, how pleasant would it be if he could join a local municipal club, and perhaps play a policeman at golf? Are you listening, Mr Caborn?

12

COLONIAL COUSIN

Digby, my colonial cousin, hails from the Republic of Texas where Things Are Big. So is he, and when he hits a ball, it stays hit, as the saying goes. I am quite big,[55] but definitely not a student of the game the same way he is; when not playing well, he will often be found muttering about knowing what he *should* be doing with the club face but not doing it. In contrast, I continue to remain mildly amazed that I manage to hit the ball at all. Occasionally, when I out-drive him, I will say something like, 'Was that your 2 iron?'

'Naw. 5, I was laying up.'

Coming from a land where they do have occasional frost in winter but in June it starts to get "uncomfortably warm", Digby adores British golfing weather. The first of our short golfing breaks included a visit to Carnoustie. As we were to play two of the three courses on the same day, the consequence of an irresistible green fee deal, a colleague and I had arranged for caddies to help us round the championship course. We had hoped for traditional types hopefully with impenetrable Arbroath accents (said to make Glaswegians sound eloquent), but the three gentlemen who served us were respectively a mature PhD student, a chartered accountant taking a year off, and a former local planning officer seeking an outdoor life. I had never before played with a caddie; would I be intimidated? Intimidated to the extent that, when I birdied the 6th hole, I "went back to level par". OK, we weren't playing from the championship tees, but Carnoustie is Carnoustie. Eventually, the gods – in their manifestation as an impossible bunker – got me on the

---

[55] Digby is in fact so big that some people think he should be called Bigby.
[56] Dreich, perhaps?

12th hole, and as the weather became something Scottish[56] and drifted, so did my score. This is when Digby came into his own, his game actually improving as we played what our caddies proudly called the toughest finish in championship golf.

So, when I met Digby off the red-eye from Dallas at Gatwick one morning on the sort of typical day in early spring which would make most arriving passengers shudder, he was delighted. As we travelled to Rye, he announced that he was interested in acquiring some English – then he changed it to British (I am slowly educating him) – wet weather gear; I was surprised. 'Isn't it the same the world over?' I asked.

'No, I mean those funny kinda pants to wear with my long socks.' Digby was proud of the long socks he had been obliged to purchase when he turned up at some snooty club in the Midlands, and carried them everywhere. 'Not pants, trousers,' said I. 'The ones you want are either plus twos or plus fours.' I had to admit that I did not know where he would be able to buy any. The people I have met who wear them seem to be the types who were born with them, or perhaps inherited their grandfather's pair. I recalled a fellow countryman of Digby's who had briefly led The Open wearing what he called "knickerbockers", sometimes abbreviated to "knickers". I suggested that they might often be tailor-made, perhaps a traditional present when a youngster "came of age" and joined his first adult golf club. Otherwise, he might try Lillywhite's. 'I think I want a tweed pair,' said Digby. I explained that I was referring to a large sports store in Piccadilly Circus and, tempted, added, 'That's it, Digby. Go into Lillwhite's and say you are after some tartan knickers.' As someone put it: two nations divided by a common language.[57]

By this time, the weather had improved a little, but the same could not be said for the traffic, and we eventually arrived at Rye 50 minutes late.

RYE

The antiquated Clubhouse at Rye Golf Club is atop a twenty foot plateau which, we are to discover, runs for the length of the

---

[57] George Bernard Shaw, in fact

course. We have to report to the Secretary. According to *The R & A Handbook*, Rye does not admit unaccompanied visitors, so I had asked The Secretary at Sherborne to provide an introduction. There had been no problem. We find The Secretary's office, sort of tagged onto the end of the building, and introduce ourselves. We are welcomed, taken into the other part of the building, given coffee, and asked to sign in. There is no mention of money; only when we are ordering sandwiches for the end of the round are we somewhat apologetically asked to pay for the golf as well. We stroll over to the pro shop – it is on the other side of the road and has its own post box built into the wall – to add to Digby's collection of souvenir ball markers. There is a long rail of plus fours for sale.

The card of the course looks a little daunting. I should not disclose the yardage, as the exact number is also the security code for the locker room entrance, but it is SSS 71, and only par sixty-eight. I set Digby a target of 30 Stableford points; if he beats it, he must treat himself to a pair of plus fours. 'And if I don't beat it, do I have to buy two pairs?' he adds. We leave the locker room, on the door of which is a detailed notice advising us inter alia that golf is a game to be enjoyed amongst friends, that only twoball matches are permitted without the expressed permission of The Secretary, and that matches should take no longer than three hours to complete. As Digby sometimes plays at courses where three hours would be a reasonable time for the first nine, he is impressed.

The 1st is the only par five hole on the course, and the yellow tee is on the plateau, looking down on the fairway. There are a couple of players ahead, and from their position we cannot tell whether we will make the carry straight ahead. They appear to be playing third shots, but they also appear to be as old as the clubhouse. They are wearing plus fours. To add to the romance of the scene, somewhere out in the English Channel a foghorn is sounding. This noise remains romantic for all of two minutes, as the fog rolls in, and the players up ahead disappear from view. We play the 1st hole, missing the green in three shots, and missing it again in four, although both our balls are on it at some stage. The slopes and pace are awkward. I point out to Digby that as he is waiting for laser correction to his eyesight, the fog is not so much of a problem. He assures me that he is accustomed to seeing the flag on a par three of 180 yards, which is what we now face. In fact, we can see it intermittently. We both miss the green to the left. As we arrive there, we comment that this is the sort of course where caddies would be useful. They would tell you, for example, not to miss the 2nd hole on the left.

The 3rd hole plays alongside the plateau towards a row of cottages at the end of the course, and we turn back and play on top of the plateau quite unable to see where our balls finish. As we walk along, we see one ball in the fairway. It is Digby's; it is about fifteen yards from the edge to the right, and fourteen to the left. Would he have played the shot if he had been able to see it? He successfully hits the green and records the first par. Having missed the plateau, I take eight. This is, I remark, a match play course. Soon, we see four players, playing only two balls. 'Foursomes,' I explain to Digby, 'alternate shot, to you.'

The front nine continues back and forth, beside, on or over the plateau. At the short 7th, I am in a crater; the correct term is bunker, but today's modern usage inadequately describes a hole in the ground which is only a club's length or so in radius, but needs four steps down to the bottom. It is also below the green, and I have to hit the ball about 30 feet vertically to get it out. I hit it about 30 yards vertically. When eventually we find it, there are two players in plus fours on the tee, whom we wave through. One hits the green, the other the bushes 20 yards short, and concedes the hole. Match play. We explain that it will be easier for us as visitors to follow them. As we are visitors, they apologise for the fog.

At the 8th tee, we wait while a group playing foursomes attempts to complete a hole on the adjacent Jubilee Course (nine holes, shortly to become thirteen). As Digby has never played the format, I explain that the first rule is that the word "sorry" shall not pass the lips of partners. As if on cue, the player in front of us with 30 yards to go to his green hits the ball 15 yards, making a sort of "grrooff" noise in response. It is still his side's turn so his partner then – to use P G Wodehouse's immortal expression – foozles the ball into a bunker to his right, saying something like, 'Oh dearie me'.

The back nine at Rye uses less of the plateau, gives more shelter from the breeze, and significantly for us, being further inland is free of fog. Nevertheless, it is challenging, with six of the seven par fours being over 400 yards, the exception being the 11th, which is only 324, but curls round a lake, inviting you to cut off as much or as little as you fancy. The need for Digby's eye surgery becomes evident when initially he thinks that some of the balls on the practice range we pass are moving about. They are seagulls. I point out the view of sheep disappearing into the middle distance, but this is the only reminder that we are on Romney Marsh, except that the 12ᵗʰ tees are tidal – little islands next to the estuary surrounded by marshland which the presence of flotsam indicates is flooded at high tide. I hit a "magnificent" 3 wood onto the green at the 12ᵗʰ, but unfortunately my ball is in about the position of the number 2 on my watch face, while the flag is where the 8 is. I take three putts. My last three rounds have been played on recently hollow-tined, top-dressed greens which have not been cut for a couple of weeks, and I cannot cope with the pace here. Neither can Digby, but he cannot believe how much slower they are than they appear. He has a state-of-the-art $300 aluminium putter which he is only using because he won it. It looks like it was designed by a retired cattle-rancher who needed something to do with his branding irons. Neither of us deals well with the contours.

Hole Number 13 plays over another ridge, through a long saddle-shaped gap. There are unusually two marker posts with which to align the second shot. I assume that if you line them up so the further one is obscured, then you will hit the green. If you are off line, you use the parallax effect to choose your line. If, like me, you have hit a poor first shot and a foolish second, you are in the rough at the foot of the saddle, hopelessly trying to get over with a sand wedge. Digby hits a screamer, though, but can still only manage a five on this tough hole. Another two points, and he is still on course for the plus fours.

After another change of direction, we arrive at the 17ᵗʰ, and Digby needs to finish 4, 4. Into the wind, this should be no problem, as the holes measure a mere 222 yards (par three, index 18) and just 439 yards (index 8). Alternatively, 3,5 will do. He makes 6, 6. My second shot fails to slice round the dogleg on the 18ᵗʰ and hits a building, obviously a painted portacabin, with a resounding clang. It is the back of The Secretary's office.

We pop into the pro shop before it closes, but they don't have Digby's size. Can we go back some time? It may depend on whether The Secretary knew it was me who hit their office...

I like to entertain Digby with tales of life in the Old Country, and he seems quite happy for me to do so – either that, or he uses the time I am speaking to recover from jet lag. We have established that the Pilgrim Fathers were not terribly well educated, so that, on seeing a red-breasted bird in their new country, they called it a robin, even though it is the size of a starling. I also reprimand him for talking of a creek in front of the green. Talking of creeks, have you ever wondered about Rae's Creek at the Augusta National? Properly speaking, a creek is "a narrow inlet, especially of the sea" and this was what it meant in 1620 when the Pilgrim Fathers set sail. Because they came from Devon, they knew a creek when they saw one, because there were plenty around, particularly south of Dartmoor. But, as noted, they were not terribly well educated, so they did know that narrow *inland* watercourses were called streams, or brooks, or bournes, or becks, or burns – but not creeks. They are now, in America.

On the other hand, I am humble enough to acknowledge that words such as "burglarise", "gotten" and "normalcy" are all more "correct" than the versions used this side of the Atlantic. American kids speak something called "Pig Latin", but they have no answer to Cockney rhyming slang. In an exchange of emails, I once informed Digby that we were to play at Minchinhampton, but not to worry, it was not as painful as it sounded. It was subsequently necessary to explain that, in rhyming slang, "Hampton" was short for "Hampton Wick". If he understood, he had forgotten by the time I met him again at Gatwick, with a trip planned to Littlehampton, a resort town between Bognor Regis and Eastbourne. It was, I explained, very popular with Londoners, and when the decision was made to open a nudist beach at Brighton, Littlehampton decided to follow suit. It rapidly became very unpopular with Cockneys.[58]

When Digby finally understood, he told me about a friend of his from Texas who had an extended series of assignments in Bismarck, North Dakota, which though a state capital, has a population of only 50,000 and a mentality to match. Digby's friend Dave used to frequent a bar, where the regulars became interested in the imminent birth of his son back in Texas, and held a sweepstake on how much the infant would weigh. When Dave returned after the birth, no-one had got near the actual figure of 25 lb, so they decided on a rollover, on how much he would weigh on Dave's next visit. No-one got near that either. '18 lb,' said Dave. 'I had him circumcised.'

---

[58] It would have been popular with the Carry On team. 'Where d'you meet your Dennis, Marge?' 'Oo, on the beach at Littlehampton. His charm stood out a mile.'

LITTLEHAMPTON

Littlehampton Golf Club is two miles by road from Littlehampton town, though only a 7 iron or so through the air, or a stroll across the swing bridge over the river Arun. The land here is quite fertile, being part of a plain below the Sussex Downs (it always amuses Digby that something can be "below downs"). The tree-lined lane down to the club passes by a couple of closing holes, which are attractive enough, but not typically seaside in appearance. From the clubhouse, the 1st hole plays a quarter of a mile beside the road down to the beach, which can be deserted in winter, but lively in summer. From the elevated 2nd tee, there is a good view of Littlehampton beach proper, and the river entrance. It looks fun on a nice day in August when I have seen it, and rather less so in November, when we played it.

If memory serves, there are no other views of the sea, as the course is separated from the beach by magnificent dunes. Perhaps because this is not linksland, the course looks a little manufactured, the lips on bunkers probably having been formed from the earth removed in their excavation, for example, and there is a fair amount of scrub around. The 2nd hole plays under the shadow of the dunes, and is followed by a short 3rd. Digby and I then followed two old-timers (D's term) to the next tee, which turned out to be the 6th hole, also a par three. The crafty blighters had missed out consecutive par fives, which take one back up towards the clubhouse, and back down to pretty much where we were. This cuts out 11% of the course by holes, but 17% by length, so perhaps it is no bad thing if one is "not as young as one used to be". Or maybe, if you're having a bad round and the arthritis is playing up, the temptation to walk in after the 4th is too much.

Digby and I played both these holes, parring 4 and birdying 5, so we liked them. After Number 6 came the curious incident of the clanger. The 7th green is in the far seaward corner of the course, looking into the afternoon sun. I lost sight of my second shot, but it appeared to be travelling left into the dunes, and much too far, but then we both heard a curious clanging noise. On arrival at the green, there was a fence to the left, and a footpath beyond, and on one of the fence posts an ancient, cast iron notice (probably once upon a time reading "keep out or else") but now devoid of paint. I then looked back, and saw my ball just short of the green on the landward side. It had not just hit the sign, it had somehow bounced backwards in the direction of the hole. This proved to be a good omen for me, as I forged ahead in the match. Digby got a few holes back when he caused my game to stutter by talking about work (at that time the company of which I was a director was making an embarrassingly bad fist of fulfilling the licence we had for the use of Digby's firm's products) and my memory of the course suffered accordingly. Once through that ritual, we played the rest of the course, mostly inland, in good spirits. Digby later apologised for having talked about work, saying he did not need to personally but rather felt I expected that we should, and I had to admit there was an element of truth in that. Shortly afterwards, I resigned, which ensured that the problem could not spoil our golf again.

Playing a seaside course, one wants either to see the sea, or to play on seaside terrain, and preferably both, but sadly Littlehampton offers neither. That is not to say that if I lived there I would not happily play there regularly, just that it did not stand out as a seaside course. But, talking of standing out, whoever would live at a place called Little-hampton? The village along the coast is called Climping. I am not sure exactly what that name evokes, but it doesn't sound much better.

I was surprised that Digby had not heard of the Texan who determined to become an Alaskan upon learning that it was now the biggest State. He made his way to the capital, Juneau, and walked into a bar, asking aloud how he got to be an Alaskan. 'Easy,' said the barman. 'Just drink a quart of Alaskan moonshine, shoot a polar bear, and make love to an Alaskan woman.' 'Is that all?' 'Yup. But you gotta do 'em all tonight, and you gotta down the moonshine in one.' 'OK,' said Tex, and proceeded to put away the booze and, tottering a little, went out of the saloon doors. Three hours later, the doors crashed open, and it was Tex. His clothes were torn to shreds, he was bleeding in several places, and some of his hair was missing. He looked a serious mess. 'OK, wheresh thish Alashkan woman I gotta shoot?'

Digby is fond of bad weather, but I doubt that he, or even the toughest Alaskan, would have fully appreciated my trip to Littlestone. One of the cleverest advertising slogans has to be for an anti-dandruff shampoo – you never get a second chance to make a first impression. On many occasions in this book, I will be able only to account for my first impression of a golf course. It would be nice to get to know them all, because I am reminded that Bobby Jones disliked St Andrew's on his first encounter, but ended believing it to be his preferred place on earth.

However, there are plenty of other places besides the coast of England to play golf: New Mexico, for example, where Digby has returned the compliment, and where the weather is better, and the desert courses are strangely reminiscent of classic English links, despite it being at least 600 miles to the nearest ocean.

LITTLESTONE

Thus excusing myself, I can only tell you what happened on the day I visited Littlestone Golf Club – January 31st, 2004.

I was late, and I was meeting friends who lived nearer. I would probably have been late anyway, but what delayed me as I drove along the south coast was the spray. I could only go at about 40 miles an hour, and the wind blowing off the sea buffeted the car to the extent that I actually thought about turning back. Eventually, I arrived, and then we only played because we had booked into a hotel that night in Sandwich, with a plan to play Prince's the next day.

Most of the front nine holes were downwind, but consequently leading away from the clubhouse. It did not actually start raining until the 2nd fairway, after which I don't believe it stopped. There was little chance of controlling the ball. In fact, I struggled to control my trolley. The plastic cover I used acted like a spinnaker, until it blew off, and was only saved by a rugby tackle from Mrs P, my partner's wife, who was playing with her friend P, behind Mr P and me. (Littlestone is a "twoball course", as The Secretary put it on the phone.)

The trolley itself was lightweight plastic with a third, front wheel, which generally made it much easier to handle as there was no need to fight gravity. The wind was a different matter. If it had been a dinghy, I think it would have been jibbing, as it kept literally overtaking me. The bag also kept blowing off the supporting brackets, so we strapped it on tight, whereupon the wind snapped the brackets off where they joined the shaft. Thereafter, I effectively wrestled it to the far end of the course, but once we turned into the wind, there was nothing for it but to abandon it. It was only then that I realised I had left the carrying strap on my bag behind. I "waltzed" with the bag for a couple of holes, and was then rescued by Mrs P's friend P. She lent me her heavyweight power trolley, as the girls had decided to walk in. On the way, they met an amateur meteorologist (how's that for an anorak pursuit?) who said he was recording wind gusts of 60 mph. One such managed to blow P's heavy duty trolley into a bunker!

I think Littlestone was probably a decent links course but, as we know, when it comes to links courses, much depends on the wind. The 18th hole is a par five, dead into the wind. Mr P and I both played driver, 3 wood, 5 wood, 4 iron, each of us hitting each shot well – and we were still short of the green!

Later, driving along the sea front at Dover en route to Sandwich, a wave broke on the sea wall, splashed up, and completely obliterated my vision. Somehow, it summed up the day.

Digby's response to the saga of the disintegrating trolley was to arrive for his next visit with a Sun Mountain Speed Cart™, the state of the art in personal ambulant golfing equipment logistics' solutions. Ready to use in two easy actions, it has three wheels with wire spokes and pneumatic tyres. The single front wheel folds out from the tubular steel frame, and has a calliper brake, which it needs. The upper section also folds out, adjustable to a height and angle to suit the owner, and in addition to the brake lever, offers places to keep balls, tee pegs, score-card and pencils, as well as a repository for a drinks' can, and possibly a lunch box.[59] On the frame there are clips holding a pump, an umbrella, and a device which screws into the handle to hold the umbrella when it is up, protecting both clubs and player. Adjustable supports cradle a golf bag, which is secured with fast action easy clip strong elastic belts. It does not need go faster stripes, it goes quite fast enough, even when pushed with a single little finger. Yes, it is pushed, that is the twist, or rather the lack of twist. *Pulling* a trolley is hard work; it is behind you, which basically means that you are twisting all the time, and if it has only two wheels, you are also fighting gravity.

Not with a Sun Mountain Speed Cart™ you aren't. It is derived from the "jogger's buggy" for the parent who has everything – you load the baby into the buggy, put on your trainers, and go out for a run. It sounds like a brilliant piece of marketing. How long would the average child tolerate being pushed round at speed, I wonder, the way they grow up so fast these days? In case you're wondering, the jogger holds onto a dead man's handle type of device. Let go, and it stops.

---

[59] Actually, a compartment for unspecified use. I am sure that the instructions, sadly mislaid, would have stated its purpose. They explained how to steer it!

Not so the Sun Mountain Speed Cart™. At Royal Cinque Ports, I soon found out why it had a brake.

ROYAL CINQUE PORTS

With a name like Royal Cinque Ports Golf Club, you would expect to find some old world charm, and we were not disappointed. The ancient clubhouse must surely have been there longer than the 112 years since the club was founded. It is equipped with high ceilings and wood panels, and the whole fabric of the building seems to be gently perfumed with the aroma of roast beef. Everyone was very friendly, as they usually are at seaside golf clubs. I think this must be because while the rest of the world dashes up and down motorways leaving mobile phone messages for people they urgently need to speak to about something they will have forgotten tomorrow, life at seaside golf courses just lets this sort of thing pass it by. Indeed, the fact that generally it does not pass anywhere near such places adds to their charm. There is a lane between the clubhouse and the course at Royal Cinque Ports, but it leads nowhere now (it did in prehistoric times, perhaps). They are so relaxed in the clubhouse that, when I phoned to inquire if I had left a sweater behind, they offered to post it back to me free of charge, and in due course, I received an application for schoolboy membership (very generous terms, but I was a little too old). I got the sweater at the second attempt.

The course is a great place to try out a Sun Mountain Speed Cart™ which could have been designed with this kind of terrain in mind. It wasn't, of course, because they don't have courses like this in the USA. Think of linksland and you think of mounds and hummocks and tussocks liberally interspersed with bunkers with greens appearing as and when required to make eighteen holes. This is exactly what you find here. They didn't bother to look for flat places for the greens; several are basin-like in form, both upright, to gather the ball, and upturned, to spurn it. A couple that come to mind are the long 3rd, where the green is almost hidden in a hollow even for a third shot with a wedge, which is immediately followed by a short hole to a plateau green which might have been the inspiration for crown green bowls. Apart from the 1st and 18th, which are less tucked away in the sandhills, and boast a meandering water hazard instead, this is the only hole without bunkers.

Otherwise, they are all over the place, meaning that there are lots, and they also appear in unlikely places, as if they are relics of the natural phenomenon from which they are descended, rather than placed in a particular spot to catch a certain sort of shot. They also, like in some kind of fairy tale, seem to be filled not with sand, but icing sugar. There is no need to plant the feet firmly, they sink for themselves. The accolade for having the most bunkers goes to hole Number 8, which has nine. It is a 165 yard par three! The only short hole on the back nine, Number 14, has another fantastic green which gives the impression that the ball simply *must* release down to the hole if only you can hit it. Unfortunately, it measures 222 yards.

By the time Digby and I reached this stage of the course I had more or less mastered the art of using a Sun Mountain Speed Cart™. I had learned that a gentle gust of wind could be enough to send it trundling down any slope that happened to be available. This is why it comes with a calliper brake. Fortunately, slopes in any given direction don't last for long here. Thank goodness I was not at nearby Walmer & Kingsdown, where I could have lost it for ever. The real beauty, particularly on an undulating course like this, is that one pushes it, and it is very easy to push. I wonder where the "standard concept" of pulling a trolley comes from? Suddenly, it does not seem to make any sense. I could however make sense of the member at Royal St George's who told us he probably preferred Royal Cinque Ports. The latter is too small for the Open now (it was held there in 1909 and 1920), and therefore just my sort of size.

As mentioned, Digby and I have some fun with the language. He likes to learn that you go up onto the downs, and ascend fells, and I insist that a creek must be an inlet of the sea. Not that we always play by the sea, as circumstances do not permit. On one occasion we went to my favourite day out near London, at the Berkshire. Digby of course pronounced it like "Turk's fire". I explained that it was "bark sheer". I attempted to add that it was one of the Shires (pronounced like fire), but it got too much for us. I must say, why is Berkshire one of the Shires, if it is (read that aloud). I think Dorset counts as a Shire, though it is not.

Not all Digby's compatriots are aware that there are languages besides their own. I have heard Americans pronounce "cinque" as "sink" in Italy, in the area known as Cinque Terre (chinkway terray). I have even heard Americans pronounce La Spezia (la spets-ee-a) as "loss-peas-ee-a". They looked like they had been to college too! Digby has travelled Europe in his conscript days, and knows that cinque means five in both Italian and French. He asked me why it was pronounced "sink" and not "sank" in Cinque Ports. I knew the answer (of course). It is French, but it is mediaeval French, the official language of the English Court at the time. It means five, but it is pronounced "sink". The Cinque Ports were special places in Kent and Sussex which by Royal Charter were granted exemption from certain forms of taxation, and other privileges. There are fourteen of them.[60]

Digby comes from one of the 21 contiguous American states which have access to the sea, but as he is from Dallas, it is still some 300 miles away. At our first meeting, I gave a business presentation designed amongst other things to impress upon our Texan visitors the small scale of the country. If I had my facts right (and no-one queried them at the time) you can fit England (not Britain or the UK, remember) into Texas 4½ times, and, if you did, you would have the population of the US contained within the Lone Star State. As Texas is exactly as "averagely populated" as the US, this means that there is 4½ times as much land per American as there is per Englishman or, therefore, four Americans have eighteen times as much land as one Englishman. So, if the estate surrounding the Englishman's castle is big enough for one golf hole, his equivalent four Americans could have a complete golf course.

So, when I asked Digby what he liked about playing in the Mother Country, I was surprised when he mentioned the twoball format (I have told him it is called singles, to no avail). It seems that at his fairly typical, 50 year old club, you have to play in fourballs, and use buggies (carts, Digby). Indeed, apparently they sometimes let fiveballs and sixballs out at weekends, just to give everyone a game. This is because Digby's "club" is a commercial enterprise, and typically so. Membership is by subscription, so there are no green fees, but the level of membership is set that such is the demand from members to play. So, a visit to the Berkshire, where one of the courses is always twoball[61] only, or Rye, where people are playing foursomes, is remarkable. And if the land at the Berkshire were allowed an alternative use and its owners sought a proper return on capital from it (which thank the Lord is not the case), they would probably have to play in tenballs.

---

[60] Alright. There were five originally, but others insisted on being included. One, Tenterden, is actually inland.

As well as the variety to be found in England (and to be fair, I have chosen some quite special courses for us to visit) Digby also mentioned walking the course as something he really liked, which may strike us Limeys as odd. Perhaps the situation will arise in the US where you may walk the course if you wish, but you will have to pay a premium for the privilege. Possibly it already has, with only expensive, exclusive clubs allowing walking.

Incidentally, if you want to play abroad just as a pair and want to avoid being matched up into a four, try this: book a tee time for three, and when you arrive, claim that your third member has sunstroke, or better still, something infectious like dysentery. Unless there was a lone player matched with you, you will be able to play as a two, and word of the infectious illness should discourage anyone else from joining you. Good luck. I haven't tried it myself. Let me know how it works.

I mentioned that the day after our visit to Littlestone, Mr and Mrs P and I had booked a tee time at Prince's, at Sandwich.

PRINCE'S

Prince's is the third literally littoral stretch of linksland on the Kent coast between Dover and Ramsgate, and at one point only an out of bounds fence separates it from Royal St George's. Like that club and Royal Cinque Ports, Prince's has hosted the Open Championship, in 1932. Unlike its neighbours, it is not a members' club, but in proprietary ownership, by a company which also owns the Bell Hotel in Sandwich. Sufficient time has now elapsed for me to mention that Celia and I came downstairs one morning in that establishment to find that there were no spare tables available for breakfast. When we drew this to the management's attention, someone pleaded that they had not known how many people to expect for the meal. Breakfast, in a hotel? Since those days, nothing has ceased to amaze me about British catering, nothing negative, that is.[62]

---

[61] Pedantic note: not singles only. Foursomes would be OK.

As noted, the occasion of my visit to Prince's was the day after the car wash experience at Littlestone. Mr and Mrs P and I had booked a hotel/golf package so we were determined to play. The weather had abated somewhat; there was probably a strong wind blowing, because the longer par fours into it were out of reach. It was February 1st, and we had arranged tee off times which enabled us to start with breakfast (at the club), play the Himalayas, followed by the Shore, and then lunch, leaving enough daylight to add, if we felt so inclined, the Dunes. These are the names given to the three loops of nine holes, each of which starts and finishes near the "new" clubhouse. One passes the derelict "old" clubhouse on the way in. What with practice facilities, car parks and the like, the area around the clubhouse is confusing, and it took us a while to find the right tee. Actually, I would not have been entirely surprised if we had each played off a different tee. We were still suffering from the after effects of yesterday's wind and rain. Mr P remarked that he felt more like he had been playing rugby the previous day, and his normally elegant swing suffered accordingly. I definitely ached in places not normally associated with the swinging of a golf club, but it took more than that to disturb my normally inelegant swing (or to make it look any worse, anyway).

The three loops appear to have equal status, which in effect means that Prince's offers three eighteen-hole courses, each "semi-detached", and prints cards accordingly. The cards show white and yellow yardages, but my memory is that there was only one set of tee markers, and we could not tell which it was.[63] But, if like Mr P and me – when acting in the image of my late father – you want maximum value for a day's golf, you can add the missing loop as a visitor for an extra tenner. Mrs P declined. I would in fact have been happy to decline so inevitably, I ended up playing my best golf on the Dunes' loop. I think I liked the Shore best being, as its name implies, closest to the shoreline. Hole Number 6 on the Himalayas' loop is also a very nice par five along the shoreline, but it is also into the south-west wind. We started on this nine, which begins with two awkward doglegs. I found a hidden water hazard with my opening drive, and massively overclubbed to the

---

[62] On another occasion, we walked out of a pub in Sandwich because the landlady was unacceptably rude. It had a full entry in *The Good Pub Guide* at the time!

[63] Wentworth does this. If they put out whites and yellows, people try to play off the whites. Once, in a friendly match there for The Bucks, we were all set to play off the set (yellow) tees when the captains agreed to play off the actual tombstone yardage markers. Not even Ernie Els plays from there.

2nd green. We should perhaps have invested in a course planner. Overall, there was little to choose between the three loops. Checking the cards, Himalayas is a couple of hundred yards shorter than the others, and par thirty-five. Shore and Dunes combined make a nice 6690 yard par seventy-two.

As well as the derelict clubhouse near where Prince's meets Royal St George's, there are some other abandoned houses which have an air of mystery about them. Apparently the golfing nature of the terrain was rudely disturbed during the Second World War, when it was prepared to withstand a German invasion, and has had to be reinstated mechanically, so there is not always the seemingly natural appeal of its near neighbours, but if you want somewhere to be welcomed as a visitor for weekend links golf of a championship standard and within 100 miles of London, this is undoubtedly the place to come.

13

STORMY WEATHER

Death is different when it happens to you. Perhaps this was what Stalin meant when he said, 'One death is a tragedy; one million deaths is a statistic.' Mind you, he had a fairly relaxed attitude to large-scale deaths; spilling blood in "glorious revolution" is one thing, but eradicating the Kulak class because their success exposed the flaws in the Soviet method of collective farming is another.[64] Over 20 million Soviet soldiers died in the Second World War (which the USSR regarded as having started only in 1941. Nyet. That was just when you joined in, comrades.), a staggering figure, statistic, indeed, which always seemed to mean little...

Until Boxing Day 2004, when the Asian tsunami killed 300,000 people in the course of a few hours. With television, we were able to see the devastation wrought by this phenomenon, but even so, 300,000 people are an awful lot to imagine. What made the whole thing more "real" is that everybody seemed to know someone who knew someone who was on holiday in that part of Asia. The nation responded in its modern, feeling way, by holding collections and fund-raising events, to help it feel better. No amount of fund-raising would make the bereaved feel better.

So, what do you make of these statistics: 400,000 British, 200,000 French, 500,000 Germans? These were the casualties of the battle of the Somme in 1916. Not all of them died, but about a third did, more than were killed by the tsunami, and get this: it was not a natural phenomenon, "mankind" did it. You can pretty much bet that, back in

---

[64] If you have ever been to Russia, you might share my view that he must also have killed off all the plumbers after they had done their initial work.

Blighty, everyone knew someone who knew someone who died at the Somme. Many years later, one single death occurred shortly before the 2005 general election, of a British army officer in Iraq. His widow publicly accused the Prime Minister of being personally responsible; it became part of the election agenda. Now, I too have lost my spouse in death, so maybe I ought to be willing to extend the benefit of the doubt to this lady, but I am sorry. It may be that the Prime Minister was responsible for the war, and thence the presence of the woman's husband in Iraq, but he was not responsible for the man having the *occupation of army officer* in the first place, something of a prerequisite to his misfortune in being in the wrong place at the wrong time. Packets of cigarettes carry messages saying "smoking causes death"; what, I wonder, does it say on an application form for Sandhurst? To put this in perspective, *the men who died at the Somme were conscripts.* Death is different when it happens to you.

I need to mention this for two reasons: firstly, if there is a little violence between supporters of German and English football teams during the World Cup in 2006, let those people who use it to roundly condemn sport as a pointless and undesirable aspect of modern life dwell for a moment on the role sport has taken over from war in today's society. I do not condone it, but would you rather have a few punch-ups in a stadium, or hundreds of thousands of young men murder each other in a poppy field? Sport has an enormous importance for world peace, and it is not stretching the imagination too far to claim that America's problems in relating to the rest of the world stem from its not playing the same sports...

...except golf, of course. The second reason is that I cannot possibly write this book without reference to the death of my beloved wife which, amongst many more important things, was central in my resolution to undertake this littoral peregrination. But, I don't mind if you miss the following bits out, and just read about the courses. Death is different when it happens to you.

One death which seemed to reach out to the nation was that of Princess Diana. Probably everyone remembers where they were. Celia and I were in Thurlestone in Devon. It was August, so the weather was pretty awful...

THURLESTONE

We once spent a week on holiday in South Devon, not entirely devoted to golf, in which I played three times at Thurlestone Golf Club. I got drenched seven times in all. I could see the storms sailing in from the English Channel, and had plenty of time to prepare, and after the drenching, the wind would dry me out again very quickly. Celia spent the time on the beach reading a novel, sheltered from the wind behind a large umbrella, and apparently dry. The beach is magnificent, and there is nothing between it and the course which sweeps alongside Bigbury Bay for about 2 miles. The golf course grows on you, both figuratively and literally.

The first six holes call for precision, with three par threes, and the longest hole measures 360 yards off the yellows. On one of these rounds, I played a 9 iron second downwind to 3 inches, with a green-keeper watching. On a corresponding hole back into the wind, I hit a full pitching wedge apparently over the edge of the low cliff, and watched it sail all of 25 yards onto the green. Were these shots flukes, I wonder, given that I "played for them"?

The second group of six holes proceeds up the rising cliff with an in-land loop, mainly heading south-west and therefore into the prevailing wind, and there is a noticeable change of pace – the shortest hole is 346 yards. Hole Number 12 is the first of the four par five holes, at the highest point of the cliff, playing inland. We stay on this rough plateau for a while, before coming back downhill and downwind to the club-house. The final six holes include only one par four – 421 yards – and two par threes. Overall, Thurlestone is par seventy-one, but the halves are 33 and 38. If ever a golf course can resemble the Tour de France, this does, in the sense at least that you have to survive the climbs...

During my best round of the three I reached the summit at the far end only six over for fourteen holes, notwithstanding double bogeys on 9 and 14. I turned triumphantly to play the downhill, downwind par five 15th – and was hit by the last and worst of the four fierce showers to drench me that day. There were too few holes left to dry out after that, I could hardly hold the club. I took a 9, and finished like a drowned rat. I must return.

I have since visited Thurlestone again with a "girlfriend", a term which signifies the spirit if not the letter of the description of my young-at-heart but nevertheless fifty year old companion. It was only for a weekend, and the course was chock-a-block with fourballs, so I did not get an opportunity for vengeance. I suffered no awkwardness or qualms about having been there with my late wife – but nor can I, or anyone else, pretend that I was not married for twenty-four years. This may seem thoroughly obvious, but you don't go round planning for death, and the subject was not on the agenda back then. My father, and both of Celia's parents had died, all within a year of each other, but one expects one's parents to die. There will still be shocks involved, but at least within a marriage, you have each other. When one of you dies within a marriage, the person you probably need most is not there to help. In most cases, it is the man who dies first. Women have a longer life expectancy, and tend to marry slightly older men.

MARYPORT

I never like to say unkind things about a golf course, and I need to be guarded in my comments about Maryport Golf Club. I will say that I caught it on a bad day, for the weather was certainly foul, and at its foulest when I played "the most challenging" part of the course. It starts and ends with the original nine holes on flat linksland, but has been converted into an eighteen hole venue by directing it inland across poorly draining pasture land not, in my opinion, terribly suited to golf anyway. For me, the contrast did not work. I am sure this opinion has little to do with scores of 37 out, 47 back. They did well even to fit the original nine holes into the land. I liked the way the first four holes were laid out in echelon. I parred them all, and was perhaps a little bit unhappy to go 4, 6 on the following short and long holes. It is obviously a good driving course, as I hit seven of the first eight fairways. The fact that I hit no more during the round, even when I got back onto the original linksland, is unlikely to have clouded my judgment. You can definitely see the join. One half drains well, the other does not. True, there are not exactly many alternative eighteen-hole venues nearby, but I would have kept it as a nine-holer (when I would not, under my rules, have had to play it at all).

But, I am sure that the members love it, and that on a fine summer's day the views from the cross country section are incomparable. What was it the Italian footballer Christian Vieri said when asked about his favourite goal in the 1998 World Cup? 'Goals are like children, they are all beautiful.' I am not sure that sentiment would translate easily into the rich dialect of the Cumbrian coast – they play rugby league up there – but something very similar has to be true for golf as for goals.

Actually, just as one innocent child with unfortunate timing can cop a load of grief from a parent whose nerves have been strained to breaking point by a sibling, what really got me about Maryport was Grange-over-Sands. I normally respond well to the smell of roast lamb, but when I arrived for a second visit to Cumbria in the March after Celia died, I was greeted with the stench of burning carcasses, a response to an outbreak of foot and mouth disease.

I had something of a geographical problem about whether Grange-over-Sands is actually by the sea. It is on an estuary, upstream from the peninsula of Furness which protects it from the Irish Sea proper. I decided to play it anyway, en route to the northern end of The Lakes. There were notices stating that if anyone crossed a boundary of the course into a neighbouring field, the club – and possibly the person – could be fined £5,000, and the right for *anyone* to play golf suspended until further notice. I could see why this might be a useful measure to help prevent the spread of the disease, and certainly a powerful threat, but driving the car over a disinfectant pad, and standing in a bowl of the same stuff – in steady drizzle – seemed about as effective as trying to put out a house fire with a tooth glass.

As well as the time of foot and mouth, this was the wettest winter on record, and Grange-over-Sands golf course was suffering so much that I nicknamed it Grange-under-Slime. It was low tide, and the sands of the estuary which with the best will in the world look decidedly muddy, receded into the middle distance and merged with the grey sky. The course is rather flat, and though its entry in *The R & A Handbook* claims the services of the great and good Dr Mackenzie as architect, this clearly was not one of his best. At times, it felt like I was playing in a drain. I was certainly playing like one. What is more, there was a road running alongside, not the road I had approached along, the presence of which almost certainly indicated that the course did not qualify anyway. After a nice little par three to an elevated green in a corner of the course, the round reached its nadir[65] on a sweeping dogleg return towards the clubhouse, where I played towards the wrong green. I know, because someone came and told me.

I could not work out why there were two greens, whether one was for winter use, or the course layout had been changed, because they were both decent and in good condition, but I was sure of one thing; the round was rubbish, the course did not qualify, the drizzle had changed up into third gear, and there was a group of men standing under the shelter of an open shed door, watching me. A couple of hundred yards beyond them lay the shelter and warmth of the clubhouse, and I knew what to do. I putted out, turned on my heel, and made my way to the 10th tee. Having clearly established myself as a lunatic, I might as well get fully certified in their opinion. The rest of the round was very miserable until inevitably, just like the bad date, I got a goodnight kiss with a par on 18. Indeed, I got rather more, a birdie on 17, but perhaps I'd better not pursue the analogy. Read about another golf course instead.

TORQUAY

I played at Torquay Golf Club with The Lodger who, encouraged by the previous year's good English summer, invited us to join for a few days his family entourage which was encamped in a Torbay Hotel for the duration. Unfortunately, the duration concerned was that of a thick bank of cloud which settled over the English Channel and did not budge. It was odd to sit in wet gloom, listening to test match commentary from Trent Bridge. Nottingham was about as far north as the cloud drifted, but Newton Abbott a few miles north of Torquay remained the southern limit. One day, floods caused the A30 to be closed at Exeter. It was terribly sad to see all the bed-and-breakfasters with nowhere to go in the rain. Another nail in the coffin of English seaside tourism.

Torquay Golf Club is on the cliff top in Babbacombe, or rather, we supposed it to be. We had been told we needed to get off early, so we did, notwithstanding mist which restricted visibility to just about the length of a good drive. The opening holes play through tree-lined fairways, with the trees more reminiscent of a landscaped garden than the traditional heathland of say the Surrey/Berkshire border. It felt claustrophobic, but perhaps that was the mist.

---

[65] I always distinguish between zenith - the highest point – and nadir – the lowest – by noting that nadir is an anagram of drain.

Around the 6th hole, there is a change of elevation of about 50 feet, and it became apparent that we were not so much in mist as cloud. Indeed, after playing another uphill hole, we could not work out the direction in which to hit the ball. As to whether we were now on the cliff top, we could only have found that out by stepping off the edge. The lack of visibility did not stop us (though it slowed us down somewhat), but being in cloud means that the moisture is not so much falling as circulating, and it soon gets into everything: clothes, shoes, hair, and golf bags and, apart from not knowing where to hit the ball, it became equally challenging to know how to hold on to soaking wet clubs.

Now, the Lodger and I are proud of the fact that on at least two occasions we have been the only two people to play a particular course despite adverse weather conditions. (One was in Sheringham in December, which was not surprising; the other was La Manga in October, which was.) Nevertheless, this Devonian cloud cover was a definite reason to abandon the round. The trouble was, *we could not.* We had a course planner, but it showed only individual holes; there was no map, and we had long since lost any sense of where the clubhouse lay. We had no choice but to keep playing until we heard traffic on the road bounding the course to the north, and we were able to walk in.

I have since revisited Torquay GC; I wanted to find out whether we had in fact risked stepping off the cliff while playing the "elevated section" but there is a big patch of wasteland between the course and the cliff edge. In daylight, the course is rather "pretty", but I still found it claustrophobic; you have to be terribly straight on an awful lot of holes, which is not my idea of a seaside golf course.

I could not find out anything about how people's feelings of sexuality respond to bereavement, but there were certainly some peculiar sensations passing through my head during my stays in Cumbria, though rather less so when I was back at home. Perhaps there is the phenomenon of life trying to assert itself in the face of death. If you cut a branch from a tree which is in bud, it will flower rather than die. Given that I live in a village and travel to play coastal golf courses, I have not met a large number of unattached ladies since I have been widowed, but I have occasionally subscribed to introduction services. Someone I met recently told me that she had spoken to a man looking for a new partner after only two months of widowhood. She declined the offer, because she thought it would feel more like an extramarital affair than a new romance for the man concerned. Later, he confirmed that this was indeed the case, but I can understand why he might have wanted to proceed, nevertheless.

On another occasion, I made contact with a divorcee of my age group who was looking for a new partner with whom, amongst other things, to play golf. Normally you are advised in these blind-dating situations to make the first meeting brief in case it is a disaster, but we met for dinner. As she said, "we can always talk about golf". Well, we did, and we arranged to play the following week. On the morning we were due to play, she phoned to call it off. She had a headache, runny nose, and so on. The fastest romance in history, from first acquaintance to head-ache, without so much as a kiss. What I think happened is this: she had taken up golf in response to her husband leaving her, a deliberate act of defiance because she had wanted to earlier but he prevented her doing so. Playing golf was her choice, and her own, confidence-giving pas-time, and she realised she did not want to risk her relationship with it through sharing it with me. Either that, or she was worried about play-ing with a 12 handicapper when she played to a 32.

I prefer the former explanation, because I concur with it. One day, I may meet someone with whom I am willing to share a home, and a bank account, and other things that go with being married, but not my golf. That is mine!

MINEHEAD & WEST SOMERSET

To get to Minehead & West Somerset Golf Club, head for the sea front and turn right. Be undeterred by the presence of the institution on your right, and you will find the clubhouse on a narrow strip of land behind dunes, with the 1st tee outside the pro shop and the 18th green overlooked by the lounge. There will probably be a wind, in which case you can have the unusual experience of driving through the 1st green with a 5 wood. It is a par four, though only 235 yards off the yellows. Actually, the achievement may need a serious wind in winter as it can be a little damp underfoot (drainage has been improved recently), but there is plenty of run along the turf in summer. You can take a driver on the 353 yard 2nd and maybe get close, but again you have to be fairly straight. Then the fun stops temporarily as you turn back and play into the wind, an early reminder of what is to come. After a good par three across a ditch, there is a nice dogleg par five, and a second reminder with the 300 yard 6th hole back into the wind. The 7th is a straight par five, and if you score a four and two fives on these three holes, you are as likely to have some combination of birdie, par, and bogey as three pars.

The 7th tee is by the farthest corner of the institution. They are not called holiday camps any more, the signs just read "____ins". The trees have grown up more than I remember them, but the 20 foot fence is still there. The moat is concealed by lots of foliage, but still doing its job – keeping intruders out, not holidaymakers in, of course. Personally, I never believed the stories of alligators. For the enthusiastic holiday-maker, everything is provided and everyone included. "Once you're in "____ins", you're never let out".[66] The mind still boggles a little.

The 8th hole plays across the corner of a field, and I thought the 9th did too, but it turns out to be a ditch with reeds which runs first across, then alongside, and finally back across the fairway, making this stroke index 1. On this landward side of the course, we appear to be signifi-cantly lower than the line of dunes which hide the sea. At the far end there is a nice short 10th hole, still downwind, to start the back nine, and we finally see the sea. You can also see across to Wales, and the shoreline is attractive when the tide is in, apart from what I believe is the now decommissioned Hinckley Point nuclear power station in the far distance. Inland, there are views of the Quantock Hills and/or the rump of Exmoor, the town set against a giant mound, and the upturned sow effect of the pleasure dome within the institution. Still intact are two gun emplacements built from the large flat pebbles of the beach. Did the authorities really believe the German navy would sail up the Bristol Channel, or were they built to make people feel something was hap-pening?

Of more recent construction is an attractive row of fine beach huts – grade II listed perhaps, or maybe they are cabins – the nearest bears the name "Edge O' Beyond". And that's where you are for your golf. Woe betide any tendency to slice, as the tees mainly line up on the edge of the beach, inviting – or perhaps that should be demanding – you to drive onto tight fairways. There is a gentle convex shape to the shoreline here, so the wind will be more or less blowing your ball onto the beach depending on which hole you are on. In truth, one hole – Number 15, 299 yards – turns back to be wind-assisted, but it has a very tight approach particularly if the flag is at the front of the green. You are probably too windblown to take advantage. I hit my next drive onto the beach, and it was retrieved for me by a dog who was helping his owner to stock up on used Titleists. The closing hole is a par three, 215 yards off the whites. You'll need a lot more club than you took on the 1st. In fact, you may not have a club for this hole – always assuming you have any balls left. According to the card, it's a par seventy-one course – 37 out, which is a little generous, and 34 back, which could be a misprint for 43. Perhaps next time I'll settle for a week at "____ins" – or would that be a fate worse than death?

---

[66] I think that should be "left" – Ed.

14

LANCASHIRE HOTCHPOTCH

I am self-taught at golf and, seeing me play, anyone who knows anything about the mechanics of the golf swing will recognise this immediately. My American cousin Digby says that I am the best "bad" golfer he knows. He didn't put it like that exactly, but I was too pleased with the compliment to worry about the insult. I wonder though if this is because he has not seen many self-taught players. Do Americans learn golf at high school, like they do typing and driving?

When I first attempted to play, golf was considered an expensive game, and one certainly didn't spend serious money on a course of lessons. I used to hitchhike to my nearest municipal course, hire a half set of clubs and buy a day ticket, all the time desperate to keep enough balls in a spherical shape to survive the day without the ultimate ignominy of having to walk in "OOB" (out of balls). I used a book by Sam Snead which I got from the local library, and "mastered" most of the techniques enough to be able to get round a course. I had a terrible slice, because Sam's advice on turning versus tilting was to liken the swing to the act of chopping down a tree. I didn't have experience of that. Where I grew up, boys who chopped trees down ended up in approved school.

I was pretty faithful to his advice otherwise, though. I remember the section on putting, and trying very hard to read not only the slope, but also the grain on the greens. Eventually I decided my muni course didn't have grain. It was about twenty years later that I learned that we don't have that kind of grass in the UK! It was around the same time that my rounds of golf began to be marginally coherent, as I played more than occasionally. Then, where I really made a "quantum leap" was on a series of trips to La Manga to contest the Cochinillo Cup with The Lodger, as detailed elsewhere.

I play quickly – that is, I tend to step up to the ball and hit it – and this is one reason why I much prefer to play with one other person or indeed, alone, rather than in threes and particularly fours. With more than two people, there usually seems to be somebody who didn't realise I was going to hit the ball so soon, with so little fuss, plus I have to wait that much longer, and I do tend to rush after waiting. I am trying to learn to wait until everyone is ready for me to play – but changing the habit of a lifetime is not easy.

The reason I play so quickly is simple and, to me, makes near perfect sense. I do not know how I succeed in hitting the ball, and the more I contemplate the challenge, the more unlikely the prospect seems, so best get on with it! The words I choose are important – "know how I succeed". Something within me obviously "knows" what it is doing, but it does not allow my conscious mind to be privileged with the information as to what happens, and never the twain shall meet. Admittedly, this state of affairs does not provide great scope for improvement, but on the other hand, if it ain't broke, don't fix it, as they say.

So, I never had a lesson. I would occasionally read golf magazines or books, but actually I developed an aversion to advice such as "where most amateurs make mistakes is by going for the green with a 3 wood when they could lay up and leave any easy wedge to the middle of the green and two putts for a net par". So speaks the three-time major champion; well, I have news for you: for the majority of us real golfers, there is no such thing as a simple wedge to the green. My 3 wood is more reliable than my wedge, in the sense that I am more likely to hit the shot I want with it. Actually, that is probably not true, but the point is, it feels as if it is. I play with people who would much rather be off the edge of a green than on it, so they can face a chip instead of a long putt, and some players do not even carry the kind of middle irons Mr Champion would have them use for laying up, on the grounds that they "cannot get on with them". But the real point is this: I don't want to score a routine net par, I want to hit the damned green on this blasted hole and birdie it, gross, if it's the last thing I do. That's what we play for, isn't it?

This philosophy may not make me the best of initial playing partners for newcomers to the game, but it has been my privilege to accompany a number of novitiates on their first round, including my father and The Lodger. I have learnt to distinguish between tilting and turning, and I exhort them to do likewise, though the words "watch me" never pass my lips. If there is a pattern to how first timers play, it is this; they do as requested for about three shots, and then revert to instinct, and as we know, the one thing you cannot hit a golf ball with is instinct. It must be murder being a teaching pro.

I was a formative influence on my nephew Harrison who took up the game in his early teens, as I gave him a 6 iron and some balls with which to practise. These days, aged 33 rather than 13, he has a swing which when slowed down to about half his instinctive pace looks good and performs reliably. It is great to learn when young. I have also maintained that young players learn to get the ball in the hole on the greens, but this does not appear to be the case with Harrison, as witnessed by our round at Fleetwood.

FLEETWOOD

Fleetwood Golf Club is located at Rossall Point, the north-western tip of the Fylde peninsula north of Blackpool, where it is most exposed to what the Irish Sea can throw at it. Harrison and I played it the day after our "adventure in a wind tunnel" at Knott End. Having seen what the wind could do with the waters of the River Wyre, we were probably grateful to see a giant sea wall the whole length of the seaward side of the course. The land here is generally flat; large areas of sand are exposed at low tide, but you cannot see this from the golf course, just the wall. You can certainly hear the sea, or you could on this day. Finally, to complete this weather report, it was mercifully free of rain – merciful, because it saved us from any jokes about Fleetwood Mac.

I asked Harrison what he could remember, but the answer was, 'Not much'. Some time later, Knott End had taken its toll. Given the foulness of the weather the previous day, we were surprised that we seemed to be about the only people playing the course in the middle of this Sunday. I had made a reservation for an eleven o'clock start – in the charming old-fashioned way of writing to The Secretary with my request, and receiving his written confirmation in due course. Apart from a group of boys loitering at the southern boundary I don't remember exchanging words with anyone except Harrison. The land is what I call "dusty", the sort of straw-brownish grass which covers the ground in a manner that, were it the head of a male, might cause a certain concern about the possibility of the dreaded b-word. There are mounds and bunkers and some modest slopes, but it is flat rather than bumpy linksland. It has its fair share of bunkers, but otherwise I seem to recall that the holes are unusually straight. I had not really thought about it before, but most links courses boast at least a couple of dogleg holes. Fleetwood saves that treat up for the closing hole.

The unusual feature here is the difference in length between the outward and return halves. It is not an out-and-back layout, so the wind is fairly evenly distributed across each half, but the front nine measures 3000 yards from the whites, par thirty-four, and the back nine 3557 yards, par thirty-eight. The differential is proportionately even greater from the yellows – 2890 yards out, and 3418 yards back. Given that the 9th hole measures 508 yards, one could express this as: first eight holes, 2382 yards, average 298; last ten holes, 3926, average 393 – almost one hundred yards longer.[67] Just to see how that works out per "unit of par", the first eight have a figure of 82 yards, and the second ten, 91. I am not sure if this means anything. Try instead taking off two shots per hole for putts, and the relative lengths are 183, and 171. It's all in the par.

Whatever this means, the lengthening of the holes on this occasion favoured the regular golfer. Harrison twice took a lead early on but four holes in a row from Number 10 (when my opponent took three putts when he could afford only one) saw me home comfortably. We were on our own as we approached the clubhouse, and speculated about whether everyone was too knackered to play after yesterday's weather, or on a strict roast-beef-and-yorkshire pudding[68] regime at home. In fact, they were all in the clubhouse. Those who had played must have gone off early, and would all have been at the northern end of the course when we set off initially southwards. They were all watching telly – the final of the LDV vans trophy from the Millennium Stadium, featuring Blackpool, the local team. There is usually a good reason for most things.

It is interesting playing with Harrison. Because he does not play often, he tends to need a generous handicap, but if he then plays to his

---

[67] The figures for the whites are 2454, average 307, and 4061, average 406.
[68] Surely not "Yorkshire" pudding in Lancashire? – Ed.

real capability, he beats me easily, so we sometimes adopt the flexible handicapping system whereby on top of what has been agreed, if one player gets two holes up, he gives the other a stroke, and if he nevertheless goes three up, he concedes two strokes. Somebody has to be having a real nightmare for the game to finish early.

HANDICAPS AND PLAYING FORMATS

It is interesting that we use a method designed to stop someone winning too easily. Is golf the only game where there are distinctly different forms of scoring? It is certainly hard to think of another game in which the scoring system has changed as radically as in golf. In rugby, the focus is now on the points awarded for a "try", which is so named because originally, it simply meant that the team touching down were entitled to try for a kicked goal. Even so, the teams still face up to each other; they don't line up facing the same way and race each other down the touchline...

Which is more or less what happens in stroke play golf. Originally, opponents played each other, at match play, where stroke count only mattered for the hole in play. The combination of increased numbers, and the fact that for the very best players, anyone can beat anyone else over eighteen holes,[69] ultimately led to the standard competition for the world's best golfers being 72 holes of stroke play. The fact that this format is necessary to separate players is clear, when a two shot victory is considered comfortable. Two shots in say 270 is a margin of considerably less than one per cent.

As a consequence, we club golfers are obliged to play eighteen-hole medals. The fact that this format is inappropriate is demonstrated by the regularity with which club members, in their own friendly competitions, use the forgiving Stableford system, which preserves the element of damage limitation of match play – the worst that can happen is you lose the hole – to a limited negative score per hole of zero. Stableford has pretty much replaced the Bogey competition, where everyone "played the course" at match play. Stableford rewards "natural bird-

---

[69] A statement much employed by US Ryder Cup players, and demonstrated by their European counterparts.

ies" i.e. net eagles, which Bogey does not, but they are not terribly common...More to the point, it rewards failure, since losing the hole to the course by only one shot still scores a point. No wonder it is popular.

The idea that anyone should be able to beat anyone is nevertheless at the heart of most competitive club golf, which is where the handicap system comes in.[70] In a singles' match, conditions are the same for both players and, provided the handicap genuinely adjusts for the difference in the essential skill of the players, whoever plays better on the day will win. Note that the handicap should reflect the player's best, not average, form. Under the English system, almost any round better than handicap will result in an immediate reduction, whereas a round over the mark leads to the very modest increase of one tenth of a stroke, no matter how bad it was.

Tom Pegg[71] of Sherborne suffered something of a shock when a freak winter round in a Christmas competition of 49 Stableford points led to a three stroke handicap reduction from 15 to 12. Basically, he had no choice but to accept the new handicap, since to get it back to 15 he would have needed to submit cards from 30 competitive rounds, all played badly. Somehow, he succeeded, which speaks volumes about the psychology of the handicap: 'I am a 15 handicapper, so I play like one'.

This is not quite true. It is more like, 'I am a 15 handicapper, so I expect to beat 15 over par, even though I know full well that most of the time I cannot'. Is this uneasy state of mind brought about because we see Vijay Singh regularly winning tournaments with a score of 20 under par, perhaps? Maybe we should remind ourselves that tournament pros are freaks, bearing as much relationship to a real golfer as a formula one Ferrari does to a Fiat Punto.

So, in the purest form of the club game, handicap match play, where only the *difference* in handicaps matters, should one go for a difficult

---

[70] Handicapping is not unique to golf. It exists in croquet, for example, but is thought by some to be less equitable. For each "shot" a player receives, they are allowed to miss without losing their turn. Often this knowledge is enough to ensure that they do not miss. It is said that the handicap can be used many times over.

[71] Obviously, when his parents christened their son T. Pegg, they did not have golf in mind.

shot to a green unlikely to come off, or lay up and leave a you-know-what? The answer surely depends on who gets a shot from whom, and if it's a difficult hole, the chances are someone will. The state of the match may also be an influence, depending on whether one is seeking to win holes, or playing not to lose them.[72] Someone once said that one should play the course, not the opponent, but I think it was Ben Hogan who, if he beat the course, undoubtedly beat the opponent as well. He doesn't count.

So, when receiving a shot, I should make sure of reaching the green in three and at least make my opponent birdie the hole to win it, and when giving the shot, I am effectively obliged to go for it to put my opponent under pressure. Unless of course I go for it when receiving the shot, because if it comes off, my opponent needs the birdie just for a half. Come to think of it, if I make sure of being on the green in three when giving a shot, this may put my less capable opponent under too much pressure, so maybe I should lay up. Or not. With a bit of luck, one of us (preferably him) will hit a bad tee shot and take the option out of the equation.

******

There are some good golf courses on the Fylde Coast as I believe it is known, including the Open venue at Royal Lytham, but they do not qualify for my peregrination as there are also lots of roads between the courses and the seashore. I continued north after the weekend with Harrison and visited Heysham Golf Club, but found subsequently that I remembered little about it. Indeed, my two main memories were that I ended up playing with someone whom I found annoying, and that there was a strange winter ritual in operation, which I also didn't care for. Two white lines were painted transversely across the fairway, some distance apart, and if your ball landed between them, you picked it up and dropped it in the rough, about two clubs' length from the edge of the fairway. This might have preserved the fairway, but it did not do much for the rough, concentrating the divots from an area say 25 yards wide into two, each about six feet wide. What happens in summer if the ground gets hard and the ball tends to run through the fairway? We also played off mats, so I hope the greenkeeper moved them around (al-

---

[72] Personally, I have found it very useful in match play to try to get ahead, and then stay there – that is, play to win holes while my opponent is perhaps merely playing, and then play not to lose. The match situation overrides the "golfing" criteria.

though most do not, I suspect) so as to vary the landing area. But then, if you vary the landing area, can't you risk using the fairway anyway? I didn't get it.

I also didn't get whether Heysham was actually a literally littoral course, as the sea seemed a long way off, so in due course I looked up its web site. It had a link to the relevant ordnance survey map, which showed that there was a holiday camp nearby (not unexpected, perhaps), an industrial estate (rarer) and a track bounding the golf course linking this area to another marked "nuclear power station". Technically, I should go back and establish that the track is paved, which would then disqualify the course properly, but I think I'll just give it the benefit of the doubt.

TAKING LESSONS

By the time I next visited Lancashire, I had undertaken a series of lessons. I noticed during a week playing with Digby in the USA that I hit about ten fairways per round, but only six greens in regulation (scratch). As I am a fairly reliable two-putter and reasonable chipper, it was pretty clear that my weakness is iron play, or "approach shots" as P G Wodehouse would refer to them. So, I decided to enrol in a course of lessons with Big Al, my club pro.

He came with a good reputation for respecting his students' existing style, and I have noted that he had previously helped me out during the onset of the dreaded unmentionables, where something had to be done. The solution for that problem, when distilled down to a single thought, was at first "start your downswing with your right buttock", later translated as "hit the ball with your right buttock". This was to become a source of great hilarity with two of my greatest golfing friends who for technical reasons – they live in France – do not otherwise get a mention. Madame, having been taught the game later in life, is a keen student of the swing, and she was also trying to use this tip. She looks pretty sensational in full swing, and I have to admit, there is plenty to admire from behind the ladies' tee even when she is standing still. What made things particularly entertaining in this context was her tendency to mix up left and right! I would think that many a hula dancer would find it interesting trying to start the downswing with the left buttock.

My first lesson with Big Al was a raging success. It was bucketing down, so we drank coffee in the clubhouse and talked about the game and our approach to it. Subsequent lessons did not go so well. We first established that I was using the "two wrongs make a right" approach – lining up badly, and attempting to swing badly to compensate, something to do with hitting through the line of my left knee which therefore had to jump out of the way – and to be fair, Al may have succeeded in improving my alignment. The next stage was the biggest challenge. If I can paraphrase, a less polite teacher may have said something like, 'The golf swing may be likened to a round hole; the movements you make, sir, resemble a square peg'. Al tried to work his way round the misfit, metaphorically shaving a little off a corner here, or thickening a side there, and I could manage to do what he asked while he stood there next to me, as if I was "feeling" what he wanted, but left to my own devices, well, put it this way; I have three options for swing thoughts: none, one, or too many. My preference is for none.

******

I was to discover that I had not managed to bring any of these thoughts with me on a second trip to what I thought was Lancashire – or was it? The West Lancashire Golf Club is in Merseyside – according to *The R & A Handbook*. Now, I have a problem with this. As you know, I hold the *Handbook* to be definitely reliable,[73] but my understanding is that "Merseyside" (as an official geographical area and not just meaning Liverpool, Birkenhead, etc) has ceased to exist. It was one of the Metropolitan County Councils created by the Conservative government of the early 1970s, and abolished by the Conservative government of the mid 1980s. (Younger readers may wonder why this should be. The officially-cited reason escapes me; the popular view is that the Metropolitan CCs were "collateral victims" of Mrs Thatcher's resolve to abolish the Greater London Council, whose then leader persisted in displaying a large banner from County Hall showing the number of unemployed people in the country. County Hall is directly across the river from the House of Commons, so anyone using the Terrace could not fail to see the banner. When the figure rose past 3 million, the irony for Mrs Thatcher – who had come to power using the slogan "Labour isn't working" – became too much. That GLC leader was of course

---

[73] But the editor has obviously got fed up with clubs not sending in details, and so does not carry them forward in the 2005 edition.

Ken Livingstone, as I write still Mayor of London, despite rather than because of his own party's efforts to put him there. I wonder if he or Mrs T had the last laugh?)

I consulted *The Good Pub Guide* about counties. This does not list a separate section under Merseyside, though it makes barbed comments about the Post Office which, it claims, attempts to mislead people into believing that certain pubs are in Lancashire when they are (and always have been) in Yorkshire, which is where readers should look them up. It includes both Manchester and Liverpool in Lancashire, where they have not been administratively for 30 years. Is this all to do with postal addresses? I don't think so; counties do not feature in postal addresses, it is all about "post towns". Amongst other things, this means that if you want to write to me, you have to put "Sturminster Newton" instead of "Dorset", and in so doing, you may well be none the wiser about which part of the country I reside in.[74]

The Good Pub Guide had no entries with accommodation in that area of England bound by the Mersey and Ribble estuaries, the M6 and the Irish Sea, where I wished to stay, other than a lucky dip in Southport. I happen to know Southport's postcode is PR8 – PR for Preston, home of the University of Lancashire. Great, Lancashire it is. I phoned directory enquiries for the number of the hotel. My adviser confirmed the address: Lord Street, Southport, Merseyside. Oh well.

Does it matter, I hear you ask? Well, it does if like me you are looking forward to playing some literally littoral Lancashire linksland. As noted in the "rules" section, Royal Birkdale and the other Southport courses are excluded because of minor roads between them and the shoreline. When you drive south out of Southport and see the big sandhills to the west, the adrenalin flows. Then passing Hillside Station, right next to the entrance to Hillside Club, I am reminded of visiting the Open in 1991 (train is by far the best way to get there, you can even go in spikes). The first group I saw were at the par five 17th; Nick Faldo and Nick Price both got eagles. I forget who the third guy was, he only birdied it. So, let's hope West Lancashire does not disappoint.

---

[74] *The Guide* contrives to list The Wirral under Lancashire. I asked Len at Leasowe about this. He was pretty certain that if it was anywhere, spiritually it was in Cheshire.

WEST LANCASHIRE

It doesn't. Firstly, West Lancashire Golf Club is very well sign posted, though it needs to be because the area is quite urban, until housing is suddenly replaced by flat, very black arable fields. (From an historical perspective, I suppose that should really be the other way round.) Will it be too flat? There are dunes in the distance and a flattish but nevertheless enticing looking links golf course; I have a tee reservation with no-one either side of me for some minutes, and time for a coffee. Upstairs, in the Harold Hilton Lounge in the modern clubhouse, I can see beyond the dunes to three horizontal layers of grey. I am informed that these are, from top to bottom, the sky, the sea, and the "sand".

I want to make sure that I am genuinely next to the sea, and as I play the par five 2nd hole, I see the superstructure of a ferry go past (either that or I am looking in the wrong direction and some likely Liverpool lads are towing a hotel down the M57). The 4th tee is elevated, and I am at last able to confirm that the middle layer of grey is the sea. It is moving about. The course so far is fine; the fairways are perhaps a little flat compared to the mounds that accompany them, and the grass is a little meadowy, perhaps because the soil, rather than being sandy, is black but soft and fine, like the fields. The holes seem to become more interesting, and the weather less so, as I proceed. The drizzle is making it harder to play in a straight line, and I have to admit to becoming confused by the temporary scorecard, in which the front "nine" finishes with hole number 10, and the back "nine" begins with 10a, all because number 6 is out of commission. Having looped back at the clubhouse, I think I have played the 10th but someone kindly tells me it is only the 9th, my 8th.

As my navigation brightens, so does the weather. The sky is blue; what colour, I wonder, is the sea? The direction of play is leading inland, towards terrain more reminiscent of Birkdale. The par three 12th green is edged with sandhills, and it is on the 13th tee that I begin to fall in love. I can see the sea again, but the sky is covered in white cloud, and the sea is a whiter shade of pale grey. I can also look down on a great curving right to left dogleg hole, with bunkers and mounds waiting to catch drives attempting to cut off too much. The next two holes are also doglegs (left to right) and I fancy that put cleverly together, they could form the shape of a traditional black pudding. You cannot see the fairway from the 14th tee, and strangely, there is no marker post. There is a church spire in the distance, and I wonder idly if that is the target, but no, that sort of thing only happens in books. From the cut of the tee, it looks too far right, so I aim left, hit even lefter, and catch the edge of the fairway on the wrong side. Still 280 yards to go to an elevated long green surrounded on the sides by scrubby banks. From the divots near where I play my third, I understand this is a tough hole. Looking back, I bet you really should aim at the spire; that's why there is no marker. The 15th is shorter, and there are "bullseye" targets painted on the stone wall on the left edge of the fairway, from which you can choose how aggressive you want to be. The nearer the "sur-rounded" green the better, as this is a "birdie chance". (I say that with confidence, because I got one!)

These doglegs must be particularly difficult in high winds, because whatever direction the wind is in for your first shot, it will not be the same for the second, and so on for each hole. I thought they were great. There have been frequent changes of direction so far, but strict-ly between holes, and these three dog legs now form a "crescendo". There follows a par five, a par three, and a par four, which are roughly, and I guess thankfully, a straight journey home, to complete a great round. From the 18th tee, you can see the sea, and as the sky above was blue, it was too. I hit a good drive to a "semi-blind" landing area,[75] and as I followed over the dunes, I could see a number of bunkers, characterised throughout the course by being quite small, but no ball. This was when I noted mentally that I had not visited a bunker, and you can guess what happened next. I found my ball, it had been hidden in a swale, and I played a good second shot, only slightly off line – into the small bunker protecting the green. The "sand" was a very odd colour. Nevertheless, I "got out" well, and two putted for a net par.

What a great place to play golf – and for much of the round I had appeared to be the only person playing. OK, it was a Thursday in February, but this is one benefit of playing in the winter. Here is another – the winter green fee was £35, down from a published £60. The following day I am set to play at nearby Formby with a green fee of £55 (down

---

[75] You may well ask what is a "semi-blind" landing area. Either you can see the ball land, or you cannot, in which latter case the landing area is designated, somewhat ungrammatically, blind. Well, I know that. I was just trying to distinguish between a hole where you cannot see a fairway or green from the tee, and one where you see most of the hole, but not the part where the ball lands (but you sort of know it will be OK). Put it this way, this shot would not have been "blind" for John Daly.

from £85). Can it be £20 better? Mind you, the fee does include soup and sandwiches...

Talking of sand, I popped back up to the Harold Hilton Lounge. If the sky and sea were both blue, what colour would the sand be? Well. The tide was in.

Sadly, I concluded that my lessons had achieved little. I played much better when I became involved with the course and stopped thinking about trying to hit the ball. It does occur to me that this might be the point. When Nick Faldo famously remodelled his swing, it was so that he could rely on it not to let him down in a crisis. Doesn't this basically mean that he could hit the ball without thinking about it? I don't know. I am not him – although I believe I am the same height as Faldo, and he once said that he was really too tall to be a golfer, which is a useful quote when the going gets tough. Does it matter that my lessons have achieved nothing tangible? What about the money? Well, as I write Big Al hasn't charged me for them...

Back in my hotel bar, I see a poster, issued by an odd collection of bodies including the NHS, Brewers' Association and Police, advising me not to drink alcohol in the streets because in parts of Merseyside it is illegal. Further references to Merseyside – a territory, but not with uniform laws? The buses and trains have a big M for a logo; an ornamental litter bin is designated Sefton MBC; and on the way south, I pass a sign to the County Cricket Ground. What county is that, then, Merseyside Mid Offs?

I also note this time that I actually pass right by the entrance to Royal Birkdale and its sandhills. Now I am here, it does seem a shame to be missing out only because of a minor road – but I have an important littoral peregrination to complete. Formby Golf Club is not evidently signposted, but my hopes rise as I pass the Cricket, Hockey and Squash club (people hitting balls with sticks anyway). I follow signs to Formby Point, together with a symbolic oak branch logo. I end up at a National Trust forest and, turning back, find a lane called Golf Road up the side of the railway line. There it is.

FORMBY

Despite the hints, I am still surprised that the Formby Golf Club is not sandhills, but built in a pine forest (the oak leaves are a red herring). The forest has been cleared, of course, to make way for the golf, but everywhere beyond the fairways, there are pines. The second surprise is that the course does not loop back to the clubhouse at halfway; it loops around Formby Ladies Course! There are his-and-hers' clubhouses! I had seen the reference to the Ladies Club in The *R & A Handbook*, but somehow assumed it was not for me. In the clubhouse, there are aerial photographs confirming that Formby GC, while surrounding the Ladies Course, reaches out into the sandhills, thus ensuring that I will have to return to play the latter course some day.

This is confirmed by the Assistant Pro. Members of the two clubs can play each others' course for reciprocally low fees (a frequently asked question, apparently), and both are open to visitors of either gender. The better lady players play the men's course from the yellow tees, while the men are embarrassed by the tight heather lined fairways on the distaff side. The men's club logo is a stylised pine (slightly phallic, perhaps?) and on the first few holes, large logos are fixed to certain trees to help with ball-spotting. It looks great, though flat, with springy turf. What, I wonder, is in store?

I wonder for two reasons: where does the golf course lead, and what is the meaning of the sign at the 1st tee which reads "Beware of Squidge"? I certainly shall, always provided I recognise it. I play the first four holes well – in winter, there is no rough. The first sign of elevation is at the short 5th hole, the first of three occasions on which I am courteously waved through by groups ahead. From the elevated 6th tee, there is a target fairway which gives way to a series of mounds in front of the green. There are still plenty of pines, but the change in topography is remarkable. There are elevated tees; hidden, mound-surrounded, and elevated greens; and on the par five 8th, an elevated, plateau fairway. Holes 9, 11 and 12 are long par 4s I cannot reach in two. I suppose I should lay up and "play a simple wedge to the middle of the green", but I take the 3 wood. I'm only here once.

I have been driving quite well, but I missed the attractive 7th fairway, and found the mounds on the right, where there were a number of what looked like GUR signs, on inspection all bearing the legend

"Area affected by Squidge". Well, so was I. I couldn't spot anything that looked like Squidge, but given that I did not know what Squidge looked like, this was not surprising. I played a hurried shot, and the ball flew limply off the toe of the club into the pines. Perhaps this kind of shot was called a squidge. I dropped another ball, and hit rather a good shot onto the mound-surrounded green. Then of course, I went looking for the first ball. It takes more than the threat of Squidge to deter instinctive ball-hunting habits. I found three others, but not mine, and then optimistically attempted to wash my hands with my drinking water, just in case. I saw other "affected" signs, and another "beware of" at the 10th green, but no actual Squidge itself.

The proper 14th hole was out of commission, and with its temporary replacement, level ground returned as abruptly as it had departed. At the far end of the course, you are actually briefly in the treeless sandhills, and can hear, and catch glimpses of the sea. But now I was back in the pine forest, looking forward to my inclusive soup and sand-squidges in the clubhouse. Was it worth the extra £20 on the green fee? Well, the two courses are not directly comparable, but while I found the intermediate mounded section very interesting, the opening and closing flat holes were, dare I say it, a little easy. The soup was good, though.

I think Formby might be what one calls an "exclusive neighbourhood". There were some seriously big houses, and no road signs, as if to indicate that only people who have good reason to be there should be there, and that all such people should naturally be fully cognisant of the dangers posed by Squidge... I was glad that I will have to return, though (to play the Ladies' course). Now to find a botanical dictionary...

15

SCARBOROUGH FORE!

Undeterred by its limited success on the last couple of occasions I have used it, my first action in planning a trip to Yorkshire is to reach for *The Good Pub Guide*. I know there are lots of entries in the Yorkshire Dales (where there are almost zero golf courses), but there is very little to show on the coast. It begins to occur to me that the editor does not play golf. It would interfere with his lunchtime sessions, I suppose. Still, I need to go to Yorkshire, because it is the last remaining area I have yet at least to make plans to visit, and while not losing faith in my peregrination, I would sort of like to get it over with, if you know what I mean. There are not even any lucky dip pubs, but there is a full *Guide* entry in Flamborough, very close to a golf course, and not far from another, in Bridlington. It doesn't have bedrooms, but trying an "inverted approach" I nevertheless phone it and ask the lady who answers if she has any bedrooms. When she answers in the negative, I enquire further and she tells me that the Ship Inn has, but she doesn't know what they are like. Never mind, I phone and book anyway; thirty quid a night, en suite, with breakfast.

It is dark when I arrive, and being certain that whichever directory service I had contacted had given the address as Cliff Road, I drive hopefully down whichever road looks as if it might lead to a cliff. There are a number, because Flamborough Head protrudes into the North Sea like a carbuncle on the eastern forehead of England. None leads to the Ship Inn, which turns out to be located on Post Office Street, in the village centre. Post Office Street must be all of 50 yards long. Still, the room is tolerable, and the mixed grill in the dining room for £8.50 more than tolerable, and Flamborough Head Golf Course awaits in the morning, five minutes away.

FLAMBOROUGH HEAD

It was a hazy Monday morning when I arrived at Flamborough Head Golf Club, so I don't know if you can see the sea from the clubhouse. You can certainly hear it. It was otherwise quiet in the car park, expect for one man who was loading his clubs onto a trolley. Another paused as he pulled his trolley towards the 1st tee, possibly at the sight of the "no trolleys" sign on the clubhouse wall. Up ahead, a fourball was playing the 2nd hole – three trolleys and a ride-on tricycle.

I went into the pro shop: 'Is it no trolleys?' 'It says that, but no-one takes any notice. We can't really stop them these days, with all this health and safety stuff about. Anyway, it's fairly dry.' Oh well. I bought a green fee (£15) and took my trolley to the 1st tee. The haze made seeing difficult, and when I found my drive, it was 30 yards from the green – marked at 371 yards on the card! I hadn't noticed the tee being forward, but I hadn't noticed hitting the ball really well, either. I only managed a par, though. No-one had removed the dew from the greens – perhaps it was pointless in the conditions. The inside of the holes had been whitewashed, but rather sloppily, spilling over onto the grass.

I followed the people ahead in playing the 2nd, then consulted a hand drawn map I had picked up in the clubhouse. It showed a slight dogleg left, but the shot I faced was a sharp dogleg *right*, to a blind green. I hit it, and got another par. Now I could see the cliff edge and the sea beyond, on the opposite side of the course from where the noise was coming. There was a mat for the short 3rd hole. In trying to work out the yardage, I looked at the card – 151 yards from the ladies' tee. I looked at the ladies' tombstone marker, confusingly finished in white with red print. 148 yards. Misleading.

Clearly, the climate on Flamborough Head does not support arboreal life. There is not a tree to be seen, and any self-respecting hedgerows have long since moved inland to provide cover for hare and partridge. Apart from some scrub and a few small bunkers, the major hazard is an intermittent ditch crossing the shallow valley in the middle of the course. The holes are laid out back and forth, clubhouse to cliff, across this dip. This might be where the original idea for a skateboard park came from. The wind today is in the south-east and directly behind the cliff-ward, "forth" shots. The mind boggles if it regularly blows from the south-west, across all these holes.

Eventually, some variety arrives in the form of a downhill par three 10th to a large sloping green, followed by an attractive par five hole along the cliff edge. Here we have reached the end of the headland, and there is sea on three sides. Also attractive, though not to look at, is the concrete toilet block. It is necessary. There ain't no cover on the course. (Only the ladies' toilet has a combination lock – no pun intended – which might just be evidence of positive discrimination.) The 12th hole is different, a short par four with ponds and a stream protecting the green, but then we go forth and back again, right up to the far cliff edge. This however is fascinating; there are two coves with vertical rock faces showing strange patterns which, on more careful inspection, are made up of row upon row of seabirds. What are they doing?

At last, the short par four 16th plays across the direction of the other holes, along the cliff edge, but now the view is disturbed by what looks like an oil depot (or a caravan park, or both) in the middle distance. Walking from the par three 17th green to the 18th tee, I pass a sign warning me of players on the 2nd tee, which makes no sense at all, until I catch sight of an out-of-service green, about a hundred yards beyond the one I played as the 1st hole. So it wasn't a 300 yard plus drive, and the 2nd hole isn't a sharp dogleg right. Misleading. Perhaps Albert Haddock would like it here.

I don't think Tom Watson would. If there are ever days when the wind does not blow – and there may not be, given how the elevated land projects into the sea – then as one of his women without clothes, sadly I fear photographs of Flamborough Head would be relegated to the "readers' wives" section of the magazine. I am told there are such things.

It was spring when I visited, and the daffodils were in flower. On a slope on the course, someone has planted clusters which spell out the club initials – F.H.G.C. – complete with full stops. In golf, everything is beautiful – in its own way.

Having made good time at F.H.G.C., I decide to play Bridlington in the afternoon. I have been looking forward to this, as I think I have some memories of seeing it many years ago, and – guess what – it is designed by James Braid. On the main road going south out of Bridlington, it appears on my left, looking rather flat, and not at all like the image I had. I turn left towards the sea at the end of the course, but the road leads to a large holiday park with caravans and things, next to the shore. There is no way through, so I go back whence I came, and this time, at the other end of it, there is a sign indicating the way to the golf club. Turning right, and right again, I now travel along a road by the beach with the golf course on my right, fenced off, or in, depending on how you look at it, until I come to a large car park, which appears to butt onto the holiday village. I retrace this route as well, but it looks for all the world as if Bridlington Golf Club does not meet the qualification criterion of being literally littoral. I was looking forward to it, but there we are. Rules are rules. I set off for Filey. And anyway, who knows where the entrance to Bridlington Golf Club is?[76]

FILEY

I had actually played at Filey, a long time ago. To be precise, it was 1980. Our stay in Filey overlapped Wimbledon Fortnight, and it was the year of the Borg-McEnroe tiebreak. (All Wimbledon fans remember where they were for the Borg-McEnroe tiebreak.) My recollections of the golf were understandably vague, but I did not recall it being a seaside course.

It certainly looks like one on arrival. Not a tree in sight on the golf course, just a green expanse interrupted by a small bunker, with a flag fluttering uphill in the distance (I am trying not to mention the out of bounds posts on the right defining the practice ground). When and if your second shot hits the green at the top of the rise, the beaches and sea making up the various little bays around Filey are to be seen in all their glory, just the width of a fairway away. However, that is hole Number 17. Hole Number 2 proceeds sharply inland, and the direction of play is away from the shore for several holes. This is roughly how I remember it. Each hole seems self-contained, its limits defined by plantations of pine trees as well as mature deciduous colleagues which make some of the tee shots interesting. It is hard to tell how long the pines have been there, but it looks like they were planted for

---

[76] There is actually a littoral course to the north called The Bridlington Links, which was founded in 1993, so it does not qualify. Using my road map, I also found the self-styled Skipsea Golf, a modern development to the south, and not listed in the handbook. It looked closed when I went past.

the golf rather than the golf being threaded through them. James Braid (for it was he) had a fairly free hand here and used it nicely. There are elevation changes, particularly towards the far end of the course, and I can only describe the fairways as sort of corrugated. They had regular low mounds running across them, as if they might once have been cultivated. This is something I have come across before, but I have never bothered to ask about...

This latter fact makes things interesting, because I have rented a buggy, and it is quite powerful with only me on board. Riding across the corrugations produces an effect similar to that created when a motor boat heads into waves and starts "slapping its bottom". It's probably not the best thing for the buggy, but I enjoyed it. (One of the great things about buggies on old English courses is that you do not have to stick to the cart path, because there isn't one.) I took the buggy because I had already played that morning, and I was "convalescing" after undergoing a general anaesthetic a few days earlier. It changed the rhythm of the round, but made it very quick as there was nobody else about, apart from a fourball I met where the front and back nines intertwine. As they looked at me, their body language seemed to spell the word "wimp".

The greens were big and getting the ball in the hole is probably more of a challenge than hitting them. On this occasion, they had been top-dressed, and looked like they had been cut with a blunt lawn mower, so they were not exactly at their best. The course goes inland until it almost meets the main road into Filey. There is an attractive tree-lined ravine with a stream at the bottom – what in Dorset we would call a "chine" – but the residents of North Yorkshire seem to regard as a landfill site. There is a sign at the 10th tee stating that anyone attempting to drive the 10th green must wait until the 11th tee is clear. It is on the card at 308 yards, with a watercourse in front of the green. The wind is against, so I don't even try. I have no recollection of this hole, but in those days, my memory of courses faded fast as the travails of the round took its toll. Still, there is something about it which does not seem very James Braid-like. I remember "Tattie Bogle" – JB's affectionate name for the short 12th at Stranraer[77] – and that has a stream in front of the green. What is unconvincing here is the way the stream has been edged with timber, Sawgrass-style. It is out of place with everything so far, which looks very natural.

---

[77] The name means "scarecrow in a potato field" – as far as I can tell. Mank hated this hole.

To negotiate the hazard, I attempt my recently-tutored 54 degree wedge-shot at 70% swing, and thin the ball. It hits a willow tree it should have cleared, disappears from my cognisance (and maybe even the planet) for a few seconds, then lands with a thud on the other side of the bank. Only then do I notice that there is a forward, temporary green with one of those big cups. It is about 15 feet away, and I chip in for an unlikely birdie. A couple of holes later, the timber merchant has been at work again, this time creating what would be called in the East Midlands a "jitty" – a narrow fenced-off path – to get from the green to the next tee, and he has roped off the area of land in between to make sure everyone uses it. It is possible that before he edged the path with timber, it was wide enough but only just, for a buggy to pass. Now it is almost wide enough, but not quite.[78]

The 15th hole is only 292 yards, and after a good drive, it is time for another 70% wedge shot, and again I thin it. It flies over the green, heading for oblivion in another chine, but a tree is in the way. It rebounds from the trunk, onto the green, and comes to rest six feet from the hole. When I stop laughing, I have no choice but to hole it! The 16th is a par three – the only variation on fours in this half – played across the chine, and suddenly we are back beside the seaside, with nary a tree in sight, and two nice holes along the shoreline to finish. A pleasant experience, if a little monotonous with fourteen par fours, but perhaps in summer it is advisable to take different clubs off the tees for the sake of position. This is not summer though, and what I had forgotten is how cold one can become in a buggy, not generating any body heat. Brrrr.

Back at the Ship that night there were some people dining at the next table whose conversation I overheard, without eavesdropping, you understand. I have always heard things without appearing to listen as it were, a facility which used to confuse my teachers somewhat at school. I thought everyone did, until I worked in a bank, and sat opposite someone who heard nothing unless you first called out his name, whereupon he would switch his auditory lobes on to "receive" mode.

The people next to me talked about many things, more as strangers than good friends, and their conversation was readily interspersed with

---

[78] If you are reading this Mr Greenkeeper, I own up. I was the culprit who broke the white stake, with my buggy.

references to birds. So, when there were just two of them left at the table, I said something like, 'Excuse me, but I could not help hearing you talk about birds.'

'That is because we all work for the RSPB.'[79] 'Ah,' said I, 'perhaps you could...' and I told them about the birds on the cliffs. 'Almost certainly guillemots,' they said. 'Fine, but why are they doing it? They're not going to nest together, are they?' It turns out no-one really knows *why* they do it. They just sort of hang about, literally.

After dinner, I went out for a stroll, actually a drink in the Royal Dog & Duck, just along round the corner from Post Office Street, in Dog & Duck Square. Well, it was dark and cold. There were some teenagers vaguely assembled at the corner, not really doing anything, just hanging around. I wonder why?

The following day I drove to Scarborough, a town of two halves, North Bay and South Bay. It has two golf courses, North Cliff and South Cliff, and a very bad traffic system round the outside. I popped in to look at the South Cliff Course. It looked interesting, but it was not by the sea. The town was, though, and it seemed an interesting place with its Arts' festivals, its own symphony orchestra, and many theatres. I believe the playwright Sir Alan Ayckbourn lives nearby, and his plays are premiered in Scarborough. Talking of premieres, it is self-proclaimed as "England's warmest welcome and oldest resort". I think Weymouth and Brighton would have something to say about the latter, and although I was warmly welcomed in the pro shop when I finally found Scarborough North Cliff Golf Club, I was also told to come back later, as it was ladies' morning. I went back into the town, where it started raining.

When the time came, I returned and the pro told me that North Cliff, as the locals call it, is very popular with visitors, as evidenced by the fact that a lot of them come back again. I am more concerned about locals. 'Oh, I think this rain's set in for a while, so if you're going to go out, happen you'll have the place to yourself...'

---

[79] Royal Society for the Protection of Birds.

SCARBOROUGH NORTH CLIFF

While the pro is telling me this, the rain has eased and a small throng has gathered by the 1st tee of Scarborough North Cliff Golf Club. Three juniors tee off and set off after their balls – in three different directions – leaving behind another threesome, whom I am to come to know as The Marx Brothers. Not for any physical resemblance, you understand, there is just something about their coordination and organisation skills...

Groucho takes up position 20 yards left of the tee. 'Is the tee over there?' asks Chico. 'No, I can see the green clear from here,' is the reply. It is a 240 yard par three, so nobody plays until Groucho gives the word, even though Harpo takes an iron, "for safety". This is a bad sign. It is a symptom of diffidence, and a total lack of aspiration to par the hole, or indeed, a total lack of aspiration. Harpo's safety-first strategy is questionable, as he hits an infield fly to shortstop (roughly translated, a lobbed catch to midwicket).

It's going to be a while before I can tee off, and a fourball has now emerged from the locker room. I ask if I can go first – it is a bit of a liberty, but they don't object, and I could run the risk of being there all day – so once the Brothers Marx reach the green, I hit a "three-quarter driver" nicely towards the hole. I am little bothered by the situation, so I do not take in the view of 240 yards of coastline, which turns out to be all there is of the eponymous north cliff, as the 2nd hole turns inland. It is a while before I can play that, however, as it has come on to rain again. The Marx Brothers have limited protection, but they take their time applying it; only Harpo has an umbrella, and no-one has any headgear. Now, if there is one county where one expects men to grow up learning at their grannies' knees of the perils of going "baht 'at", this should be it. (I don't think Ilkley Moor is nearby, but this is surely a Yorkshire principle.)

I clear the green so the fourball can play, and watch Harpo continue his iron play – a simple caught-and-bowled this time. Groucho disappears into the trees on the right, and when he re-emerges, finally I can play (the fourball are putting) – this time, a "seven-eighths' driver" nicely down the middle of a well-defined, flat, lush fairway. When I get to the ball, it is so nicely in the middle of the narrow fairway that I would like to pace it out to find out how far off centre it actually is, but the fourball is on the tee by now. It is a long hole, so I hit a "controlled" 3 wood which ends up in the greenside bunker. As I walk slowly forward, Chico takes an age over a putt, which he misses. He tries again, with the same result, and picks up. Harpo emerges from the woods without a ball, and they go off across the road to the 3rd tee, all except for Groucho, who fiddles with his bag for a short lifetime. From what I have seen, it is his honour. Meanwhile, the fourball is coming relentlessly down the fairway like the posse in Butch Cassidy and The Sundance Kid. I won't survive in this sandwich...

...so I switch to the nearby vacant 16th tee and play the last three essentially straight, flat, medium length holes on the course, hoping for once that it doesn't stop raining before I get back to the 1st tee to start again, all by myself. I have actually interpolated myself into a gap in the ladies' competition, as groups appear ahead, and eventually behind. They all have sensible, waterproof hats.

So, at length I cross the road to the 3rd tee, where begins one of the finest thirteen-hole golf courses I have had the pleasure to play, notwithstanding the rain. With well-defined lush fairways edged with mature pines, and lots of changes in elevation, each tee invites you to put a ball down and hit it straight down the middle (or perhaps to the desired point on a slope). If you do not succeed, you are advised to take another ball and repeat the exercise with it. The rough is lethal, even in March. The direction of play changes between holes, each of which is a variation on this theme. Sometimes a course like this can produce boring golf, but here, there is a touch of class, where everything is in balance. It does not seem to matter that houses and bungalows have been built up to the boundaries of the course, there is that quality of "one hole at a time". There is no hint that the fourball or the Marx Brothers ever existed...

...until the 8th tee, when my elation from a birdie two is deflated as I glimpse three shadowy figures some 500 yards ahead on the green. Surely not? As I get to the green myself, I see through the trees a group of four approaching what the course map shows to be the 11th green. The fourball has clearly been waved through. I take another look at the map. I still have eight holes to play, but there is no obvious way of avoiding the inevitable. I slow down, appreciating how the umbrella-holder on my Sun Mountain Speed Cart™ keeps my hands free. As I approach the 9th, also a par five, I see them about 100 yards from the 10th tee, together – one umbrella, no hats. Harpo is playing his second. He has the umbrella, but definitely no waterproofs.

I start rehearsing. I hope they don't call me through. I am not sure I can bear to see them stand there in the rain while it happens. What if they invite me to join them? The words 'You'll be even slower' form in my head, which I quickly change to 'Thanks, but it would slow us all down'. The inevitable begins to happen as I see them play the short 11th. Harpo hits, and looks anxiously after his ball (I'm sure I hear someone shout "catchitt!", maybe extra cover). They set off for the green. I arrive on the tee to see a delightful, downhill, ditch-protected, sloping green. It is devoid of balls. Taking his time, Chico plays a difficult bunker shot quite well, and another ball appears from a spinney followed by Groucho, who raises his arm for me. I know what to do; play quickly, but not hurriedly. Take aim. It's not the best of strikes, but the ball hits the green, pin high, 15 feet right. I take my trolley to the next tee, thinking they might play on, but they have stood courteously aside in the rain. I suppose they may be as wet as they will get.

I walk over to the putt, mark and clean the ball, repair the pitchmark without having to move, and address the putt. Downhill, right to left, and inside my head a voice says 'Y'know it would be nice..' It was – rolling gently down the hill, turning left as it slowed down, into the middle of the hole. I had not rehearsed this scenario, and the words came out of my mouth: 'Easy game.' 'If only,' said Groucho. 'If only,' I echoed. 'Many thanks.' It was the eve of my birthday, and this was an early present. I made sure I hit a cracking drive down the middle at the next – in fact it was so good from the forward tee that I overshot the dogleg – and then took another five to get down. That's golf.

I finished the remaining three holes "across the road" and walked in. There was no sign of the fourball; if it had been thirty-six holes, they might have lapped the Marx Brothers. The pro had told me people come back. I could see why – if only to look for their lost balls – or perhaps because they are playing all the courses designed by James Braid...

As well as its Arts' festival, Scarborough is also famed for its cricket extravaganza, being the place where they all let their hair down. Yorkshire is of course the land of tough cricketers, and I am sure that it is no coincidence that the England team's fortunes have improved since the tyke Michael Vaughan took over the captaincy. I stopped at a pub in the North York moors on a Tuesday night. They were holding their regular weekly clay pigeon shoot, a sign of how tough tykes are. In Dorset, we have skittles, and that can be dangerous enough after a few pints. Don't let me near anyone with a shotgun after six pints of Theakston's Old Peculier.

The barman was recounting the tale of a recent cricket match. All had been going well, until the pub team's fast bowler hit the opening batsman with a beamer, 'Ere,' said the barman, pointing to his lower ribs. 'When somebody bowls a beamer, it's a mistek, so you just apologise and gerron wi it. Well, e dint. E swore at t' bowler an threw iz bat attim. T' bowler were so upset, we ad to tek im off, an they knocked t 'runs off.' Well, I thought, we don't get incidents like that at golf.

The next day, I drove past Whitby Golf Club as someone drove on it, on a tee right next to the road. Instead of finishing his turn, he continued with a pirouette and launched his club after the ball. It was really quite bad to see. The hammer-throwing technique is useless for golf clubs – they do not have sufficient counterbalance. Much better the discus method where the one-handed release is easier to time, and with the correct launch angle, 80 yards is easy. I nearly hit a playing partner once, on the head.

PLAYING OTHER SPORTS

It was on the side of the ribs that the offended batsman was hit, for cricket is a game played sideways by both batsman and bowler, in which respect it is said to be good for golf (once one has learnt to hit across the line, as it were). I think it is possibly good mentally for golf; as a batsman, you must avoid mistakes, and as a bowler, you must be patient and not expect each effort to be successful, despite your best endeavours. Probably. I was a wicketkeeper.

Actually, I played tennis as a youngster. My hand to eye coordination was not well developed, except with a racquet in hand. When it came to cricket at school it was obvious to me, and whoever was the captain, that I was not much cop with bat or ball, so I announced myself as wicketkeeper. You stood square on, with a good chance of seeing the ball, and gloves to catch it and pads to protect you if you missed it. And, you were involved in the game all the time. I was right on every score except the last; some kid would always come in to bat and hit every ball all over the place, and none of the fielders would ever throw it in.

Later on, I developed some skill, and I believe there are those who know me as a competent wicketkeeper, and it is true that you are involved in the game more. It is said that cricket is played with 2 versus 11, but I have been in many games where there are only two people on the fielding side as well – the captain and the wicketkeeper. I developed a distaste for people who voluntarily turned up for cricket matches, but when required to field gave the impression that they would much rather be elsewhere, whether at home doing some embroidery, or in the garden perhaps demolishing an outside toilet. If they did happen to be paying attention and manage to field the ball, they would never throw it in; the latter wouldn't, and the former couldn't. For these people (fielding in an arc through mid-off – in first class terms, this would be called "saving one" – ha, ha), I developed the lob return. It was polite to give the ball to slip to return through the field to the bowler, otherwise he never got to touch it, but after about the fourth over, I had to return it myself, as slip was fielding on the boundary. I discovered that you can sort of roll the ball along the glove, and with a relatively slow action and clean release, send the ball to significant height, and with it distance – towards whichever of these fielders had the sun in his eyes.

The other thing I was good at was appealing. You have to back up the bowler, and if I caught a deflected ball, I appealed. The umpire might give it out, and the quality of the umpiring is as much a part of the game as the batting or bowling or the surface of the pitch. What I was really doing though was saying, 'look, I caught the ball'. Often, the umpire was one of the batting side anyway, not guaranteed to know the lbw rules, so I appealed if it hit the pads. Sometimes a batsman would tell me it was missing leg stump etc, to which the reply was, 'If you saw it so well, why didn't you hit it?' Someone asked me once why I appealed when the ball hit the stumps. I explained that from my position, I could see that the batsman was going to miss the ball, so I started appealing in case it hit the pads. There is a debate in the first class game about appealing and walking. With the standard of umpiring around in my sort of cricket, the idea that anyone should ever "walk" is laughable. Judging by TV replays, the same is true at international level.

From an adjudicating point of view, tennis looks strange to watch at professional level; two players accompanied by an umpire, eight line judges, and six ball kids, but when it is played at club level, players call their own lines. In this respect, it is like golf in that it depends upon the integrity of the players for the scoring system to work. Disputing line calls is not part of club tennis. This is the only respect in which tennis is useful preparation for golf.

When I took tennis up again after moving to the country, I was struck by the confrontational aspect of a competitive singles' match. In golf, you play alongside an opponent. In tennis, he is opposite, hitting the same ball as you. It's either your point or his; there is no such thing as a half in four. There is no running in golf, nor any anticipation (except possibly fateful anticipation)[80] but in tennis, while it is true that some points are critical, and the whole match can sometimes be seen to hinge on just one, the fact is that most points are unimportant. If you hit more good shots than bad, you will win more points than you lose, and with it, the match. Would that were true in golf!

WHITBY

After likening the calm sea of Robin Hood's Bay the previous evening to the Med (much to the disgust of an Italian waiter who muttered something about temperature) I was alarmed to be woken by a howling wind. When Neff and I met later at Whitby Golf Club, we felt its full force. My windsock handkerchief pointed directly at the sun, which at 1 PM BST was due south, meaning the onshore wind was from due north, straight from the Arctic. The course looked splendidly green between the road and the cliffs, and quite challenging enough without a gale. This was Neff's first cliff top course, and he thought it was great (ish). Although it is one of the oldest clubs, it has to be the newest course, dating from 1st April, 2005. The members had chosen it from various layout options, having acquired some new land to replace that which had fallen into the sea. It was a good decision by The Committee to let the members choose, as they will now only have themselves to blame, and not The Committee.

Numerical confusion started as we drank coffee in the clubhouse, next to which appeared to be the 18th tee. There were impressive works of monumental masonry on each tee, and what we were looking at had

---

[80] That is, the more confident you feel that something will happen, the more probable it is that it won't.

a giant 1 engraved in it. The 18 figure, visible from about 100 yards, was the stroke index. The point about these is that sadly only two or three of them are correct now. (I tried to keep a note of some of the changes. See below.) Our 4th hole was marked Number 17, but a sheet of A4 paper affixed to the tombstone confirmed the change. Two people had gone out in front of us, and Neff had used their fairway when playing the 1st hole, so I feared the worst when they invited us through at this point. I hit an acceptable drive up the right, and to his credit, Neff hit a screamer down the middle, and kept it fairly straight with his second. He wasn't as much of a challenge to me on this occasion, because he kept hitting screamers through the green from 30 yards out, but he was driving well. We had now arrived at the principal "feature" of the course, a ravine which runs through the course down to the beach. Hole Number 6 (formerly 7, unless it was 5), stroke index 1, plays across the ravine, 435 yards from the yellow tees, and 317 from the ladies', which is on the other side. It is non-trivial.

There was a notice forbidding play if anyone was walking in the ravine. Three people were, but they stopped when they saw Neff on the tee, so he had no choice but to play, and hit another screamer. Perhaps he has always needed a gallery. We then had an extended and in my case awkward walk across a remarkable long narrow footbridge. The ravine was deep enough to have a small wrecked ship in it, and the extra wind produced by the fact that we were more or less in midair kept blowing my Sun Mountain Speed Cart™ off course into the bridgework. With this same wind assistance, I subsequently hit onto the uphill green for a satisfying par. We then played up and down this slope for a couple of holes before crossing the road to the newer section. While the newest holes were obvious (there was no masonry), the rest also looked fairly new, not really matching those on the seaward side of the road. It is disappointing when this happens. For those readers who have played at Whitby, I made a note of some of the changes. Hole 14, 201 yards (white), 201 yards (yellow), is now by coincidence also stroke index 14, having previously been the 12th, when its stroke index was 9, so a fair number of members no longer get a shot there. (The tombstones also give distances in metres, but I will leave you to work those out for yourself. Multiply the yardages by 0.914.) The old 15th hole, which used to be stroke index 7, is now number 17, stroke index 6, a mere snip of a 249 yard par three into the teeth of a gale. This is also the club thrower's hole, the first one back over the road, with the ravine down the left side. I can guess where his ball went. Finally, the 18th, which is 491 yards from the yellows, 501 yards from the whites, but only 368 yards for the ladies, who tee off from the clubhouse side of the ravine of course (so you can probably work out that it is a good 130 yards carry) is now stroke index 10. It used to be hole Number 16, stroke index 11, of course, still a par five for the men. I hope that is clear. As a test question, what colour socks was I wearing?

Neff hit his third screamer, a hooky sort of draw which used the wind and went miles past my rather weak fade. I was feeling rather stiff, battling against the wind. Impressed, Neff put down another ball and hit it with his talisman driver (normally he carries it round but does not hit with it for fear of offending the gods). Yet another screamer. We both missed short putts for closing pars. The next day, we played a few holes on the short course at our hotel. His longest drive was 70 yards. That's (occasional) golf!

16

THE FINAL COUNTDOWN

As you are aware, this book is not compiled in chronological sequence. This is for a number of reasons, the most obvious being that I do not know when my littoral peregrination actually started. When I took my dad out to play his first ever game at Sheringham in September 1971, it was not at the forefront of my mind. I did well to aspire to get us round the eighteen holes in front of us, never mind England. Once I was well into it, it did seem feasible that one day I would finally play the last eligible course, so there was the distinct possibility of an end, but there was no real concept of a middle, or other staging posts. Consequently, I was never able to ask myself the question, 'What do you think of it so far?' which may have been just as well. In fact, for most of the time, I did not know exactly how many courses there were. Until I went there, I believed Seaton Carew to comprise two different lots of eighteen holes, and I didn't know the whereabouts of Formby Ladies, or the unmarked road which ruled out Bridlington. But, overall it was a good thing, and we know that all good things must come to an end.

The original format of weekend trips to play two or perhaps three courses started to wear a bit thin. It was fine in the West Country, and OK for a while going further afield, but the novelty started to wear off when the elapsed time driving the car exceeded that spent driving the golf ball. There had been periods when I had sought a publisher, and decided not to pre-empt matters by collecting any more courses for a while, but of course no-one was willing to advance my green fee money, despite my assurances that it was most unlikely I would be struck simultaneously by the Burnham hook and writer's block, and thereby unable to complete the project. While the obligation to complete the total round never became a millstone, I began to fancy the "freedom" to play inland, or revisit nice seaside courses. Happily, a nephew announced his wedding date in Gateshead (not a golfing nephew, I am pleased to say; I cannot afford to lose too many of my protégés to parenthood) the Saturday before an already scheduled golfing visit to Northumberland, so I filled in the intervening week with the outstanding venues: seven golf courses in six days.

The longest time I have spent on a golf trip is the nine days The Lodger and I once passed in La Manga. Apart from an expedition to Villa Martin, which we did not like for all the villas lining the fairways giving the feeling that we were being spied upon, we nevertheless only played the three courses we knew. This would be a different kind of expedition. Usually, in the duration of a La Manga week, there was a high spot, but it was likely to come not so much from playing good golf as playing good holes: avoiding the usual downfalls, getting the odd lucky bounce, accidentally hitting a part of a green where the flag had been placed, etc. There was also a corresponding low spot, usually brought about by alcohol. The "nine days wonder" trip was memorable in that it was during Lent, for which period, for (non-religious) reasons which escape me, I had forsaken beer. We were obliged to dine too often at the Indian restaurant[81] which was not great, and I was forced to phone Nellie (my mum) to have her explain that Sundays do not count as part of Lent. They don't. Count the days from Ash Wednesday to Easter. I may not be religious now, but I paid attention at Sunday School.

Seven different courses in a row were going to be different indeed. I fancied that events afterwards at Seaton Carew and Goswick would be alright either way.[82] If I played well, it would be because I had just played seven different courses, and if I played badly – well, it would be for the same reason. Either way, my partners ought to be impressed. The question was, since my play of holes could not improve through finally getting it right for that course, would my actual golf get better? Having recently tried "technical input" to limited avail despite the best endeavours of Big Al, here was a chance to try something mental, like striving to achieve a sharply focused target, and taking dead aim. What I needed was a competition to play, an incentive with which to reward

---

[81] Indian meals do not exist without pints of lager, and were thus exempt.

[82] I was actually scheduled to play nine courses in eight days, ending with the visits to Seaton Carew and Berwick-upon-Tweed (Goswick) which you have already read about. For the seven courses in six days, I would be alone except when Neff joined me at Whitby.

myself, and a system to stop me from cheating on the grounds that I "wasn't ready". How on earth can you be "not ready" when you are hitting a stationary ball?

By the time I got to Teesside, after the wedding, I had not come up with anything, other than the usual – try and beat eighty, if not, come in under your handicap, if disaster strikes on a hole, switch to Stableford and, if the problem persists, try to beat the course at match play.

CLEVELAND

It is not difficult to find Cleveland Golf Club. Take the A1085 from Middlesbrough to Redcar, and after the last steelworks on the left, there it is. Actually I only found this out the second time, having first followed signs to Redcar racetrack, which appears to be in the middle of a cemetery – an appropriate metaphor for the peripatetic version of that sport. At the clubhouse, you can only see the opening par three hole and the final green, and it seemed quiet, but it was Sunday afternoon and the car park was full, apart from the conspicuously empty spaces in front of the clubhouse reserved for the voluntary and honorary officers of the club. As this was "invitational day" perhaps they had not been invited.

I was actually called up from the 1st tee by the ball-hunting pair ahead and played a good shot onto the green. As I was leaving the tee, an elderly man asked if he might join me, and I indicated the need for some urgency, which he ignored. We therefore waved the group ahead back on, and took our time. From the elevated green (which turns out to be the only such one), you can see the whole course, and it was seething with fourballs, so Ray and I settled down to a slow rhythm and some entertaining conversation. His lack of speed was excusable. He was wearing a strange yellow mask over the top of his spectacles, because a year or so earlier he had had a stroke, which had affected the way his brain processed signals from his eyes, meaning that he was unable to follow the flight of his balls. This device was to be the antidote. Because of this same problem he could not drive (a car, that is; he drove a golf ball well, once upon a time reaching the 557 yard 4th hole in two when assisted by a gale, as he proudly informed me). I asked how he had got to the course today – bicycle! He gave me the line on the first few holes, each a different chimney of the steelworks which hummed and occasionally clanked away. It is a continuous production process, apparently. Ray told me that they have to toast the iron ore to stop it rusting. I am not sure if this is the correct technical expression, but I got the message that it could be unpleasant when the wind blows from that direction.

Ray pointed out that the chimneys were more distinct than the trees you might have to aim at on a parkland course, and asked me if we had views like this in Dorset. I was particularly taken by the tall chimney with the flame burning as if from some giant Bunsen burner. Ray claimed that you got used to it, but then he had been a member since 1961, and – it was he who mentioned it, not me. It was one of those warm but dull days with greyish white cloud cover, and not at all easy to see the ball, so we could not pass sound judgment on Ray's light-enhancing device. The car breakers' yard across the road added a little colour, as perhaps the ball I hooked into it will do when some-one finds it.

Titleist 3, reg no PRO V1X, approx 1000 yards, fsh,[83]
one careless owner, free to a good home.

After a while, we turned and played back towards Redcar, its sky-line dominated by a church spire. This seemed to be the driving line on holes 5 and 7. Ray got a par three on Number 6, his first of the year, and left me after the 7th to "get home before it was dark". I should think he made it, as it was about 4.30 PM in the middle of May. I hope his eyeshade works while he can still remember how to hit the ball. I played on. The course is flat linksland with firm greens, and the main challenge is to keep the ball out of the rough when the wind is blow-ing. Even when playing away from the steelworks (towards the church spire) you cannot forget its presence, as it can still be heard and smelt (no pun intended). The tees of the 11th and 16th holes are quite near each other. As I stood on the 11th, I thought the people on the 16th might be hitting towards the steeple, but when I got there, I found that you have to aim left of it, and right from the 11th. Normal service was resumed on both 12 and 17 – you aim at the steeple. Both chimney and steeple give good lines from the tee, but when you get near the ball, it is so flat that you cannot really see where the tee was anyway. I bet the membership are typically straight drivers.

---

[83] Full scoring history – par, par, oob.

The 14th hole seemed for a while to be a bonus. The card said it was a 152 yard par three, and there was indeed a short hole. I had "a butcher's" at the tombstone on the tee, but it merely advertised a family butcher. Thereafter, numbers 14 and 15 on the card were marked as 13 and 14 on the course. I went out of bounds again in the big dunes near the 15th green, where a path paved with slabs appeared out of, and led to nowhere – except an abandoned tee for an abandoned but still apparently maintained short hole. The mystery was solved, and I am sure it has nothing to do with the steelworks. There was a pond nearby, but I bet it was safe. As Ray had said, 'They keep telling us it's alright.' The course ends with a pleasing par five played from an elevated tee where everyone seemed to have to wait to play. Probably, everyone goes for the green in two, so waits for it to clear, and then fails to reach it. There are no prizes for guessing the line from this tee. My question would be this: the steeple was there long before the golf course, but whatever did they aim at before the steelworks was built?

As you know, I never travel without *The R & A Handbook*, *The AA Easy Read Britain Road Atlas*, and *The Good Pub Guide*. I often use *The Guide* to locate possible accommodation, and I have consulted the relevant pages of the *Handbook* where hotels are listed, but it was a surprise when the *AA Easy Read* came up with somewhere to stay. There is a blue flag between Scarborough and Whitby, to the south of Robin Hood's Bay, but no corresponding entry in the *Handbook*, so I investigated. It turns out to be a stately home, now a hotel, on the cliff top on the southern corner of Robin Hood's Bay, and it has its own nine-hole golf course. It is not in the *Handbook* because it is not a club. The morning after Neff and I battled with the elements at Whitby, we played it. It is a little eccentric, laid out on the side of a cliff, well above sea level (with the corresponding implications for wind) with lots of changes of level. My body was feeling my age, and the slopes did not help, and for once my Sun Mountain Speed Cart™ struggled to make its way through the grass, and it was easier to carry the bag. I finished with two threes, though, the second a birdie, which shows that there is always hope.

The problem was tennis, a match I had played a week previously. As a youth I adored Beethoven's 9th symphony, despite the fact that it seemed to last about half a day. In fact, it runs for an hour and a bit, and these days, if my attention wanders, I can easily fail to notice a movement or two. On the other hand, a big hour is just the right length for a tennis game, whereas to a youth, that is just a warm-up. Sometimes, if my feet turn up on the court and cooperate with my eyes and brain, I can still perform, and a week previously I had, for three hours. The effort had taken a week to work through my system.

I have to admit that I played later that day at Hartlepool under the influence of a performance-enhancing drug, acetylsalicylic acid, better know as aspirin. It worked.

HARTLEPOOL

Hartlepool's reputation in the south as a less than attractive town (although it may also be the jewel of Teesside) may have registered with the locals, because the only signage appeared to be to help people leave. Or they may have some well-kept secrets. I was trying to avoid somewhere called Headland and, navigating by the sun, attempted to steer myself towards the sea, but I kept circling housing estates, only to come up against an impressive and forbidding green embankment about 10 metres high, which I eventually realised must be a railway – with the golf course the other side? Eventually I saw a sign to the Golf Club, but still ended in an estate, so I asked a man doing his garden. The language was not easy, but with the help of pointing, he literally showed me the way. There was a second sign, obscured by a tree and pointing at such an angle that it would not be noticed by a passing motorist. There was also a tunnel under the embankment, and beyond it (on a day when my newspaper reported the Italian carabinieri uncovering a secret racecourse) a hidden gem of a golf course. After the journey, which had included negotiating the transporter bridge in Middlesbrough, it had to be either brilliant, or an anticlimax. It was both.

If there is a golf course in Fort Knox, it might be harder to get into, but Hartlepool Golf Club, protected on its landward length by the embankment, is fenced off on the approaches, and at the clubhouse has a double entry system of mechanical security gates. I spoke via an intercom, and a gate opened for me, but I learned I would have to wait until the person in the pro shop returned before I could buy a green fee. Meanwhile, I was trapped in a secure compound outside it, with no access to the car park or the course, until someone else came along. Eventually, with the help of a young man practising, I established the

13th tee was nearby, so I set off to play, intending to buy the green fee when I got back to the 18th.

It is a brilliant seaside golf course, with elevated tees all over the place (Tees are plentiful round here, of course), good fairways inviting you to hit the ball into them, and fabulous greens. I played the six holes round to the clubhouse in level par and then panicked somewhat when I saw people on the practice green, so I hurriedly paid a green fee and botched the 1st hole despite a good drive. Two ladies had started their round behind me, and looked ominous. They had power trolleys, and were much better players than the two ladies which misfortune had placed in front of me. The unpleasant prospect of a sandwich – one of those ahead looked like Laura Davies though the resemblance ended there, and she was the best looking – plus the change of pace disturbed my rhythm, but I still thought it was great, particularly when I birdied the par five 2nd hole to match my four on 17.

I suppose that imperfections must be admitted. A purist might just complain at some of the slopes in the middle section of the course which is set among the sandhills, and an enthusiast would observe that the opening and closing holes on the landward side are rather flat. In this respect, Hartlepool is rather like Formby, but with no hint of a pine tree. There were good views of a deep blue sea with white breaking waves and yellow sand, and from most points of the course, only a tall chimney hints at the industrial devastation to the south. The par threes are fun: 149 yards across a crater; only 90 yards across a ravine; all of 208 across another ravine, which you traverse over an Indiana Jones-style footbridge, and a fabulous downhill 175 yards 12th, my last. Unable to see in the sun, I hit two balls. I found them four feet apart, on the green, and holed the furthest – and first – ball. Brilliant.

Thanks to helpful signs, I left via the A19 and avoided the town. I would go back, except that I doubt I would be able to find the way.

The next day, I drove down to Merseyside to play the two courses outstanding on my list. As a rule, this kind of expedition would not be recommended, but I enjoyed the golf if not the journey. I still could not easily come up with a format which would make me aspire to play "a hole at a time", which is reckoned to be the secret of good scoring, instead of as an eighteen-hole sequence. I thought I might play two eclectic rounds, taking say the best three scores by hole number, and the best three by stroke index, and play them against each other, but even to my convoluted mind, this seemed complicated, and flawed. So long as the indexes rated the relative degree of difficulty of a hole, the hole number version would always win.

I reverted to a concept The Lodger and I used to employ at La Manga. After the competitive morning round for the Cochinillo Cup, which was the best of seven Stableford eighteen-hole rounds, we would play a Texas Scramble in the afternoon, again Stableford, but off scratch. Our purpose was to add two zeros to the points we scored, and this became the number of pesetas we could spend on the wine list at Jose Maria's, our favourite restaurant, home of the *cochinillo asado* after which the trophy was named, and a fabulous wine cellar with prices which appeared not to have been updated since Franco's time.

I settled for a pound a point towards a luxurious case of wine for the three best Stableford scores by hole added to those by index, but I never spent the money. I found I actually was playing hole-by-hole, because when each is different, you have never played it before, and there is a sequence of 126, that is how you must play. Also, it seemed that I had played through the stiffness, probably just as well with its potential for innuendo as next on the menu was Formby Ladies.

FORMBY LADIES

Formby had literally blossomed since my visit in February, with the yellow of gorse and white of may accompanied by all the bright new greens of the deciduous trees. It looked delightful, even though there was no sunshine. I had reserved a start at the Ladies' Club at 1 PM, but was late. (Memo to the people who put up road signs: if I am going to Formby, I am not aware that I am taking the scenic route to Southport when I come off the M57, am I?) Not terribly late, and with the sparse number of entries in The Secretary's diary, not apparently a problem. 'No, it will be fine now,' she said, 'as long as there is no-one on the 2nd tee.' This seemed odd. If there was anyone on the 2nd tee, it should have been me.

In my hurry to get started, I almost forgot, but managed to add, 'Is there any Squidge about?' 'No, I don't think so.' 'Good. Do you mind my asking, what exactly is Squidge?' 'It's sort of slippery. Maureen,' she said to a player, 'is there any Squidge?' 'No.' 'What is it?' 'A kind of moss.' ' Gets very slippery.' 'Dangerous.' 'Bright green.' 'Dissolves shoe leather...'

There was a sign at the 1st tee, "Warning. Fairways sprayed with fertilizer." I had been going to eat a sandwich as I played, but I went hungry. The course is a scaled-down version of the men's, with fewer elevated areas, but lots of different tees, heather lined fairways, and really nice, flattish greens. It measures 5374 yards, which makes it both par and SSS seventy-one for ladies, but the three par fives are between 415 and 430 yards. It was not really windy, I was driving straight, and putting well. It was a delight to play. From the 7th green, the clubhouse clock is visible, and I fancy I played the first seven holes in a little over forty minutes. Then I came upon a pair of young men, playing genteelly behind three ladies, and the pace slowed. I saw what the young pro had meant about accurate driving. The guys ahead were hitting it close to 300 yards, which was fine if and only if they pointed the club straight... (Mind you, I saw plenty of men on their own course wandering around in the heather, which was pretty thick.)

There was a shorter (literally, and for fewer holes) elevated section than on the men's course, but some of the tee shots posed definite questions about length and accuracy. All the par fours on the back nine were over 300 yards, so it was not a pushover, but I finished with a 74, say 6 over a men's par of sixty-eight, and the ball I started with. I was left with two thoughts, one speculative, and one certain. Possibly, playing here gives a player like me a grasp of what it must be like to be Ernie Els and have a course more or less at your mercy, with just short irons and wedges to greens. You still have to play it, but it is there for the asking. The greens were small, so just hitting them was the equivalent of hitting it close on big ones, but I suppose the difference would still be the relative width of the fairway.[84] Hence, my speculation – but it is nice to be in such control.

The certainty is that, of coastal golf courses of England (a subject upon which I am becoming expert) Formby Ladies' is the best Ladies' course. As for the Squidge, it was nice of them to warn me, but I was just as much in the dark about what to look out for after the warning. Now, that's really unsettling...

---

[84] To hit a 30 yard fairway at a distance of 200 yards, you have an arc of error of about 9 degrees. At 300 yards, the same width of fairway requires accuracy within 6 degrees.

I gave up on *The Good Pub Guide* in this area as a source of accommodation after my experiences in the Wirral and Southport, as I wanted somewhere handy for one of the courses I had to play. I thought there might be good chances of a hotel in Formby, and I decided to turn to good old Google, usually a very present help in trouble. After all, Google had given me 55,000 references for the word squidge, although none was actually helpful. The third was the name of a dead cat, for example. Most were actually created by a web address www. squidge.org. I added the word "golf", and the number reduced to 1,120. I then included "danger", and the total declined to 52, including a reference entitled "A man and his latrine". I wondered if adding "Formby" would give me a reference to a small, dangerous, slippery golfer with a ukulele, but there was nothing.

When I tried "hotel" and "Formby", Google produced 33,200 references, but – and this is remarkable – none of those I chose indicated a single hotel in Formby itself. One offered an establishment in Wallasey which would have been ludicrous, except that I was to play at Wallasey the next morning. It was an unusual place, next to a much bigger, derelict hotel building, with its entrance in a different road from its address. There was a sign apologising for disruption as parts of the floor were being restored to the original Victorian floor tiles, but when I came downstairs in the morning, men were putting in pvcu windows. The landlord was a friendly scouser with an unfortunately loud voice. There was a poster advertising Tranmere Rovers who had been beaten on penalties the previous night in the play off semi-final by none other than Hartlepool. I asked if he supported Rovers, but he did not. He said he spent a lot of time in Milan, and supported A C Milan. Oh well. Two weeks later, Liverpool beat Milan on penalties to win the Champions League, having been 3-0 down at half-time. The hotel was handy for Wallasey Golf Club.[85]

---

[85] I was also served at table by a gorgeous local girl called Maria. This is a joke which only Celia and Jim would get.

WALLASEY

Wallasey Golf Club was magic. I had caught glimpses of it from previous visits to the Wirral, and on arrival this time, but as I walked through the clubhouse, the view from the lounge was of the most fantastic dunes and sandhills, with the 18th fairway funnelling its way along to an elusive, sunken green. I could not wait, but I had to as there were people scheduled ahead of me. When the time came, I played rather hurriedly – after all this time, I still have a little of that "let's get away from the clubhouse" feeling when I am alone. The following wind carried my ball on the full into the furthest fairway bunker – well, it was distinctly beside the fairway in fact, not particularly deep, but small, and what you could call a "sand iron" bunker, because no other club is going to get you out. This is a characteristic of the course; it certainly was of the six bunkers I visited. With my left leg practically behind my back, I just managed to get the ball out, and into a clump of grass from which I could only hack out. An opening six was not a good start to a medal round.

The holes are named, and number two is called Stableford. In 1931, Dr Frank Stableford, captain of the club two years later, devised a form of scoring that would acknowledge the fact that, with the wind against (as it was today), he could not reach this 458 yard hole in two shots, in which case, he reasoned, five was a good score, and deserved some reward. I suppose you could say he had a point. Apart from a few commemorative plaques and the legend "Home of Stableford" on the card and flags, the club does not make much of a fuss of it.

I did not see my first drive, so I hit a provisional, and found both balls, either side of the fairway which doglegs right. I thought I had sliced my second shot, so I played another provisional, off the heel of the club into deep rough and oblivion on the left of the fairway, but I was delighted to see my first ball some 20 yards short of the green. The hole doglegs more than I had thought. My chip-and-run left the ball seven feet six inches from the hole (I measured it); this was a putt I must hole – but I missed. I tried the two-for-one compensation – hole two more balls to cancel the miss – but I still missed. In fact, I missed altogether seven times, and I had to accept that my score was a five, the same number as the hole's stroke index, and therefore worth two Stableford points.

From the elevated 3rd tee, I saw the three men ahead searching the right hand rough. They waved me on. Important to find the fairway, I thought, and the ball started left, but drifted into line on the wind, and hit a downslope as if I had been playing there all my life. If only. They played up to the green, but still called me on. Now to hit the green. My iron shot did, but it was fading, and it kicked into some nearby rough. One of them found it for me as I walked up, not in a good lie. 'Shall I just settle for three more from here?' I asked, meaning to pick up, but he did not get my drift, so I hacked at it, and it flopped out, to about 7 feet 6 inches, I would guess. This time, I made no mistake. As I walked away saying thanks, I fancy I heard the comments: 'I think I'll pick up', and 'Yes, why don't you play alone, and let him play for us?' I did make a mistake from the elevated 4th tee, a straight but great par five next to the shoreline, and found the right hand rough (if you have not formed an impression yet, there is rough on this course). Because of the guys behind, I was obliged to throw another ball down, which I then hacked across the fairway into a bunker, giving cause to a seven, but still a Stableford point. The next hole was the first par three, and three mates of the guys behind invited me through. The tee is shared with the 17th, and when I arrived back at it, it looked really intimidating, but I was in "playing through" mode. All I saw was three men and a green waiting for me. A 7 wood to the back, and this time I asked them to give me two putts and walked on.

From the flatter, inland part of the course you must inevitably see houses and hear traffic, as this is essentially an urban location. In fact, the most penetrating noise known to, and made by humans was in evidence, that of children in a school playground. You can also see the cranes of Liverpool Docks, but apart from that, Wallasey Golf Club is a wonderland. I was having a wondrous time too. I thought my approach to the par five 7th had cleared the bunker I could see, and it had, but there was another lurking behind, which swallowed it. I had to take a stance with my left foot tucked up behind me as if impersonating Long John Silver, and my speculative splash lifted the ball out to run down to about a foot from the hole. As I was playing the 8th, I thought that the course was getting perhaps a little flat. The hole appeared to be named, incongruously, but perhaps after some seafaring tradition, "Hammocks", but I looked again, and it was "Hummocks", and the course stopped being flat again.

I could write a short eulogy on every hole and how I played it. I judged the 10th needed a drive to start left and fade into the middle, and produced one, where a shot down the middle would have faded into trees. I played up the severe slope to the green alright, only to find the flag was seven paces onto a thirty-two pace green with my ball at the back, but I managed the par. The greens were beautiful. The short 12th is one of the most beautifully bunkered greens in English seaside golf, with seven hazards, all probably equally penal. Every hole had something special. If I must find a minor criticism, it would be the back and forth par five 13th and 14th holes. The former was a 544 yard bumpy monster into this wind, the latter a flatter 485 yarder which, with wind assistance I reached in two, only to take my only three-putt of the round. The next hole, called Plateau, is a dogleg right followed by an elevated green, only 351 yards. I inevitably found the middle of three brilliantly placed fairway bunkers. I thinned my escape, usually OK in this situation, but here the ball finished in thick rough on a bank. Hack followed slash, followed by hack, and I was on the green en route to a triple bogey. Still, I loved it.

They say you will know when she comes along, the one for you. In 1975, I met a girl from Mossley Hill, Liverpool which is, as the crow flies, about eight miles from Wallasey Golf Club. This makes Wallasey Golf Club the nearest literally littoral course to Mossley Hill, birthplace and childhood home of my wife. Despite liberal trends, you cannot marry a golf course, not even in California. This may have saved me from a rash decision.

UP THE JUNCTION

On my way to the Golf Club at Wallasey, I came upon the sort of junction which Merseyside planners seem to specialise in. The road I was on bent through 90 degrees before giving way to another road, similarly bending. Close to this point, another road came into mine from the left. A double decker bus, which should have had the right of way, stopped to let me pass.

Celia and I used to joke about Liverpool road junctions. They were never straightforward; there is always at least one extra road joining in, at a different angle from the others, at least one road is a dual carriageway, and the junction is at a bend. There probably used to be trams, as well. The directions are just as bad. As I've noted, to get to Formby, it was clear from my road map that you go to the end of the M57, where you are offered a choice of St Helens & Manchester, Bootle & All Docks, or Scenic route to Southport. I now know that I need the last of these. If I had been local, of course, I would have known that Formby was on the scenic route to Southport, but then I wouldn't have needed the sign to tell me the way, would I?

It was fun leaving via Liverpool, too. The Wallasey tunnel was blocked, so I used the Birkenhead one instead, not without difficulty. I fancy there may be some people still looking for it. When you get through, someone had told me, you follow the signs for M6 North. I did. It looks like a good road system until you are halted at traffic lights which are green for 15 seconds and red for 150 to allow umpteen different traffic flows. But then, you still have to cross over a major traffic stream to head for M6 North. This is actually the traffic heading south through the Wallasey tunnel! Then, with traffic lights every 200 metres, you are routed thoughtfully past Everton football stadium and onto the famed A580 East Lancs road. This has three lanes, but because of re-generation work it is down to one. Further along, it is being resurfaced in both directions, causing mayhem at the intersections which are every half mile. You keep following the blue M6 North signs, and if and only if you are wide awake and very lucky do you spot a left filter with M6 North in green ("M6 South" is in blue on this sign). About three miles on a glorified country lane follow, and finally, you join the M6. Almost immediately, there is a junction, signed to M59 Southport and – wait for it – Liverpool.

The answer to why do so many comedians come from Liverpool is, 'Well, you have to have a sense of humour to live there.' They must have one in the highways' department: 'Why are you signing the traffic that way?' 'Why do you ask?' 'Because I wouldn't go that way myself.' 'Exactly.'

******

To avoid being consumed by simmering road rage – Celia used to call it IDS, not Ian Duncan Smith, one time non-playing captain of the Tory party, but Irritable Dowell Syndrome – I thought it was time to evaluate how I had played so far. Excluding the nine-holer, and subject to the vagaries of my scoring when alone, I had had a sequence of Stablefords as follows: 37, 30, 41, 45, 34.

Adjusting the par fives should perhaps make the 45 at Formby Ladies into a 42, and that could be explained by the shortness of the course. As I was short of length, often I could not drive into trouble when others could, but I still had had to get the ball in the hole, which

I appeared to be doing well. I felt that I had played quite well at Wallasey, particularly out of bunkers, but being in them in the first place was the reason for the poorer score compared to Hartlepool. There was promise, particularly in how I felt out on the course, which was pretty relaxed. After the blow-out at Whitby, I was broken in, wind-wise, as it were.

I was undoubtedly playing well despite lots of motoring, which is not the best preparation for a round of golf, but I have always seemed to play well on a first visit to a course, pips, mulligans etc notwithstanding. I came up with a theory; whatever happens on a hole, you have to forget about it, or at least put it to the back of your mind, in order to play the next hole, because you do not know anything about it. Contrast this with your home course, where after a triple bogey, you are most likely to treat the next hole with contempt. This could explain the seemingly successful habit of a Sherborne member of talking to himself about the shot he wants to hit next. Some people find this nauseating, but it seems to work. Perhaps you do this anyway. I must try it, try and treat each hole as if I have never seen it before. Maybe I should watch the movie 50 First Dates. Whatever, I felt relaxed about things.

Things were also fairly relaxed when I got to Seahouses, the centre of gravity for tourism and commerce on the Northumbrian coast, where I met up with the happy couple whose wedding I had attended three or four weeks earlier. (Actually, it was five days. It just felt like three weeks.) I thought that Seahouses was a fairly naff name, until I remembered that I went to school in a town called Coalville, a memory brought home as I made my way through the disused coal fields to Newbiggin-by-the-Sea.

NEWBIGGIN

Newbiggin-by-the-Sea. How my industrial/ mining school town might have been? If it had been by-the-Sea? Modern, low clubhouse. Advertising beer. Brewery Money? Cheapest green fee in county. A quid less than Seahouses. People's golf.

Seaside fairways. Flat, featureless. Semi-rough dotted white. Daisies. Main stuff likewise yellow. Buttercups.

Ominous white posts, blue tops. For ball spotting, not OB. Also spot walkers; dogs off leads; grazing horses, tethered; motor bikes crossing fairway. People's golf.

Windy. Greens OK. Hard to get ball close in wind. Next hole a few degrees westerly. More into wind. And again, twice. Elevation change. Mounds. 6 and 7 towards aluminium plant. 8 and 9 back by power station. Waved through. Two men behind. Wind strengthening. Fourballs coming out after work. On wrong fairways. People's golf.

Hole 11, called "Prevailing wind". Into its teeth. Stroke 1. Third shot in bunker. First double bogey. Rats. No birdies. Hard to get ball close. In this wind. Hole 12. First par three hole. Get one. Hole 13. Two women behind, in buggy. Hole 14. One left-handed man behind. Play your own course? Scramble bike on shore path. Two girls. Blonde, brunette, no helmets.

Windier. Sun Mountain Speed Cart™ under own steam. On gentle incline. Uphill. Wind blows sound over. Ice cream van, touring housing estate. "Raindrops keep falling on my head". No way. Will be blown out to sea before landing.

Last 3 holes. Wind against. Par – good. Par again – second and last par three. Last Hole. Double bogey. Bugger. That's golf. People's golf.

Newbiggin Golf Club. Founded 1884. I wish my town had had a golf club. Gets in the blood. How good would I be now?

This round followed one at Seahouses, and after this climactic thirty-six hole day, I finally fetched up at the C J's in Gosforth, and you know about the remaining courses. Afterwards, as I drove on to Cumbria and then home, I reflected on the experience: 171 *different* holes in eight days. First, there was too much driving, particularly the trip to Liverpool, but then I wouldn't have done that in normal circumstances; a two centre holiday in the north-east would have been fine, though. Second, though I liked the variety, there was too much change; for eight days, two pairs of good courses played more than once each would have been better. Doing two different clubs in one day – apart from being expensive compared to buying day tickets – leaves little time for digesting the experience. Also, there were so many particular holes that if time had permitted, I would really have liked to play again, once I had seen how they were built. Third, I was particularly pleased with my application on the last two days – the weekend. Having been mostly alone, when I finally had people to talk to, friends I had not seen for a long time, it had rather got in the way of my golf at first. At Goswick, feeling that I had had a poor first nine, I applied myself on the way back, and scored twenty points which could so easily have been twenty-two. Could I remember the feeling and conjure it again?

Finally, I was tired. I could probably do with some rest; something like a week in Cornwall.

17

A WEEK AT TREVOSE

You might think that after such an intensive period I would want a rest from golf, but I knew that I had a lot of writing to do, and I wanted to be somewhere where I could do just that, but also "relieve myself" from writing about the great game with a spot of playing, as and when the need arose. I headed for Trevose. I had played there a total of thirteen times – once in March on a trip to Cornwall with Celia, and twelve subsequent times, being four annual visits with teams from Sherborne for a three day event in the name of the charity CLIC, always held at the beginning of March. On the very first visit, I was invited to join in the members' weekly Stableford and played round with two chaps who were recovering from a family party the previous night, or perhaps they were planning one for the following night. Either way, they were good company, and amongst other things, they explained that Trevose is a resort, a prototype of its kind, with summer houses and holiday accommodation as well as golf and lots of visitors, and thus becomes quite a different type of golf club during the summer months. I hoped it would be quite a different type of weather too, for although we managed to enjoy our trips in early March, it also seemed to be the case that on at least one of the days we had dreadful weather. So, I booked into one of the "cabins" at Trevose for a week in June.

On the way, I recalled the last visit Celia and I had made to Cornwall, when we stayed at Falmouth. I played two golf courses, at Falmouth itself in the south, and West Cornwall on the other side of the peninsula.

Feature	West Cornwall Golf Club	Falmouth Golf Club
Location	Between Hayle and St Ives, North Cornish coast	South West of Falmouth, South Cornish coast
Distance apart	8 km north of Falmouth GC 30 km crow wise	26 km east of West Cornwall GC 30 km crow wise
Ease of finding	High if you spot the sign	Remarkably difficult
Date founded	1889	1894
Yardage	5884	6012
Par	Sixty-nine	Seventy-one
Par fives	494 & 521 yards	531, 526, and 502 yards
Par threes	229 (hole 1), 179, 191, 135, 194	152, 175, 191, 116
Is that the difference?	Yes, there is a comparable range of par fours	… but they seem to look longer here
Space available	Compact	Spacious
Terrain	Bumpy	Sweeping
Changes in elevation	Continuous	Likewise
Changes in playing direction	Frequent	Likewise
Chances ball will be above or below feet	You bet	Depends on fairway – either certain, or low
And uphill/downhill lies?	You bet	Don't even ask
What about the bounce?	Wizard (as in Pinball)	Depends on season
Vegetation	Some patchy scrub No shrubs	Healthy scrub Verdant shrubs and saplings
	Nary a tree	Many mature evergreens

(*continued*)

Feature	West Cornwall Golf Club	Falmouth Golf Club
Any sandhills?	Yes, two or three impressive ones	No
Appearance in summer	Brownish	Green and pleasant
Winter condition	Probably drains wells	Possibly muddy
Overall impression	Like playing golf on the surface of the moon	Landscaped by Capability Brown
Confusing layout	Yes	Not really
Duck at the shout of 'Fore!'?	Definitely	Mostly not necessary
Shared territory?	For much of first nine you wait for players on other holes	No. Fairways well defined
Greens	Roundish Grassy but fast Some tricky	Long, plum-shaped Slick, but not too pacy Potential for nasty pin positions
Number of greens with steps for access	None	One
Number of greens adjacent to churchyards	One	None
Times churchyard in play (as OB)	Three	None
Number of railway lines running through course	One, first cutting, then embankment	None
Number of holes with sea views	18 (approx)	6 (approx)
Number of holes contiguous with shoreline	Five	One
Minimum height above sea level	15–20 feet	80–100 feet (guess)

(*continued*)

Feature	West Cornwall Golf Club	Falmouth Golf Club
Aspect	90 degrees of coastline	180 degrees of coastline
Views east	Working town of Hayle, but no longer hearty. Rusting buildings. Headland with pylons, strewn with buildings as if some giant lost his temper at Monopoly	Impressive town of Falmouth, looking wealthy and well-maintained. Inland and beyond lots of housing, to Carrick Roads,[86] inlet of sea
Views west	Pleasant aspect of leeward side of St Ives, with "The Island" beyond	Superb untouched coastline, possibly as far as Lizard Point
Wind effects	Exposed. Best in easterly?	Some shelter. Worst in easterly?
Result of comparison	Buy house in Praze-an-Beeble Join this club…	Or Prospidnick (both equidistant) and join this club

The contrast between the terrains for these two courses, and also my experiences of playing there, set me back to thinking about the unanswered question of what makes a great golf course. In the context of this book, this has been outstanding since the consecutive visits to Seaton Carew and Berwick back in Number 4 (although rather less time elapsed in reality). There are quite a few wind farms in Cornwall, and they do not do a great deal for the landscape. Perhaps they are justi-fied in the name of renewable energy, but people tend not to want them "in their back yard" as the expression goes, but then, neither would they want a coal mine. At least with wind farms, you do not have to send men underground to extract the energy. On the other hand, how much energy do you get from a wind turbine? I have seen them station-ary, to which I address this question: if in a normal state, they rotate

---

[86] Don't ask me, I haven't a clue.

253

and produce energy, then when they are constrained not to move, where does the energy come from to stop them? Is it being wasted?

Anyway, the point about these windmills is this. They are indeed mills; they are not dark, because they always seem to be white, but there is something devilish or satanic about them and, as William Blake would have noted were he here to see them, they are in England's green and pleasant land.

Now, for a number of years at home, from time to time we would buy a selection of wines and ask guests to help us "taste" them. You have probably come across all the sophistication which can go into wine tasting, ending in the expectoration of the sample. That has always struck me as odd. Isn't the ultimate point of wine to drink it? In our house, we soon abandoned complex measures which amongst other things make comparisons difficult, and came down to two significant criteria – "wineness", and "drinkability". The first is a single measure of the structure of the wine, and the latter sums up the experience of drinking it. A Gran Reserva Rioja will score high on wineness, but you probably wouldn't want to drink your way through a bottle while watching a cricket match, whereas a simple Valpolicella would do well for recreational purposes but struggle to complement a roast sirloin or game pie.

So, here are the two criteria for golf courses: golfability, and green-and-pleasantness. Hopefully, after such a contorted preamble, they speak for themselves.

Trevose definitely offers both. In June, the sun does not set until around 10 PM, and it descends gloriously across Constantine Bay beyond the golf course, finally setting over the headland. On the first couple of days I played in the evenings, but then switched to 7.30 AM. Given that my cabin was almost part of the clubhouse, this option offered the minimal intrusion of modern life before I set off onto the course, just ablutions, breakfast, and a walk to the 1st tee. No radios, cars, traffic, or people even. There was warm sunshine, and a beautiful golf course, and not too much wind. During the course of the week what wind there was changed direction a number of times which added interest, but my principal objective was in trying to "feel" my way around, particularly on the greens.

The greens are big, not flat, and fast. In March, they scare us to death when contrasted with our inland winter putting conditions. Here in June they did not seem quite so quick – but I have spent enough years on the fast greens of The Bucks to believe that I am readily adaptable to speed. What was definitely the case was their fidelity. Start the ball on a certain line, and that is the line it follows and, from 10 feet inwards, don't think of "hitting" the ball, just start it moving. From 20 yards away, there is no possible means of calculating how hard to stroke the ball, you just have to feel it. It is magic when it turns out right, and if you can keep repeating the task, it seems to reinforce belief in the rest of the game. I could even feel how I was going to hit my iron shots onto the greens. Golf is a mind, body and spirit game, and on these mornings, the spirit was leading the way.

I had a 39 and two 38s on the front nine, one of which included three consecutive birdies, but sadly I never managed to sustain the enhanced state for a whole round. Whether it is possible, or whether the tension would mount, I cannot say, but in one sense it is meaningless since it would be a solo round anyway. Trevose appears to have the admirable policy of no fourballs allowed before 11 AM, but for reasons of longstanding friendship, three groups were allowed out from the 10th tee during the week I was there, and somehow their appearance and ultimately my having to wait for them broke the spell. I actually complained mildly to the management on the last day, despite my non-status as a lone player, as I followed a group of four which hit three fairways out of sixteen attempts. The players had bona fides, I was told, coming from places like Hunstanton. I have played at Hunstanton, and I can tell you that if these men had been as far off line there as they were here, they would have drowned! Two things emerged from my complaint – they had actually kept the pace they were allocated, so the problem was mine for being too fast, and they had been on a big night out for their last evening!

Having played Trevose intensively, I sought to summarise our experiences playing in March, tempered with a little summer sun:

TREVOSE

The wind seems to be capable of blowing from just about any quarter, and presents a challenge, as does the layout of the Championship course at Trevose Golf and Country Club:

Hole 1 – 440 yards Par four Index 8 Direction W

There is nothing really intimidating about the opening drive, if you ignore the people milling round the elevated tee next to the putting green and those looking on from the clubhouse as the starter calls out your name over the PA system. The challenge is to thread a long second shot between grassy mounds to run down to the green.

Derek's tip: The road in front of the tee looks nasty but it's not far and downhill, so even a half-decent top gets over.

Hole 2 – 359 yards Par four Index 14 Direction W

Pretty straightforward par four if you hit the fairway. KPMG often birdies it, emphasising its false promise of routine golf for the remainder of the round.

Derek's tip: If you line up for the green, then notice that the fairway is to the right and try and compensate, you usually end up in the right hand rough. Well, I do, anyway.

Hole 3 – 156 yards Par three Index 16 Direction N

A great par three across a valley, with a "half saddle" green throwing the ball in from the left. KPMG also birdies this, but only in the practice round before the two spot competition starts.

Derek's tip: If you miss the bunker on the right, the ball runs miles down the bank, leaving an unpleasant wedge shot. Better to risk the sand.

Hole 4 – 465 yards Par five Index 6 Direction N by NW

One of my all-time favourites (if only it were eleven yards longer and a "proper" par five). If you can miss the big bunker to the right and drive up onto the ridge, you have a nice fairway wood shot which might end up on the green. It seems easier for being played to a marker post over a ridge than a clear target.

Derek's tip: the second bunker on the left is even deeper than the first. Usually, it's a Hamlet cigar job. If you're bringing a picnic, this is the spot to enjoy it, right down by the beach.

Hole 5 – 445 yards Par four Index 2 Direction E by NE

Dogleg left round an out of bounds, uphill to an elevated green with slopes that don't guarantee a par even on the rare occasions when you reach it.

Derek's tip: I usually pick up on this hole.

Hole 6 – 319 yards Par four Index 18 Direction SW

Innocuous short par four, except we never seem to come away with more than three points in a best-two-scores-to-count round.

Derek's tip. Try to miss the fairway right. The rough on the left is terminal.

Hole 7 – 367 yards Par four Index 4 Direction SE

What a classic hole! A good drive gets reasonably close to this magically contoured green, where the pin position, and getting close to it, is critical, but difficult.

Derek's tip: Club selection is vital. Go short, risk straining and find the front bunker, or go long, hit it easy, and bounce over the back?

Hole 8 – 149 yards Par three Index 12 Direction SW

Elevated tee shot to an elevated, but fairly flat green. Gives you a much needed chance of something.

Derek's tip: If you manage to find your ball in light rough and not the water in the valley to the right, there is quite a lot of green to work with for your second. Be bold!

Hole 9 – 454 yards Par five Index 10 Direction E

Downhill drive, uphill second, decidedly elevated green. We've never seen anyone reach it in two, so probably don't try, but leave a comfortable third shot.

Derek's tip: Keep left, and you have a good chance of par. Go right, and you have a good chance of hitting the bank, and getting thrown off the green to the left.

Hole 10 – 472 yards Par four Index 3 Direction NW

Fabulous driving hole if you hit it straightish. Long second over a stream to a two tier-green. The tiers are left and right, not front and back. From the wrong one, three putts are a formality.

Derek's tip: Given three putts, this plays as a par six, so don't lurch at your second shot and top it into the water.

Hole 11 – 197 yards Par three Index 7 Direction NW

Elevated green with sloping front that throws anything short back off. Wind against, the club choice is driver, driver, or driver. Expect to be short.

Derek's tip: I don't think I remember this hole.

Hole 12 – 440 yards Par four Index 1 Direction NE by N

Fine par four where you're likely to be chipping to the awkward green to have a chance.

Derek's tip: It is actually possible to play this hole via all three bunkers up the left hand side.

Hole 13 – 504 yards Par five Index 15 Direction SE

Downhill alongside ditch and out of bounds left. Depending on the wind, the first reasonable birdie chance of the back nine.

Derek's tip: Actually, if I can get a drive away, I quite fancy this hole. Providing I'm not already knackered.

Hole 14 – 307 yards Par four Index 13 Direction W by SW

The back nine's answer to the 6th, though more bunkers. Usually, the same result.

Derek's tip: I usually forget that there is a second line of bunkers behind the first. Something of an oversight if playing a pitch and run second.

Hole 15 – 330 yards Par four Index 17 Direction NE by N

This is the third of three holes which should be known as Hallelujah Corner for their relative ease. Tricky green, however.

Derek's tip: It is amazing how a bunker as small as the one on the right of the fairway can gather so many balls.

Hole 16 – 206 yards Par three Index 9 Direction SW

The only par three at ground level. Despite the length, a chance of par.

Derek's tip: A bad slice actually finishes on the 12th fairway, giving a good lie for the second shot.

Hole 17 – 375 yards Par four Index 5 Direction SE

If you can drive over the fairway mound, there is a relatively short shot over the stream in front of the green which slopes nastily from back to front. You need to be below the hole. If you can't clear the ridge, we suggest laying up, remembering the golden rule of laying up.[87]

Derek's tip: I usually lay up to leave a "simple wedge to the middle of the green". Unfortunately, there is no such thing.

Hole 18 – 430 yards Par four Index 11 Direction SE

Uphill, and always longer than it seems. A tough closing par.

Derek's tip: My only chance of getting up in two is a high bounce off the road that crosses about 90 yards in front of the green. I haven't succeeded in hitting it yet, though I scared a cyclist last time.

(With thanks to Derek, who represents our collective misfortunes over the years playing in the CLIC event.)

The total experience of spending a week in Trevose was great. Despite the men from Hunstanton, I enjoyed everything; the golf, the writing, food and drink, and I was made to feel really welcome and part of the Trevose community, one of the few areas in the land which is free from mobile phone signals, and where people still talk to others that they are with, therefore. If I had been making a TV documentary, the high spot would have been the replacement of a washer on my Sun Mountain Speed Cart™, which involved several members of the maintenance crew, most of their tools, and a man who had come to read the electricity meters. As a single occupant, the accommodation was perhaps a little overpriced, but it was more than compensated for by the cost of the golf. If you can, keep this fact secret. We don't want them to start charging more.

In assessing the overall experience of a round of golf, there is a third factor besides the golfability of the course and the green-and-pleasantness of the environment, which is the amount of "click", or what in the context of a relationship one would call the chemistry of it all. Some people may allow this to cloud their judgment of the first two factors, just as many a romance has proceeded despite being formed on what to onlookers is decidedly unstable foundation. I have tried not to do that in this book, but if my judgment has been so clouded, I apologise to anyone who feels that I have somehow misrepresented their beloved golf course.

At the end of the day, there are three dimensions: mind, body and spirit, with which we play the game, and if "click" is chemistry, then golfability could be the physics of the game, and biology the equivalent of the green-and-pleasantness of the land. The more usual order of these would be physics, chemistry and biology and, if you will, throw in a little mathematics, but hopefully not too much. We want to keep the scores down.

As I drove away from Trevose, vowing to return – though whether it will be in March again now that I have tasted June remains to be seen – I wondered if I could draw any scientific lessons from the week. I looked back at those special moments when I had been playing well. I wanted to condense the feelings I had then into a single thought, to carry round with me for future times.

First there is *concentration*, but the word carries with it a feeling of intensity, which is not right for golf. In the days when there used to be the Ring at Twickenham, and you watched the rugby from about scrum height, I once saw into the eyes of the great Irish player Mike Gibson as he tracked the ball and his man. I had never seen anything so fierce. It was probably the look that Mike Tyson's unsuccessful challengers saw in his eyes, split seconds before he despatched them. Such intensity is fine when you are moving, but it kills if you are standing still. The kind of concentration needed for golf is to be *calm*, if that is possible.

Actually, you might say you need *relaxed* concentration, which is clearly a contradiction in terms. Coming up behind the fourballs spoiled the *rhythm* of the round as I ceased to be relaxed. But, though I don't like it, it is possible to maintain a relaxed rhythm when forced to play slowly, say when playing as a two amongst threes, if someone fails to turn up for a medal. Also, you only need to take one look at Ernie Els to see what a relaxed rhythm does for a swing.

The next point was about hitting the target. Generally, I was in the groove off the tee, but I noticed that if I made exaggerated allowance

---

[87] When laying up, lay up; that is, do not take too much club and hit a nicely timed shot into the hazard.

for the wind I would sometimes hit nasty hooks or slices, because the stance was plain wrong. The question of alignment is perhaps more complex than it might sound. The less frequent periods when I was hitting greens reminded me of the importance of *accurate alignment*. If you do not set up to hit the green in the first place, you are unlikely to hit it. As Harvey Pennick says, take dead aim.

Finally, there is the question of getting the ball into the hole. The greens at Trevose are scrupulously fair. The ball goes where you hit it. They are also fairly big. I tried to recall the feeling when I was rolling the ball up to the hole from 60 feet to 6 inches or, if I should have misjudged the line, rolling the ball into the hole from 4 feet. Thinking of alliteration, I called this a purple patch, but I don't think "purple putting" does the trick. You will notice that when a tournament player hits a green, he gives the club to his caddie, who gives him a putter, and he walks up to the green. I once overheard someone say he did not know why the players do this. I am sure I do; they want to feel the putter, and it to feel part of them, for as long as possible. Putting is about not just looking at, but *feeling* the green as one unit, from the hole through the green to the ball through the putter to the head. The putter needs to become part of the golfer. What one needs is a *prehensile putter*.

So, these are the four elements of golf: the state of one's being; swinging the club; hitting in the desired direction; and getting the ball into the hole. Calm concentration; relaxed rhythm; accurate alignment; prehensile putter. I thought I might combine these concepts into one useful acronym. Then I decided not to.

18

HOLING OUT

As Norfolk was where it all started, so it turned out that Norfolk would play host to the grand finale. This was not any deliberate plan, but rather a failure to recognise just how far England bulges out into the North Sea. Neff and I went on a trip where we stayed at Aldeburgh in Suffolk and ventured as far as Gorleston, but we called off the visit to Great Yarmouth & Caister when we worked out what time we would get back to London, even assuming good traffic conditions, on a Sunday evening. As I organised excursions to take in the other outstanding venues for my collection, so it became clear that Great Yarmouth & Caister was going to be left on its own, and would be the final, 78th course. I could try and justify this by claiming that if one calls it Yarmouth (which East Midlanders do) then it is alphabetically last, but that theory is rather ruined when they answer the phone "Caister Golf Club". But, who needs justification? I only needed a plan to go there – but first, let me tell you about the other golf courses in Norfolk we have yet to meet.

ROYAL CROMER

Quite why Royal Cromer Golf Club should be ennobled by its prefix when its neighbour is plain Sheringham is not clear. Certainly in their heyday as north Norfolk's "twin" resorts, Cromer had the greater reputation, with hotels to match – and we talk of Cromer crabs, though they also catch them from Sheringham. When it comes to golf courses, comparisons are invidious, but it would not be the case that Cromer is in any sense superior. Arguably, Sheringham is better endowed with more consistent land.

From the coast road, Royal Cromer looks green and lush, because that part of the course on the landward side, which is below the cliff top, is just that. The seaward holes up on the slopes and the top of the cliff are bumpy and rather dusty, leaving no-one in doubt of the effects of the east wind. It may also be the north wind, for this part of the coast looks out to sea due north, and the locals claim that the wind comes straight down from the Arctic without touching land en route. In the days when we used to stay in Sheringham, Mank and I would alternate our games between the two courses, until later on we embraced Hunstanton at Cromer's expense. No-one in their right mind would stay at Sheringham and not play there. When I started making winter visits to the area, I found the lower lying areas at Cromer to be somewhat muddy, so I tended to go elsewhere. Oh, and there was Larry.

In those days I was not at all adept, when playing alone, at giving out body signals saying "Please don't expect me to join up with you", and I was a sitting duck. I even heard Larry approaching up the 3rd hole chuntering to himself – 'You knew it was only a wedge, stupid _____ing prat', as I stumbled along the 4th. He scarcely paused to let me join him as he carried on cursing what I sometimes thought were quite good shots. Usually, people comment positively on their partner's shots, but not Larry, who was merely negative about his own. Well, not merely negative, he was scathing, in fact. He also walked quickly, a fact on which I commented. 'Yes,' he said, 'and you know what, I've got two artificial knees.' Apparently it was somehow less of an all-round effort to walk quickly than to stand for longer periods.

By this time we had reached the cliff holes on the first half, where it would help to have a mountain goat as a caddie. I asked him why he was playing alone. 'Always do. Need the exercise. Had a heart attack. Look at you. Wrong _____ing club again, you _____ing _____.' On the tee of the rather enticing sharply downhill short 9th hole, he showed me a bracelet he was wearing. 'Ever seen one of them? It's to warn paramedics not to give me cardio-vascular massage.'[88]

'Great,' I thought, 'here I am a mile or so from the clubhouse with a man I don't know who doesn't want to be resuscitated after he has a heart attack. If he finally hits a shot that satisfies him, he might have one, as well.' It turned out that the bracelet signified that he had had his

---

[88] I think that's what he said. It was a long time ago.

chest opened (literally) for surgery, and any attempt to "pump-start" his heart would only cave his chest in. Apparently most people would not have survived the attack he had had, but he was quite fit, having been a PE teacher. That and the fact he was "a ____ing stubborn bastard", as he put it.

He didn't bother to play holes 10 and 11, par fives below the cliff which return you to more or less the same spot we were at. 'No ____ing point, going down there just to come back.' I thought it would be churlish to mention that the whole course in fact both started and ended at the clubhouse, so instead I referred back to Larry's various medical conditions. 'Is that why you play alone?' I ventured. 'Nah, it's because I'm a ____ing miserable bastard.' And, he spelt bastard with only four letters, the first of which was "c".

There wasn't much to say after that. Whoever first said "Happy as Larry" I wonder? I should ____ing cocoa!

******

GORLESTON

My abiding first memory of Gorleston Golf Club is of an extraordinarily wide clubhouse, with the pro shop at the opposite side from the car park, and a series of treks between shop, car, changing rooms, coffee lounge and toilets before play began. Outside the clubhouse, there is Norfolk's answer to the *campus martius*, a wide flat plain. I estimate (using the course planner as a guide) that it is about 300 yards wide, after which there are cliffs and the North Sea. It stretches south along the cliff for just under a mile, getting narrower in the process. What is clear from the course planner however is not so obvious from outside the clubhouse. The 1st tees are there, but instead of the usual echelon formation, here the whites, yellows, and reds are side by side. This adds to the illusion of an already wide 1st fairway which is made doubly so by its proximity to the 9th, travelling in the opposite direction. It then gets very confusing if people are playing the 10th, as the tee is in the corner beyond the pro shop, and the fairway stretches across the 1st, and past the clubhouse at an angle of about 30 degrees. So as you wait at the 1st you may see as many as five groups in front of you, ranged out in formation, moving in different directions. The rest of the course takes on a more conventional layout – up the middle, back down the side, over to the other side (hole 9), up the other side, back down the middle. I am sure you can imagine it.

Can you also imagine circumstances when we would welcome fog? Neff and I could not previously, but we did here. It was an exceptionally hot August day and whether it was actually fog or low cloud we were unsure. It did not obscure our view, but it stayed at a nice height to keep the sun off. It probably drove the people on the beaches wild with annoyance, particularly as it was a Saturday, but we appreciated it. The story of our golf is also somewhat obscured. Neff was having one of his dog days, the dog in question being a lurcher. As I have observed, it is common amongst people who are unfortunate enough never to have had the time or opportunity to learn the real rudiments of a golf swing that they will tilt, not turn. Increasing energy put into strenuous efforts to make contact with the ball coupled with decreasing confidence in the outcome turns a tilt into a lurch. As his team's line-out jumper, Neff needed his lifters to hold him down on this occasion.

But, he is a game dog, and we had a sort of match, thanks to the flexible "self-tapping"[89] handicap system of "go two up, give a shot, and three up, two shots". Neff started with a stroke a hole, and the scores went as follows:

	Neff	Unk	Result	Match
1.	6	5	Half	All square
2.	Blob	5	U W	U +1
3.	9	5	U W	U +2 (N now gets 2 shots)
4.	4	3	N W	U +1
5.	Blob	4	U W	U +2
6.	Blob	5	U W	U +3 (N now gets 3 shots)

---

[89] I have heard of "self-tapping" screws. I have no idea what the term means, but I like the sound of it.

	Neff	Unk	Result	Match
7.	4	3	N W	U +2 (back to 2)
8.	5	5	N W	U +1 (back to 1)
9.	6	5	Half	U +1

At the turn, Unk has scored 19 Stableford points off 12. Neff, playing off 30, has scored 10 points. Neff is 1 down.

The match proceeded

	Neff	Unk	Result	Match
10.	7	5	U W	U +2
11.	4	3	N W	U +1
12.	7	7(!)	N W	All square
13.	6	3	U W	U +1
14.	8	6	U W	U +2
15.	Blob	5	U W	U +3
16.	5	7	N W	U +2
17.	8	4	U W	U wins 3 and 1
18.	6	5		

It was closer than it seemed. If Neff had gone 8, 5 rather than 5, 8 on 16 and 17, he would have lost only 1 down. Total points Unk 35, Neff 20.

I think you can see that this format makes for good competition. Just be careful to whom you suggest it. It is most condescending.

Whether because of the sea fret or not, Neff and I failed to notice that when we arrived at the 8th tee, we had just played the eastern-most golf hole in Britain. I am indebted to the course planner for this information, which seeks to corroborate the fact by stating that there is no land between the 8th tee and the North Pole. That might be so, and interesting with it – maybe Santa lands his sleigh here in emergencies – but what does it have to do with being easterly? There is no land between Toygunen in Magadanskaya Oblast in NE Siberia and the North Pole, but it is longitude 175 degrees west. Do I detect a Com-mittee at work?

Having said that the course was conventional after the start, it isn't quite. After number 12, you walk across the 15th fairway, through a gap in the hedge, and into a field with spinneys in the middle, where you play a dogleg right of 375 yards round them. Then, you play a dogleg right 400 yards round the other side of the spinneys, go back through the gap, and walk back to the 15th tee, a par five which takes you past what looks like a perfectly serviceable-looking but disused fairway. Committee?

******

HUNSTANTON

Here are eighteen things I remember about Hunstanton Golf Club.

1.   The first time we played, Mank and I wore just short of the 1st green. He putted, and we watched as the ball went up towards the hole, past it, and off the green the other side.

2.   Now it was my turn. I did the self-same thing.

3.   This green is 37 yards long, the third longest on the course, and possibly slightly uphill.

4.   A ridge runs through the course, with a number of strategically positioned benches for interested spectators. I have seen them blown over by the wind (the benches).

5.   One November, we played using tee pegs to protect the very dry fairways. Even so, the 427 yard 5th hole seemed about 100 yards longer than it is deemed to measure.

6.   This hole (Number 6) is only 339 yards, to a plateau green, the sort of plateau that you might expect to see pterodactyls landing on. We christened it the "catflap" hole, after I took six, getting on in two and four-putting from 5 feet, and Mank took nine, with only one, curling putt. He "hit" the green a few times, but failed to stay on it. It is 35 yards long, but only 15 wide.

7.   This is a great 168-yarder with another plateau green, not so severe at the sides, but excavated at the front to form a bunker fronted with railway sleepers. From inside the trap, you cannot see out, as it were. All you need is an anemometer to measure the wind speed and a set of Duckworth-Lewis tables to select the right club.

8. If the wind is in the north-east quarter, you are pleased to reach this green because (a) it is 506 yards into the teeth of the wind, and (b) apart from a par three and the catflap hole, everything else so far has been wind against. Things can only improve from here onwards. Conversely, if the wind has been following, and you haven't got at least 20 Stableford points already, take advantage of the nearby lane, and call for a taxi to get you back to the clubhouse.

9. A man once played The Lodger's ball on this hole, and ignored our comments. My hapless partner was obliged to run after him, whereupon he turned and said angrily, 'Well, why did you put it there?' Apart from being rude, this was a stupid question. The Lodger doesn't use other people's fairways on purpose...

10. ...we were playing the 10th hole. The course, though high on golfability does not rate particularly on green-and-pleasant-ness, even as linksland, but this is my favourite corner...

11. ...but not The Lodger's. Once again upset at the injustice of it all, he flung his favourite 4 iron at the ground, whereupon the shaft snapped into two. This was the first – and only – time he has ever thrown a club.

12. Purists would dislike this classic linksy hole. Unless you hit a very good drive, your second shot is blind to the edge of a ridge where you have to hope it will run down nicely to the "bucket" green...

13. ...and this appears to be the hole with no fairway, blind over the ridge. Downwind you may run out of fairway; upwind, you may end up short of the green amongst mounds which may be modelled on the Ural Mountains. According to folklore, this is the first higher ground to be found east of Beeston Stump in Sheringham.

14. This 3rd hole over the ridge is a 221 yard blind shot. People leaving the green used to oscillate the marker post to alert the group behind (no bell would be heard in certain winds) but now there is a push-button system of red and green lights!

15. This is my favourite par five, with a "tunnel" fairway alongside the ridge. People up on the 15th tee can look like Apaches or Cherokees.

16. This 188 yard hole is famous for being completed in one stroke by a player in the Eastern Counties Foursomes in 1974 *on three consecutive days*. I wonder what his partner said?

17. Twice he used a 6 iron, and once a 1 iron. That's what the wind can do.

18. There is a straggly line of beach huts to the right of the 18th fairway. At 7 PM the sun is well over the sea – in the west.[90] But this is the east coast!

And so, the end was near. There was no need to think about a plan; it was a sacred and undeniable truth that The Lodger – the man with whom I had honed my golf game in La Manga, with whom I had pioneered winter visits for English seaside golf, not only to Norfolk, but one year when the eastern side of the country was frozen, to Lyme Regis and Bridport – would have to be there, so I summoned him from retirement (only temporary, I trust). We fixed up a date well in advance and, using *The Good Pub Guide* – what else – I booked us into the Fisherman's Return at Winterton-on-Sea.

En route I booked myself into the Rose & Crown at Tring, which I located from the "lucky dip" section of the *Guide*. It turned out to be a three star hotel, practically unoccupied, with no native English speaking staff. There was a cavernous, empty restaurant, and a miserable smoky bar where you could take meals. It did not seem as clean as it might have been. Only the price reflected the three star status of the place. Will someone please tell the correspondents of *The Good Pub Guide* that while a Pub may also be a Hotel in so far as it has bedrooms etc, a Hotel is not a Pub if its reception area is bigger than its bar. I could go on, but I suppose this experience was in keeping with tradition, though it certainly was not Innkeeping with tradition.

I am trying to remember how I felt, and I think I was quite excited, but the tension within me became a little frazzled as I tried to negotiate the east-west road systems through Hertfordshire and Bedfordshire. Am I glad I live in Dorset! Apart from that, nothing in my life quite compared with what this achievement was going to feel like. This is not to say that it was necessarily the greatest, just that it was incomparable. I might perhaps have recorded things differently if I had known at the time of this final expedition that the book would be published,

---

[90] According to me. According to the weather vane on the clubhouse, it is due north!

but I did not. Thus, I was actually on the verge of finishing the journey. I travelled in hope, and duly arrived.

GREAT YARMOUTH & CAISTER

I arrive at the car park of Great Yarmouth & Caister Golf Club to wonder if I have come to the right sort of course. Dominating the surroundings are the white rails of a racecourse. This is not the only golf course to share land with a racecourse, but it is the only one by the sea, and the clubhouse is in the vee where the round course joins the straight, about five furlongs out. The Lodger is already there, announcing that he has a new swing, new clubs, but has not played for ten months. We also discuss balls, and I hand him a few spares, just in case.

The 1st hole plays across the racecourse, and there is a very strong wind in our faces. I hit a decent drive which the wind moves into the left hand rough, but we see it bounce OK. The Lodger hooks one mightily on the wind, and hits his mulligan somewhere which I won't mention for legal reasons. We set off, but though most of the rough is innocuous, there are patches of really thick stuff, and there is no sign of my ball, not to mention either of The Lodger's. Given the significance of the occasion, we go back to the tee, to start again. This time, I hook one. Mulligan. This follows the line of my first, but I find it, and hit a very good iron onto the green, and hole the six footer for a three, five or seven depending on how strict you want to be. The Lodger fails a third time to find his ball.

The wind is blowing across hole 2, but our slicing balls just manage to stay in play. My opponent hits his second just short of the green. With all my experience of seaside golf, I show just what I have learnt – nothing – as I slice two balls off the course. The Lodger wins the hole with a fine par to my eight. Hole 3 changes direction again, and the wind is off our right shoulders. After watching the Lodger hit another ball off the course, I switch to a Pro V1x which I proceed to cream. Unfortunately, I cream it left of the fairway, and it goes the way of the brand-new Srixons I started with, as does The Lodger's second, which disappears into a deep watercourse crossing the fairway. Are we just playing badly, or is this course quite tight? The Lodger loses another ball in the ankle high gorse to the left of the 4th hole which, when we

270

finally reach the green, features bunkers lined with railway sleepers. I have seen them before at the front of a bunker, but here and elsewhere on the course they are all the way round. There could be some very interesting bounces to be had.

Finally, on the 5th hole, I get my first par, my opponent gets a net par for a half, and we both finish the hole with the ball we started with. I am actually quite worried. We have so far lost eleven balls between us, and though we know that we get back to the clubhouse at the 10th green, what kind of ignominious end to an epic journey will it be if we run out of balls? I suspect this is bothering The Lodger too, as he appears to be ball hunting, reminiscent of my father in his prime. The other thing that worries me as we switch to the "seaward" side of the course is the caravan park. It is not at all pleasant to look at but more to the point, it is between the course and the shore, and if it continues all the way, then it will disqualify the course. This will be the biggest anticlimax imaginable, running out of balls on an ineligible course. However, with the wind behind us, at least we start to play a bit. The 6th measures only 256 yards to a plateau green which I reach with my provisional. The Lodger is short and right, but he plays an exquisite pitch – his trademark La Manga shot played with a wedge which pitches short and runs up – on this occasion to just outside gimme range. He holes it nicely. Easy game. I meanwhile find my first ball – a Pinnacle which I would be quite happy to lose – in some short gorse. Either this is a bonsai strain, or the wind is so bad around here that not even gorse grows to its full height.

It makes the course awkward because you can lose your ball in it without knowing it was there, and when you reach what you guess to be your landing area, it is difficult to judge where you are in relation to the tee. But it is easier downwind, and we continue to play some golf. The 180 yard 7th has a 47 yard green with a step, down which the Lodger has to putt. His ball comes to a halt on the slope, and we swear that the wind is stronger than gravity. My topped 5 wood second to the 466 yard 8th finishes pin high. The wind is strong indeed.

Thus settled down, we pass the 10th green without resorting to an emergency dash for more ammunition, and as we walk down the 11th fairway, the line of caravans – there must be several hundred, all about two metres apart – finally comes to an end, leaving an area of dunes between the course and the shore to confirm that this really is my last literally littoral links. This end of the course is bumpier, and there are some interesting holes, but the wind – and perhaps for me the relief from anxiety – is taking its toll. The Lodger is tiring, but also happy

271

when he hits two consecutive good fairway woods on the upwind par five 13th. The par five 15th is downwind, and surely offers a chance even at 534 yards, and with what appears to be a bomb crater in front of the green, but I fail to use the fairway, and take six. It is time to concentrate; I do not expect to go out in a blaze of glory, but neither do I want to finish with a whimper. The 16th is 400 yards into the teeth of the wind. The Lodger tries to play it down the middle of the racecourse, which is a mistake. Everyone knows the going is better on the stand rails. I am on the fairway, and I nail a 3 wood which is blessed with first-time visitor's luck and threads its way between bunkers to the front edge from where I get down in two. Par. Now the 17th, 187 yards in a ten o'clock wind to a green in the edge of some woodland. My 3 wood finds the target. Two putts, another par. So finally to the closing hole, played out of the trees, slight dogleg across the racecourse, 375 yards, wind off right shoulder. Concentrate! My drive goes over the right hand trees. 'Tiger line,' says the Lodger hopefully, but when we get closer, there is ominous rough. The charm that is keeping this ball in play in still active though, but I can only hack it onto the racecourse. My third shot finds the green, but I face a 30 foot putt. In dramatic closing hole fashion, The Lodger putts out to leave the stage to me and the gallery (him), and tends the flag. I miss. Well, what did you expect? This is a true story, you know.

And so to the Fisherman's Return, with such mixed feelings that could only begin to be appreciated fully with the assistance of the products of Messrs Adnams & Co of Southwold. This was a splendid little pub, with just three bedrooms, at the top of the most vertical staircase I have ever come across. The mixture within the feelings is perhaps reflected in the common question asked by sports journalists, which goes as follows:

Interviewer: 'Colin, I am sure it has not sunk in yet that you have finally won your first major, but how does it feel to know that you have finally won your first major?'

Colin: 'I dunno, Steve, it hasn't sunk in yet.'

That was it. It hadn't sunk in.

'So,' asked The Lodger at breakfast the next morning, 'how do you follow that?' How about a hole in one? Sportsmen and women these days not only warm up before an event, but also warm down after it, and there is certainly only one way to follow up a climactic golf trip like this – with more golf. We called in at an attractive nine-hole course at Mundesley and, more or less as I played my tee shot to the 4th hole, The Lodger called out, 'Good grief, I think that was a hole in one!' I thought this a little unlikely. True, I was playing a par three, but it was 200 yards and the green was out of sight in a hollow. My companion had been in fact watching the 1st hole close by, where a badly struck tee shot had bounded up well left of the target, bounced right and run sharply across the sloping green, hit the flagstick, and dropped. It had all happened in a bit of a blur, and he could not be sure, but there was no sign of a ball elsewhere.

The Lodger then played his tee shot, which went off the toe at about 60 degrees to the required line, so while he went over to play a second shot, I remained behind. The two players on the 1st walked forward, one into a gorse-filled gully in front of the green, and the other over the green to the area where the ball that had been seen would have ended had the hole not intervened. He looked around for a while, but obviously did not spot anything, all of which left me in an interesting position. What should I, unsighted colleague of someone who might have seen, but could not be certain, that the ball had gone into the hole, say, if anything? Eventually, I called out, 'Try looking in the hole.' At first, I did not think he had heard me, but he was actually moving, albeit slowly, with what I can only call reluctant enthusiasm, towards the hole. Possibly a small boy, being so excited at being announced winner of a competition that he immediately wet his trousers, might have walked forward to claim his prize in a similar fashion. After an age, he reached the hole, looked in, and raised both thumbs to me. He did not remove the ball, obviously wanting to show his mate.

It occurred to us later, that if the gorse hunter had failed to find his ball, as seemed probable, without our intervention, they might well have walked on to the 2nd tee declaring the 1st hole a half. This would have left someone else to go into the clubhouse later with an interesting story of finding a ball in the 1st hole!

We were of course on our way to Sheringham, where it all started, to make sure that it kept going, as it were, for an afternoon tee time of four o'clock. I was delighted that we could be joined by Harrison, bringing with him his grandfather's genes (but not his jeans, obviously, as he would not have been allowed on the course) so that we could celebrate fully. It could begin to sink in. Harrison had visited Sheringham many times as a small boy but never the golf course. The Lodger had played it before, but only in winter. In the June evening, with a gentle breeze, they both thought it was magnificent, as indeed did I, for it is. It may not offer the finest golfability in Norfolk (or so the purists maintain) but throw in the green-and-pleasantness factor and it's hard to match. I had hopes for the chemistry too, but there were rather a lot of people around, play was slow, and things went against me. I hit the 1st green, as is my wont, but it was slower than the practice green, and I three-putted. On the 2nd I had a putt for par from off the green and I asked The Lodger to tend the flag. When my ball hit it, he was still tending it, and it was still in the hole. He had reckoned it was going too fast, and left the flag in to give it a chance. It bounced off, of course. There's friendship for you.

Later on in the round I sort of "got back into contention" and I easily beat the others, but they were both out of practice. I remember their cheering on my final putt on 18, but not whether it went in or not, or if I did or didn't play to my handicap as a result. I do remember sitting outside the clubhouse afterwards drinking a pint of Adnams and gazing as ever up the 1st fairway. I remembered back to the days when Celia and I used to visit my parents in Sheringham in the 1970s. At the golf club, it did not matter how I had played, I would always sit there afterwards thinking how enticing the 1st hole looked, and how it might be possible one day to play the whole course really well. Back in my late twenties, much of my life and aspirations were ahead of me, of course, though I don't recall what exactly I aspired to. Whatever it was, I am mostly glad that it happened that way. Now, with Mank and Celia departed this earth and Nellie still content to be living at home at the age of 94 but doing little else, there is no point in wishing them back. It was good to be reminded of those days; these days, possibly I am still searching for something new to aspire to. On that evening, June 12th, 2005, we aspired to celebrate my achievement, and considering the relative lack of golf practice of The Lodger and Harrison, they made a splendid fist of it. I don't remember too much, except that the staff of The Two Life-boats Hotel where we stayed (but of course) did eventually come and ask us if we would mind going to bed.

The next morning on my way home, I popped into the golf club for a last look. It's true, you know. When you look from the veranda up the 1st fairway, it must definitely be possible to play the whole course well, one day...

19

REFLECTIONS IN A GLASS OR TWO

I think I know what you are going to say. It can only be one of two things: was it worth it; and, which was the best? Let me take the second question first.

It is interesting that on the celebratory visit to Sheringham, we were told we would need to produce handicap certificates (although we were not asked for them in the event). If that had been the case back in 1971, Mank and I would never have played, and who knows what might, or might not, have happened then? Without those occasional seaside games, I might not have taken up the game I toyed with briefly in my youth. Heaven knows, I might even have become a walker.

The romantic metaphor for relationships with golf courses gets into difficulty if one likens joining a club and obtaining a certificate to prove it, to getting married. The former turns into a licence to go and play away at other venues, but the latter does not exactly give one a free hand to go out and become a serial adulterer. But, just supposing for a moment, if one were to have seventy-eight lovers, could there possibly be a best amongst them? I doubt it.

Nevertheless, I don't feel this work would be complete without a review of events so, not without difficulty, and for obvious reasons without anyone else's input, I have compiled an alphabetical list of awards:

A is for *accessibility*, which without a doubt goes to Bude & North Cornwall. You simply cannot miss it, unlike a surprising number of others.

B is for *beauty*. This is in the eye of the beholder, and I fancy that linksland only looks attractive to a golfer and, even then, beautiful?

Perhaps the footballer Christian Vieri summed it up when he said golf courses are like children, they are all beautiful.[91]

Which *county* would I choose to visit for golf purposes only? Kent and Northumberland deserve honourable mentions, Norfolk is special, but I guess it would have to be the non-county of Merseyside, with two provisos; the Wirral should be included and, breaking my own rules, so should the links of Birkdale, Hillside etc.

As for a single *destination*, I would not dare nominate one single golf course, but this award can go to Saunton, as it alone has two of equal status.

Some of my *encounters* with strangers could have been briefer, but Ron's back nine at Clacton is the best golf I have ever seen live.

The best *flags* I have seen were a diagonal dark blue and yellow. On the front nine, the yellow occupied the segment from the bottom of the stick side, with the blue below, and the number of the hole in yellow on the blue segment. The colours were reversed on the back nine. The sticks themselves were blue for the bottom third, then yellow. These were on a course called Taunton & Pickeridge, which is not actually by the sea. I mention this to emphasise one last time that no-one is perfect. If I have got a fact wrong, I apologise. If you happen merely to disagree with my opinion, I'll argue with you.

G is for *greens*. They tend to be good at the seaside because they have the right sort of soil and are free of frost. Amongst many possible criteria to choose from, I have been shocked by the speed of a green on three occasions, all first visits obviously. Turnberry, which is in Scotland, The Buckinghamshire, which is inland, and Hunstanton, which wins my award (assuming they are still as they were).

Where would I choose for a *holiday* with golf (as opposed to a golfing holiday)? Cornwall is a great destination, but at the other end of the scale, as it were, so is Northumberland.

I is for (stroke) *index*. As suspected, the 224 yard 6th hole at Bamburgh Castle is the only such par three, and so the shortest stroke 1. All but 8 stroke 1 holes are par fours, usually long, and the longest of all is the 561 yard 7th at Seascale, par five. This is not the longest hole of all, which honour goes to Number 8 at Isle of Purbeck at 594 yards. (It is stroke 3; stroke 1 on that course is the 492 yard 6th, also par five). I had intended to include lots more stuff like this but then I realised it does not mean anything. If you are in the bunker on the 8th at Purbeck, it does not matter a mashie-niblick if the stroke 1 hole at Bamburgh is on the clubhouse snooker table. Stroke indexes only have a meaning within a given course, and even then thanks to the EGU, their meaning is uncertain. I also felt that statistical analysis by par or length of all the holes encountered would be pointless. What counts is that as far as possible, I played each course as I found it.

What about the *journey*? Sometimes, I have travelled in weather for which the saying "It is better to travel hopefully than to arrive" must have been devised. The worst such journey was to Littlestone on 31st January 2004. I even remember the date.

As for the best-*kept* secret, with apologies to their members by whom their clubs' charms are obviously greatly appreciated, I nominate three: Felixstowe Ferry, Hartlepool and Seascale.

Which is the most *literally littoral* of them all? Is there a course where you are almost on the beach? Thurlestone gets pretty close during the early holes. Warren is very close to the estuary, but the actual beach facing out to sea is never in sight. Dunstanburgh Castle probably swings it.

M is for *magnificent*. Linksland tends to deserve the adjective splendid but not really magnificent (St Enodoc being a possible exception). I was very taken with my companions' reaction to Sheringham on that June evening. From the 5th tee to the 17th green, you can see so much of the rest of the course. It is a magnificent spectacle.

Golf is all about *numbers*, and I can list quite a few. I played seventy-eight courses, 1,404 holes, of which 325 were par threes, 867 par fours, and 212 par fives. If I averaged 90, or five strokes a hole, I played about 7,000 shots of which, using Dave Parsons' statistic, about 2,800 were putts, or in my case, at least 3,000 after allowance for pips. But the number which really means something is this: the total yardage was 487,898. That's four hundred and eighty-seven thousand eight hundred and ninety-eight yards. Adding in the courses I played but which didn't count takes the figure over 500,000.

---

[91] He hasn't actually said this, yet, but I am sure he will when he takes up golf.

What about *oddities*? The brick steps at Bamburgh, the lampless lamp post at Felixstowe Ferry, and the Indiana Jones bridge at Whitby are nominees, but the honour goes to the church at St Enodoc.

The best *panorama*, the single best view, has to be that from Start Point to Portland Bill which you get from beyond the 8th green at East Devon, but it takes its time coming.

The *quirkiness* award, for its three, three, five, five start, its brick observation platform, and other eccentricities has to go to Bamburgh Castle.

I only really stayed at one *resort* course, but it is hard to imagine an improvement on Trevose.

What were my best *scores*? Sadly, the best rounds appear to have been when I was playing alone, but that may not be unconnected to my propensity to cheat. The best individual scores were:

eagle – Number 4 at Furness (the only one, I believe);

birdie – two nominations: Number 7 at Silloth-on-Solway, because I was waved through and it was index 1, and Number 11 at Scarborough North Cliff, with the Marx Brothers in attendance;

par – again, two nominations, holes 1 and 2 at Sheringham, the first the first ever, and the second included an out of bounds;

bogey, given my handicap, is the most common gross score. Nevertheless, one stands out, Number 2 at Wallasey, called Stableford, and finally;

double bogey – Number 18 at Littlestone. All seven shots were well struck.

And the *toughest* courses? So much depends on the conditions, and the tees used, but I would say the Royal St George's starts off relentlessly and gets worse (the members actually play to an old-fashioned bogey of 76) and Rye, being par sixty-eight but SSS 71, are literally hard to beat.

Unusual, unexpected, unexplained, unseen, and unnerving – it has to be Squidge.

The choice of best all-round *views* shows an understandable local bias. Most seaside views are good, and there are some spectacular ones in Northumberland and Cornwall but, for its combination of the rolling hills of Dorset, the Jurassic Coast and Chesil Beach, and the historic Cobb and the town itself, the winner has to be Lyme Regis.

The worst *wind* (as opposed to weather) was at Knott End. It may have been stronger at Littlestone, but at Knott End it was across for sixteen holes.

The *X-factor* is awarded for the best "click", and goes to Wallasey, the feeling being all the more remarkable for the visit coming right in the middle of a gruelling week, the fifth of nine consecutive courses visited.

For the *Y-factor*, see below.

Finally, the *zoo* award. For the incontrovertible evidence of wild animals, to be treated as loose impediments or ground under repair according to severity, this must go to the daddy of them all, Royal North Devon.

And so to the first question. Who knows "Y" I did it, but was it worth it? Can I sum up seaside golf? Well, at seaside golf courses, you do not get: motorways, flight paths, sirens, housing estates, litter, heavy industry (often), crowds (if you choose well), and claustrophobia; you do get: welcomed (because everyone is relaxed), natural surroundings, the freshest air, all sorts of weather, all-year-round greens, generous green fees (often), great golf, and that mysterious ingredient, the sea itself. That takes care of the "Y" factor.

Now, to play seventy-eight different golf courses takes a certain effort what with all the travelling, and the question remains, was it worth it? Some of the courses I have played only once but if we say I averaged two visits to compile this book, that is 156 days. If I maintained an average of three visits a week (and I did not) then it took a year of my life. So, while you spent a year in the office or at your work bench, or driving your taxi, I played golf. At the seaside. Perhaps I too should have been working, saving up for my retirement. Assuming I make it to retirement age – and I might not – it will be nice to have money. I could spend it on what I like best. I could use it for green fees. I could play my way round England – do the *English Golf Coast*. There's a thought.

INDEX OF COURSES